CATHOLIC HIGHER EDUCATION, THEOLOGY, AND ACADEMIC FREEDOM

Other Books by Charles E. Curran

Tensions in Moral Theology
Toward an American Catholic Moral Theology
Directions in Fundamental Moral Theology
Directions in Catholic Social Ethics
American Catholic Social Ethics: Twentieth-Century Approaches
Moral Theology: A Continuing Journey
Transition and Tradition in Moral Theology
Issues in Sexual and Medical Ethics
Catholic Moral Theology in Dialogue
New Perspectives in Moral Theology

Catholic Higher Education, Theology, and Academic Freedom

CHARLES E. CURRAN

UNIVERSITY OF NOTRE DAME PRESS
NOTRE DAME   LONDON

Library of Congress Cataloging-in-Publication Data
Curran, Charles E.
    Catholic higher education, theology, and academic free-
dom / Charles E. Curran.
        p. cm.
    ISBN 0-268-00625-3
    1. Catholic universities and colleges—United States—
History—20th century. 2. Academic freedom—United
States—History—20th century. 3. Teaching, Freedom
of—United States—Case studies. I. Title.
LC501.C85   1990
378.1'21—dc20   89-40742

To
Paul C. Saunders
John F. Hunt
Ronald K. Chen
Juanita A. Crowley
and the firms and associates of
Cravath, Swaine, and Moore
and
Wilmer, Cutler, and Pickering
in gratitude for
your defense of my academic freedom

Contents

Preface   ix

1. An Overall View of Academic Freedom   1

2. Catholic Attitudes toward Academic Freedom
   before the Mid-1960s   26

3. Acceptance of Academic Freedom by the Mainstream
   of Catholic Higher Education in the 1960s   66

4. Some Continued Opposition to Academic Freedom
   in Catholic Institutions   112

5. Rationale in Defense of Academic Freedom
   for Catholic Higher Education   154

6. My Personal Involvement in Struggles for Academic Freedom   192

Index   245

Preface

For almost twenty-five years I have been immersed in the issue of academic freedom in Catholic higher education in the United States. I have coauthored two books and written a number of articles on this issue. In addition I have been practically involved in some significant struggles centered on academic freedom. This book is thus the fruit of years of theoretical reflection and practical involvement. There is no need for a long preface or introduction. The book speaks for itself. Chapter 6 explains in detail my own personal involvement in questions of academic freedom that affect Catholic higher education.

I have researched and written this book while serving as the Visiting Kaneb Professor of Catholic Studies at Cornell University and the Visiting Brooks and Firestone Professor of Religion at the University of Southern California. I am grateful to the donors of these professorships, the administration, colleagues, and librarians at both distinguished institutions of higher learning for their gracious hospitality in general and their support for my research on this topic.

Since August 1986, I have struggled in different contexts to defend my academic freedom but especially the academic freedom of the Catholic University of America. My efforts were not successful. I was supported and sustained in the process, however, by many different people. I can never adequately thank all those who have assisted me in so many different ways. My earlier book, *Faithful Dissent*, tells of the ecclesial aspect of my case involving an investigation of my writings by the Vatican Congregation for the Doctrine of the Faith which concluded that I was neither suitable nor eligible to be a professor of Catholic theology. This book, especially its last chapter, recounts the academic aspects of the case at Catholic University. The two aspects are closely connected and many of the same people have supported me in the different phases of my case.

To mention personally all those who have assisted and sustained me during the last few years would be impossible, but I must record my never-ending gratitude for people from Catholic University who have supported me in this struggle over the years, especially colleagues, students, Friends of American Catholic Theology (FACT), canonical and academic advisors, those who testified for me, and especially the five graduate students who were intervenor-plaintiffs in my law suit. I am grateful to many academic colleagues and associations who have publicly endorsed my competency and standing in my field. The staff of the American Association of University Professors, especially Jordan E. Kurland, have been most helpful without ever sacrificing their impartial commitment to the principles of academic freedom. Robert K. Webb once again volunteered his time and expertise as my academic counsel. Committee A of the AAUP and particularly its investigating committee have given much time and effort in proof of their commitment to academic freedom.

I can never adequately express my thanks to the law firms of Cravath, Swaine, and Moore of New York, and Wilmer, Cutler, and Pickering of Washington. Cravath offered to defend me pro bono in both the academic and legal aspects of the case. I have dedicated this book to them and to Paul C. Saunders, John F. Hunt, Ronald K. Chen, Juanita A. Crowley, and their associates. I was in frequent contact with these people for over three years, came to admire their expertise and dedication, and am privileged to regard them as friends.

Phillis Molock and Stephen Salvatierra have typed the manuscript. John Ehmann, my editor at the University of Notre Dame Press, has continued to encourage and expedite my work. Jeannette Morgenroth Sheerin of the Press was most helpful in preparing the manuscript for publication. Julia Fleming has prepared the index.

1. An Overall View of Academic Freedom

To understand properly the debate about academic freedom in Catholic institutions of higher learning, one must first be acquainted with the meaning and practice of academic freedom in the United States. This opening chapter analyzes the principles and procedures of academic freedom as they have developed in the United States.

Existing Principles and Procedures of Academic Freedom

General agreement about some of the principles and procedures of academic freedom in higher education in the United States exists today because of the widespread acceptance of a Statement of Principles on Academic Freedom and Tenure issued by the Association of American Colleges and the American Association of University Professors in 1940. In 1958, both groups proposed a Statement on Procedural Standards in Faculty Dismissal Proceedings, a supplement to the 1940 Statement that spells out in greater detail the process to be observed in dismissal proceedings.[1] The principles and procedures of both documents have generally been accepted in the American educational community.

The American Association of University Professors (AAUP), founded in 1915, has staunchly defended the academic freedom of professors and has cooperated with other organizations to insure the recognition of these principles and procedures throughout the American academy.[2] The AAUP works in collaboration with other interested organizations and also issues policy statements on questions facing faculty and higher education in general. In the light of ongoing experience and changing circumstances, the AAUP also proposes

1

updated guidelines on the 1940 and 1958 Statements; the latest of these documents is the 1982 Recommended Institutional Regulations on Academic Freedom and Tenure.[3] In addition, the AAUP investigates alleged violations of academic freedom and censures institutions that are guilty of such violations. The 1940 and 1958 Statements have not been looked upon as policies to be implemented word for word in university bylaws and faculty handbooks, but as the standards, principles, and guides to be adapted to the nature and traditions of particular institutions and to give effect both to faculty teaching and tenure rights and to the obligations of faculty members to the academic community.[4]

Higher education in the United States illustrates well the characteristic American emphasis on the role of voluntary associations in the life and culture of the country. The order and organization of higher education come about through voluntary organizations of colleges and universities that work together for the good of the academy. For example, accrediting associations serve the academy by promoting standards and practices that assure the proper functioning of institutions of higher learning. The accrediting associations and the major professional academic societies have accepted the 1940 and 1958 Statements. Individual colleges and universities incorporate these principles and guidelines into their operating procedures.

The 1940 Statement is quite brief. It succinctly defends academic freedom as necessary for the common good of society, which "depends upon the free search for truth and its free exposition."[5] Academic freedom covers three areas: research and publication; teaching in the classroom; and extramural utterances. Correlative duties are also mentioned in each area, and full freedom in research and in publication is subject to the adequate performance of other academic duties. In the classroom the teacher should be careful not to introduce controversial matter that has no relation to the subject. The 1940 Statement recognizes that in the context of teaching, "limitations of academic freedom because of religious or other aims of the institution should be clearly stated in writing at the time of the appointment."[6] In speaking or writing as a private citizen, the professor should be free from institutional censorship, but the public may judge the professor or the professor's institution by his or her utterances. Hence, the professor in extramural utterances "should at all times be accurate, should exercise appropriate restraint, should show respect for the opinions of others, and should make every effort to indicate that he is not an institutional spokesman."[7]

Tenure is explicitly related in the 1940 Statement to the protection of academic freedom as well as to economic security. After a probationary period not to exceed seven years, a professor should have permanent or continuous tenure. Except for retirement or the extraordinary case of financial exigency, a professor should be terminated only for "adequate cause." The conditions of any appointment should be stated in writing before any appointment is consummated. During the probationary period teachers should have the same academic freedom as all other members of the faculty. The procedures for due process for the dismissal of faculty members from the institution are mentioned. If possible, both a faculty committee and the governing board of the institution should hear the case. Further protections of due process are built into the later recommended dismissal process. In its schematic development of protections of due process, the 1940 statement also recognizes three reasons for dismissal in addition to bona fide financial exigency: incompetence, moral turpitude, and other reasons not involving moral turpitude.

The 1958 Statement on Procedural Standards in Faculty Dismissal Cases spells out the guidelines for due process in greater detail.[8] The procedural recommendations deal with preliminary proceedings concerning the fitness of the faculty member, the commencement of formal proceedings, suspension of the faculty member, the makeup of the hearing committee, the committee proceeding, consideration of the case by the hearing committee, consideration of the case by the governing body, the publicity. The introductory comments in the Statement recognize the importance of the faculty and its concern over its own membership through appointments to and separation from the faculty. The processes and procedures of the hearing by peers are spelled out in detail. The governing body should normally be expected to accept the committee's decision, but the document does recognize that the governing body has the power to make a final decision overruling the committee.

The understanding of academic freedom found in these documents and incorporated into the structures of American higher education can accurately be described as pragmatic, prudential, procedural, and partial. Significant overlaps exist among these four different characteristics, but the individual characteristics can be addressed separately. These characteristics can be explained by the historical circumstances and context in which the statements arose. To obtain the approval of all involved in American higher education, the documents had to avoid what might cause division and opposition.

The pragmatic nature of the statements is evident in two ways. First, there is no detailed theoretical understanding or in-depth defense of academic freedom. Defenders of academic freedom might use different or even opposing rationales. For example, at one time, many in the United States defended academic freedom because it was in accord with the scientific method; but while philosophical empiricism can readily justify academic freedom, such a defense would not be acceptable to all. These pragmatic documents avoid giving any detailed theoretical foundations for academic freedom. Second, the documents can also be faulted for not spelling out the reasons justifying the dismissal of a tenured faculty member. Broad concepts of adequate cause, competency, and fitness are mentioned. The 1958 Statement recognizes that one persistent source of difficulty has been the definition of adequate cause for dismissal. Considerable ambiguity and misunderstanding exist in higher education about this matter. The 1958 Statement simply and somewhat illogically sidesteps the whole issue: "The present statement assumes that individual institutions will have formulated their own definitions of adequate cause for dismissal, bearing in mind the 1940 Statement and standards which have developed in the experience of academic institutions."[9]

The principles and procedures of academic freedom that have been agreed upon are also prudential. *Prudential* means ease in handling practical matters and the exercise of good judgment and common sense; the word also connotes a cautious and circumspect approach. Such descriptions aptly fit accepted American norms of academic freedom. The principles and procedures basically accept the American system of higher education as it exists and then build in appropriate safeguards for academic freedom. The 1958 Statement implicitly recognizes this approach. The distinctive characteristic of American higher education is the role played by governing boards that have ultimate legal responsibility for the institution. Unlike many other and older structurings of universities, the faculty in the university or college in the United States does not have the ultimate responsibility for the institution's governance. The AAUP documents accept the American system, since it was and undoubtedly still is impossible to change it. The faculty, however, must have "a first hand concern" with its own membership. The faculty member is entitled to a hearing by peers to determine if the institution can dismiss her or him. But the accepted approach to academic freedom does not give the faculty absolute, ultimate, and final say. While the governing board should normally accept the faculty committee's decision, the governing board can overrule the faculty. In reality, heavy moral pressure exists on the governing board to accept the faculty committee's recommendation, but the accepted process does not challenge the ultimate authority of governing boards.

Academic freedom is primarily protected through the procedures of tenure and academic due process. The standards or criteria to be employed in dismissing faculty members have purposely been left vague and undefined. The primary defense of academic freedom is the judgment by one's peers about one's competency and fitness. Very little of substance or theory has been spelled out; nevertheless the controlling documents have concentrated on tenure and due process that centers, in turn, on judgment by peers.

The defense of academic freedom in these documents is partial in the sense that they do not address themselves to the total reality of academic freedom. They cover only the threat to academic freedom that comes through institutions' governing boards and administrations acting either on their own or at the behest of other external parties. But there is no recognition, for example, of the threat to academic freedom that might come from one's own peers or from the sponsors of one's research. In addition, some faculty members are protected much better than others. Tenured professors cannot be dismissed without the administration's proving to a faculty committee that adequate cause exists; the burden of proof rests on the part of the university. For nontenured faculty members, on the other hand, the individual faculty member must prove that academic freedom has been violated by nonreappointment. Possible violations of academic freedom in the selection and first appointment of faculty members are not even mentioned.

Thus principles and procedures of academic freedom exist that are generally accepted and operative in American higher education.

These norms and practices, however, are pragmatic, prudential, procedural, and partial.

Historical Development

An overview of the historical development of academic freedom in the United States will be helpful in understanding how the present principles and procedures arose.[10] Academic freedom obviously exists in different contexts, and the context in which academic freedom arose in the States explains in part both its theory and practice.

The intellectual life has always given great emphasis to freedom. The intellectual wants freely to investigate questions that he or she believes are important and significant; freedom is crucial for intellectual inquiry. The Middle Ages saw the rise of corporate institutions called universities that carried on the task of the intellectual pursuit and dissemination of truth. Medieval universities stressed the primacy of the faculty in controlling the internal affairs of the institution with regard to academic standards, curriculum, and membership in the faculty. Church restraints on the universities did exist, but even here the universities enjoyed a great deal of independence and even exercised some political power.[11] Thus the intellectual profession and the collegial coming together of scholars as teachers and students have recognized the importance of some freedom, autonomy, and independence.

The distinctive character of academic freedom in the United States was similarly shaped by the particular context of higher education as it developed historically in our country. Higher education in the United States before the mid-nineteenth century was heavily dominated by the churches and their members. (To speak of "churchmen" in this situation is neither sexist nor inaccurate.) Administrators, faculty, and students were often associated with churches. The American college was marked by Christian principles in living, traditionalism in thought, drilling and rote memory in method, and paternalism and authoritarianism in structure.[12] However, by the end of the nineteenth century, many changes had occurred. The influence of churches and denominations continued but was much reduced. A spirit of searching for new knowledge challenged the vision of higher education as only preserving and handing down the wisdom of the past. Research became more significant and affected the way in which academicians went about their work. Competency became more significant than paternalism and authority.

There can be no doubt that the growth of the natural sciences, more specifically, the rise of Darwinism, had a great influence on the changes taking place in higher education in the United States in the second half of the nineteenth century. Most of the significant struggles over academic freedom at this time centered on the friction between religious authority and science. The Darwinian debate, according to Walter Metzger, the highly respected historian of American academic freedom, supplied a new rationale for academic freedom.[13] The evolutionists supplied impressive new support for tolerating error. All beliefs are tentative and verifiable only through a continuous process of inquiry; what is true is never fully known and never fully verifiable. The Darwinian debate also put a heavy emphasis on scientific competency and questioned the presumptions of clerics and others who lack scientific competence. Such an approach supplied new and significant justification for the need for academics to be judged by their own peers. Finally, the scientific worldview and the Darwinian debate underscored the important values of universality and neutrality. Universalism eliminates all particularist criteria such as race, creed, or nationality, as well as unearned advantages such as connections, rank, and cast. The researcher's neutrality and disinterestedness question any ideology or preordained assumption. These two scientific virtues, which came to the fore in this debate, helped pave the way for full academic freedom. The Darwinian debate proved for many the need for the communal intellectual enterprise to be free of church control.

The later nineteenth and early twentieth century produced new sources of friction in American institutions of higher learning. As higher education emerged from its denominational context in the nineteenth century, independent governing boards ran the universities. Private institutions sought and received money from wealthy industrialists to support their educational endeavors. State institutions depended on individual states for their income, and they too were subject to criticism from the legislators and others who controlled the funds. Thus faculty members were vulnerable to the disfavor of nonacademics who helped fund and support the universities and who were often members of the governing boards. Academic freedom cases in the last decade of the nineteenth century generally focused on faculty members who espoused social reform or criticized the existing social order, thereby incurring the wrath of certain supporters of the institution. A long list of martyrs for academic freedom appeared at this time. In the face of these threats, members of the American academic profession began to recognize the need for some concerted action to protect their freedom, their role in society, and their jobs.[14]

Also exerting a considerable influence on American higher education was the German university as it existed in the second half of the nineteenth century. Between 1870 and 1900, about eight thousand American college graduates flocked to German universities for advanced studies. These young scholars admired and wanted to emulate the model of scholarship and research that they found in Germany. In late nineteenth-century Germany, academic freedom embraced three interrelated concepts—*Lehrfreiheit, Lernfreiheit,* and *Freiheit der Wissenschaft. Lehrfreiheit* literally means "teaching freedom" and allowed German professors who were salaried civil servants to teach and do research without the interference of church or state; however, they were held responsible for their positions and actions as private citizens. *Lernfreiheit* means "learning freedom" and was the prerogative of German students, who had freedom about attending classes and whose courses of study were subject only to state professional examinations and teaching licenses. In addition, the German universities had no responsibility for student behavior and did not provide dormitory accommodations or residences. *Freiheit der Wissenschaft* guaranteed the university control over its own internal affairs through its governance by senior faculty. The German universities thus had an institutional autonomy.[15]

As the twentieth century began, American academics were contending for academic freedom in the light of the experience of the German universities and in light of the struggles that had been endured and were still continuing. The focal point for problems continued to be the boards of trustees, which were often composed of leaders in industry and commerce and at times tended to treat the faculty as employees to be fired at will. Nor could the academic receive any support from the courts, which later would become quite sympathetic to the academic freedom of professors. The courts at the turn of the century generally deferred to the judgment of the governing boards that the termination of a professor was in the best interest of the institution.[16] In 1913, a joint committee sponsored by three learned societies (the American Economic Association, the American Sociological Society, and the American Political Science Association) grappled with the principles and questions of academic freedom but could only issue a preliminary report on the matter. Finally, eighteen full professors from Johns Hopkins University issued a call for a conference looking toward the creation of a national association of university professors. Thus was born the American Association of University Professors.[17]

The AAUP's membership was originally limited to the elite and the aristocrats of college and university teaching. After some years, the organization opened itself up to all college and university teachers.[18] At the organizational meeting of the association in January 1915, a committee on academic freedom and academic tenure was constituted in order to formulate principles and procedures to ensure academic freedom in colleges and universities. John Dewey, the chair of the meeting, thought that the defense of academic freedom would be the primary concern of the existing learned societies rather than a significant activity of the new association. The year 1915 proved how wrong Dewey was, for the new committee considered in that year eleven cases of alleged violations of academic freedom. Despite this heavy practical workload, the committee was able to finish its comprehensive report; the report was accepted and became known as the 1915 Declaration of Principles.[19]

The 1915 Declaration of Principles sets forth the norms and terms for the understanding and defense of the principle of academic freedom in American higher education.[20] The 1940 Statement follows the same general approach. The four characteristics of the 1940 Statement—pragmatism, procedure, prudence, and partiality—are all found in the earlier document. The committee designed an approach that within the lifetimes of its members became generally accepted throughout the American academy but not in Catholic higher education. The general acceptance of the document proves the wisdom and prudence of the 1915 committee. However, some of the shortcomings of its Statement have continued to exist.

The principal threats to and violations of the academic freedom of American professors had come from governing boards and administrators who looked upon professors as employees who could be fired at will. One obvious solution was to change the nature and structure of colleges and universities so that they would be controlled by the faculty, as in Germany. The AAUP committee recognized, however, that they could not change single-handedly the course and structure of higher education in the United States.[21] The 1915 Declaration of Principles therefore does not call for faculty-controlled institutions, but rather seeks to protect the faculty from the sources of incursion, namely, trustees and governing boards. The Declaration distinguishes universities from proprietary institutions which are run to promote the specific positions of the founders and supporters. In true universities, whether public or private, trustees have a public, not a private, trust. Governing boards cannot limit the intellectual freedom of professors without making the institution proprietary. University governing boards are stewards for the whole of society; they cannot run the university like a private business, and they cannot treat the faculty member merely as an employee of a business. The independence of the professor also serves the good of society as a whole. To make this point, the 1915 Declaration compares the relationship of the trustee to the professor and his or her independence of thought and utterance to the relationship of the executive to the judge who was appointed by the executive. In universities, trustees hold an essential and highly honorable place; but the faculties hold an independent place, and in relation to scientific and educational questions they hold the primary responsibility.

The 1915 Declaration justifies academic freedom on the basis of its contribution to society in general. Universities can serve society through three distinct functions—by promoting inquiry and advancing human knowledge; by providing general instruction to students; by developing experts for the various branches of public service. All these purposes require academic freedom for the good of the community at large. The university is to be a place of intellectual experiment that serves the larger community.

Since no rights exist without corresponding duties, the 1915 Declaration proposes certain correlative obligations. The conclusions proposed by the professor must be "conclusions gained by a scholar's method and held in a scholar's spirit; that is to say, they must be the fruits of competent and patient and sincere inquiry, and they should be set forth with dignity, courtesy, and temperateness of language."[22] The document also points out the discretion and care that the professor must use in teaching immature students. The 1915

Declaration ends with practical proposals for insuring academic freedom through academic due process.

In brief, academic freedom according to this document involves three realities—freedom of inquiry in research, freedom of teaching within the institution, and freedom of extramural utterance and action. The freedom of research is safeguarded so fully that the document does not even bother to discuss the issue further. The inclusion of extramural utterance and action illustrates the particularities of the American context of academic freedom. (German university professors enjoyed no special protection for extramural words or deeds.) However, the experience of the early twentieth century in the United States indicated that the primary source of infringements and violations of academic freedom involved the extramural speech and actions of faculty members. To this day, extramural academic freedom cases have continued to dominate AAUP investigations.[23] In extramural utterances, teachers have a peculiar obligation to avoid hasty or unverified or exaggerated statements and to refrain from intemperate or sensational modes of expression; these restraints are proposed since the scholar is assumed to have added responsibility precisely because of her or his academic connections and affiliation. Within these restraints, academics must be free to participate in all aspects of public life. The 1915 Declaration proposes that the membership of the association give further consideration to the role of professors in political parties or in running for political office.

The means proposed to safeguard academic freedom are peer review, tenure, and academic due process. Official actions relating to reappointment or refusal of reappointment should be taken with the advice and consent of faculty committees. After ten years of service faculty members should be given permanent tenure. Tenured faculty can be dismissed for legitimate grounds. Professional incompetency is mentioned, but the grounds are left to be determined precisely by the individual schools. Nevertheless, tenured faculty can only be dismissed after a faculty committee has heard the case. The charges are to be formulated with reasonable definition, and other protections of due process are to be incorporated.

In light of historical development and the earlier 1915 Declaration of Principles, one can better understand the 1940 and 1958 Statements as well as the subsequent interpretations made by the

AAUP. When the 1915 Declaration first appeared, it was rejected by the Association of American Colleges.[24] However, in 1925 the American Council on Education called a conference to formulate a statement of principles and procedures of academic freedom. At this conference some compromises were made, and ultimately the Association of American Colleges and the AAUP agreed on the statement.[25] The 1940 and 1958 Statements have not only been accepted by both organizations, but by American higher education in general. All the groups connected with American higher education, many professional scholarly organizations, the accrediting associations, and American colleges and universities in general accept the basic principles and procedures found in the 1940 and 1958 Statements. Continuing interpretations made by the AAUP are also widely accepted.

The changing work of the AAUP in monitoring and interpreting the principles and practices of academic freedom in American higher education is confided to the association's Committee A on Academic Freedom and Tenure.[26] This committee monitors all aspects of the question and produces statements that are proposed either in its own name or as policy statements of AAUP. Many of these statements are not explicitly endorsed by other organizations. The AAUP follows a careful process in the writing and acceptance of these statements, and some are proposed more tentatively than others. In its briefs to various courts, the AAUP understands its own documents as reasoned argument. The court may well be persuaded by these arguments, unless of course someone makes a more reasoned argument. Thus the continuing work of AAUP, especially of its Committee A, does not have the same judicial effect as the classic documents endorsed so widely in the academic world, but these continuing interpretations are proposed and often accepted for what they are—carefully reasoned positions based on experience.[27]

The AAUP has taken as one of its major concerns the policing of the academic community with regard to alleged violations of academic freedom and tenure. The national office is willing to try to settle differences between faculty members and administrations when they arise. When mediation of this type has been unsuccessful, the general secretary of the AAUP, often with the advice of Committee A and others, makes the decision to begin an investigation of the institution in question. An ad hoc committee is appointed which then visits the institution and talks with all of the parties concerned. The report of the ad hoc committee is then sent to Committee A. Committee A may suggest changes, reject the publication of the report, or authorize its publication. If Committee A authorizes publication, it is sent confidentially to the complainant, the administration concerned, and the local AAUP chapter president for corrections. The text is then published in *Academe: The Bulletin of the American Association of University Professors*. Attempts are made to persuade the administration to correct what the report deems to be wrong. If a serious situation has not been corrected, then Committee A recommends to the annual meeting of the AAUP a note of censure of the institution in question. The action taken by the annual meeting is communicated to all concerned and published. The AAUP does not understand censure as an absolute and unqualified obligation on its members to refrain from accepting an appointment at such an institution. Through censure and through the public opinion of the academy that is influenced by it, the AAUP invokes the moral force of its action to try to obtain compliance with the accepted norms of the American academy. While an institution is under censure, the general secretary endeavors to work with the institution to take actions that would result in the removal of censure. Such removal must ultimately be accepted by the association at its annual meeting.[28]

The AAUP has had outstanding success in having its basic principles and procedures of academic freedom and tenure generally accepted throughout the American academic community. The very fact that the AAUP is restricted to faculty makes this accomplishment all the more remarkable, for the group has had to gain acceptance for its proposals from administrations, voluntary accrediting associations, and the general public.

Evaluation and Criticism

The principles and procedures of academic freedom that are enshrined especially in the 1940 and 1958 Statements can now be evaluated and criticized. The very need to gain acceptance from many different groups and constituencies indicates the necessity of compromise. The historical record bears out the existence of compromises that were made in formulating the documents. Two major types of criticism can be raised against the principles and procedures of academic freedom found in both Statements and generally accepted throughout the American academy. First, even within the narrow context of protecting faculty from the interference in academic freedom by governing boards and administrations, the existing principles and procedures have shortcomings. Second, the understanding of academic freedom is limited by the context in which the whole problem arose in the United States. The principles and procedures of academic freedom accepted in these documents protect the professor from interference from governing boards and administrations that would limit his or her academic freedom, but many other threats to academic freedom exist that are not mentioned in these controlling documents. I still insist that the great accomplishment of AAUP remains, but these two types of criticisms have validity; nothing in this world is perfect.

In general, even those well-disposed to AAUP admit that the acceptance of the basic principles and procedures of academic freedom by higher education in general and even some support from the courts do not necessarily guarantee the protection of an individual faculty member. However, blatant violations are relatively rare and are likely to be challenged in a number of ways both inside and outside the academy.[29] The somewhat lengthy and cumbersome process, with its many delays, means that an aggrieved faculty member often has had to take another position, and even censure by the AAUP has not always insured the ultimate reinstatement of the aggrieved in his or her former position. Nevertheless, offending institutions subsequently have often brought their procedures and policies into accord with the controlling statements.[30] The strongest negative criticism of the principles and policies of academic freedom in recent years has come from more radical and Marxist scholars.[31] No doubt, radical thinkers have had their academic freedom violated over the years and have lost their positions. Sheila Slaughter indicts American academics for having consistently sacrificed individuals and substantive principles in order to gain compliance with procedural safeguards from university officials for the profession as a whole.[32] Ellen W. Schrecker strongly criticizes the AAUP for not protecting the legitimate rights to academic freedom of many professors during the McCarthy period in the 1950s.[33]

What are some of the shortcomings of the accepted American approach to defending the academic freedom of faculty members from violations and infringements by the board of governors and administration of their institutions? The first problem is that not all faculty members enjoy the same amount of protection. The fullest protection is given to tenured faculty members. The rationale proposed for tenure has consistently emphasized its relationship to academic freedom as described in the statements already considered. Tenure also provides economic security for members of the academic profession. Tenured faculty members can be dismissed only for cause that bears on his or her fitness to teach and to do research, and only if the institution grants the faculty member the right to have the case heard by a a committee of peers with the institution accepting the burden of proof. The final judgment is made by the governing board, but the governing board must give significant weight to the committee report and the record. The AAUP and others have insisted that faculty members on probationary appointments have the same academic freedom as tenured faculty, but they definitely enjoy fewer protections. If a nontenured teacher is not reappointed, the burden of proof rests with the faculty member to show that nonreappointment really infringed on academic freedom. However, it would be foolhardy for institutions to give permanent tenure to people the moment they enter the academy without any kind of probationary period. Also from the very beginning, in 1915, protection was given only to those who were already members of a faculty. No protection at all is given to people who are applying for teaching positions in colleges and universities.

The argument can be made that the protection of tenure for some in the academy provides an environment of academic freedom for all. An umbrella argument maintains that the tenured members of the faculty who have full protection can provide academic freedom to the rest of the academy precisely because they are the ones who will be making decisions about appointments and reappointments of the nontenured. Those who do not have the full protection of academic freedom will still obtain benefit (and stay somewhat dry) thanks to the protection of the tenured faculty. However, such guarantees are far from perfect.[34] The existing system is probably the only feasible one in the light of the complex circumstances involved, but it is not perfect.

In discussing tenure as the protection for academic freedom, we must also call to mind the discussion about the very existence of tenure itself. Tenure is often attacked for protecting incompetent faculty members. The institutions and the students at colleges and universities suffer from the deadwood. New Ph.D.'s find it difficult to attain teaching positions in the academy. As a result, the academy loses the needed infusion of fresh blood. Women and minorities who exist in greater number among new Ph.D.'s continue to be disproportionately underrepresented in the academy. With the lifting of compulsory retirement, the problem will only be compounded. In addition, tenure does not perfectly accomplish its goal of protecting academic freedom for the whole academy.[35] Still generally accepted as an important characteristic of the academy in our country, however, tenure is defended for the protection it gives to academic freedom and for the financial security it provides.[36]

Defenders of tenure recognize some problems but maintain that the good involved in protecting academic freedom outweighs all the possible problems. In addition, stringent appointment and reappointment procedures on a probationary level can eliminate some deadwood in the future. Moreover, peer pressure in many good academic institutions stimulates faculty to continue their own growth in teaching and research. Tenure is not a perfect system even for protecting academic freedom, but it appears to be a reasonably satisfactory and generally accepted instrument for achieving its purposes.[37] It is so much a part of the fabric of American higher education that it would be hard to replace with either a better or a worse alternative. No one has yet been able to come up with a better approach that can both safeguard academic freedom and win the support of all the different constituencies involved.

A second problem concerns the important role given to the procedure of peer review. Peers should pass on faculty appointments and reappointments. Dismissal proceedings require peer judgment, although the final decision is made by the governing board. The primary way of protecting academic freedom is thus procedural, an imperfect approach at best. The more radical opponents of the present system of academic freedom point out that peer review has failed historically to protect the rights of political radicals. Ellen Schrecker has documented the actions taken against more radical faculty members throughout the twentieth century but especially during the

McCarthy period. The historical record shows that some faculty lost their positions just because they invoked their fifth amendment rights. Also in the 1950s, the AAUP for various reasons (especially due to the role of Ralph Himstead, the general secretary at the time) did not always stand up for the rights of more radical teachers. Schrecker concludes from her historical research that the traditional structure of academic freedom with its emphasis on the procedure of due process in faculty self-government did not and does not protect the rights of politically unpopular professors.[38] Recall that there was much discussion at the time over the role and rights of Communist party members in American higher education.

Schrecker reminds us that judgment by peers is not perfect and that nonconformists of all types may very well at times have their rights violated. Tenured senior faculty tend to be somewhat conservative and are as susceptible to pressure, prejudice, influence, and partial judgment as other human beings. Judicial due process does not assure a substantially just result; judgment by peers cannot always insure justice. But if not peers, then who? Certainly on the whole, judgment by peers is better than judgment by governing boards or other outsiders.[39] Perhaps some type of arbitration might work. The practical problem involves coming up with acceptable alternatives. Schrecker recognizes the problem and realizes that answers here are hard to attain.[40] Judgment by peers is not perfect, but it remains a feasible form of protection in the present circumstances.

Third, the standards proposed for dismissal are quite vague. What precisely constitutes incompetence or lack of fitness to teach and do research? This vagueness and the lack of substantive criteria are in keeping with the general bias in favor of procedure over substance. The history of the AAUP documents shows a concerted effort to remain vague and indefinite while the institution of peer judgment takes most of the responsibility. I think competency and fitness to teach should be spelled out in greater detail, but I cannot deny that the present vagueness has some advantages and fits in with the emphasis on procedural safeguards that characterizes these policies.

A fourth and final criticism of the existing policies of academic freedom within the narrow context under consideration concerns the area of extramural utterance. The founders of AAUP recognized that the area of extramural utterance and actions occasioned many of the infringements on and violations of academic freedom at the beginning of the twentieth century. At that time there was also no other way to protect academics' words and deeds. The courts were not willing then to protect the employment of one who used one's free speech to criticize the employer. William Van Alstyne has made the point that extramural utterances should not be seen as academic freedom as such, but as the civil rights of the professor.[41] In this area of political involvement in free speech, the professor is merely exercising his or her basic American rights. Today the first amendment will protect the aprofessional political utterances of the professor as a citizen. The argument as to whether the extramural utterances of faculty members involve academic freedom as such or simply her or his civil and political rights will continue. In light of the widespread acceptance of academic freedom as including extramural words and deeds of faculty, Professor Van Alstyne has to wage an uphill fight in trying to bring about change. For our purposes, however, this discussion points up a further criticism of the existing concept of academic freedom even in its narrow context. According to the present understanding, the academician has added restraints in her or his extramural words and deeds that a citizen does not have. Professors are thus subject to more accountability in their extramural utterances and political involvements than other Americans.

Thus general agreement within the American academy exists about the principles and procedures governing academic freedom in its narrow context of the freedom of the faculty member vis-à-vis possible encroachment by governing boards. These protections of academic freedom are imperfect and continue to be criticized and scrutinized, but so far no one has been able to come up with more acceptable and feasible procedures and protections.

The American academy generally accepts the principles and practices of academic freedom that protect the faculty member from infringements on academic freedom by governing boards and administrators of institutions. Such an understanding of academic freedom is narrowed, however, to one particular context, explained by the historical situation in the United States in the late nineteenth and early twentieth centuries. Beyond this narrow context, the principles and policies of academic freedom are not as well worked out and accepted. Discussion continues on many aspects of academic freedom at the present time, and the AAUP has issued its own guidelines in many areas. Some of the contexts and areas not covered in the documents and policies mentioned above will now be considered.

In comparison with the German understanding of academic freedom, the American concept proposed originally in 1915 totally neglected the academic freedom of students. Historical and cultural circumstances help to explain why academic freedom for students was excluded. In subsequent years, the academic freedom of students has been discussed at great length. Five national groups (American Association of University Professors, United States National Student Association, Association of American Colleges, National Association of Student Personnel Administrators, and National Association of Women Deans and Counselors) endorsed a joint statement first issued in 1967[42] This statement insured students' rights to freedom of expression in the classroom, to protection against improper academic evaluation, and to protection against improper disclosure. The statement also recognizes the right of students to invite and to hear on campus any speaker of their choosing. The institutional control of campus facilities should not be used as an excuse for censorship.

At the present, some discussion concerns the academic freedom of aliens. At times, foreigners invited to speak or lecture at academic institutions in the United States have not been allowed into the country. Court cases have dealt with these issues. In a sense, the academic freedom that is violated is that of the institution with its faculty and students who have invited the alien to its campus.[43]

In addition to the people who are not covered by the older and well-established norms governing academic freedom, different potential sources of threats infringing on academic freedom have come to the fore over the years. Government constituted a threat through the imposition of loyalty oaths and investigations into un-American activities. These threats existed before World War II but reached their high point in the 1950s. Some faculty members lost their positions in the 1950s because they exercised their civil rights to invoke the fifth amendment in testifying before government committees.[44] In the midst of the cold war, some people, such as Sidney Hook, argued that practicing Communist party members should be excluded from the academy.[45]

As the twentieth century continued, another potential enemy of academic freedom appeared on the scene—sponsored research. The source of funding for faculty research could become a threat to academic freedom. The potential conflict of interest between the academy and the funder is evident.[46]

In the last few years, discussions of academic freedom have focused on a new threat—the faculty itself. Some aspects of this topic have already been considered under the effectiveness of peer review. But today the academy is more conscious of the danger that faculty pose to other faculty. Faculty doing sponsored research are asked at times to trade away scholarly exchange and openness in order to preserve their findings for the companies that sponsor the research. Sometimes faculty themselves have become entrepreneurs and seem to be playing two conflicting roles. Thus today possible threats to academic freedom do not necessarily come from outside the academy, but can also come from one's own peers. David Rabban has perceptively pointed out that academic freedom is not the same as faculty autonomy in research, teaching, and publication. At times, faculty autonomy can violate academic freedom. Academic freedom puts some limits on what faculty members can do.[47]

Academic freedom is a multifaceted reality. Different aspects and questions arise in different historical circumstances. In the United States general agreement exists about how to protect a professor against violations of academic freedom by administrators and governing boards. This context characterized the first understanding of academic freedom in this country and the principles, policies, and procedures of academic freedom in this area are widely known and accepted. Criticism of these policies still surfaces, and debate continues on a number of controverted issues. However, the accepted approaches have been in place for a long time and will be hard to dislodge. In different historical contexts different aspects of academic freedom come to the fore. No long-standing policies and protections exist in these other areas. Theoreticians and practitioners try to work out the meaning and practical protections of academic freedom in changing circumstances. In this way, the entire academic community tries to be true to its own tradition in the light of changing times. As happens in many cases, the issues appear much clearer in retrospect after the heat of the battle has cleared. For example, I do not think that many people today would contend that Communist party members should be expelled from or excluded from the academy. Thus discussion and debate continue on the policies and procedures of academic freedom in different contexts as these historical situations come to the fore.

Considerations about the theory of academic freedom still continue. For the purpose of this chapter, giving an overview of academic freedom in United States higher education, a brief description of some of the more significant contemporary debates suffices.

As mentioned earlier, radicals and Marxists have attacked the very concept of academic freedom because of its emphasis on the neutrality of the institution and of the professoriate. Walter Metzger has pointed out that institutional neutrality was the means taken by the framers of the 1915 Declaration and by the subsequent proponents of academic freedom to defend the academic freedom of professors. The neutral university is open to all positions and does not place a corporate seal of approval or disapproval on a particular claim to truth.[48] Radical thinkers question the validity and the very reality of such neutrality. The professor is loyal to her or his own class interests and to the interests of his or her supporters. Professors are functionaries of the dominant capitalist class and keep an unjust system in power. They should truly align themselves with the working class and employ their energies on behalf of the working class.[49] To be sure, such an understanding radically attacks and undermines both American higher education as it exists today and the concept of academic freedom.[50]

However, one can question the total neutrality of the university without calling into question the existence of American higher education or of academic freedom. Institutions of higher education are a part of our society and have a role to play in it. Recall the recent efforts to have institutions withdraw their funds from companies that invest in South Africa. Questions about institutional neutrality will continue to be raised in our society by many who still want to defend academic freedom.

Another theoretical aspect of academic freedom that is in dispute concerns the grounding of academic freedom. The vast majority of commentators agree with the 1915 and 1940 Statements in basing academic freedom in the service provided by faculty and the academy to society at large. According to Fritz Machlup, "It is in the interest of society at large, not just in the interest of the professors, that academic freedom is defended.''[51] Recently a few scholars have proposed a nonconsequentialist argument for academic freedom that rejects the instrumental value of the academic enterprise for the good of the society as the basis for academic freedom. According to T. M. Scanlan, it would be unfair to give the professor the societally useful task of discovering the truth and then not allow the professor to accept the task. Note, however, that such an argument presupposes that the search for truth is a societally useful task.[52] A purely nonconsequentialist argument would have to maintain that the very task of pursuing the truth can be justified without any considerations of its consequences for society. In ethical reasoning, I have argued for a third approach between a deontological and a consequentialist approach. In general, such an approach recognizes the importance of consequences but does not reduce moral considerations only to consequences. From my perspective, the justification of academic freedom based on its service to the good of society at large does not necessarily embrace absolute consequentialism. The vast majority of commentators, without getting into philosophical disputes about method, continue to justify academic freedom because of its contribution to society at large.

A further contemporary discussion concerns the relationship between academic freedom and autonomy. In the context of pressures from outside the academy, autonomy can be an appropriate defense of academic freedom. However, academic freedom is not the same as autonomy. In contemporary judicial rulings, academic freedom is often defined in terms of autonomy. But the autonomy of the college or university to make its own decisions can conflict with the academic freedom of the professor.[53] Also, the autonomy of one faculty member (e.g., one who is not willing to publish one's research) can truly oppose the rights to academic freedom of other persons in the academy.[54] Thus autonomy and academic freedom are not the same things.

In theory and in practice, the legal status of academic freedom is often discussed in the literature. The courts are deciding more and more cases concerning academic freedom. Is academic freedom a constitutional right? What are the relationships between academic freedom and the civil rights of the professoriate? Do the courts accept the professional understanding of academic freedom? A detailed analysis of these questions lies beyond the scope of this chapter and book. The courts appear to understand academic freedom in terms of autonomy, but such an approach clashes with the professional understanding.[55] Further, the extramural utterances of faculty members are today protected civil rights of American citizens. Should we continue to refer to these as academic freedom rights?[56]

This chapter has attempted to present an overview of academic freedom in America. Some debate continues about the very nature of academic freedom. In different historical contexts, different aspects of academic freedom come to the fore and require new approaches and policies. However, within the American academy, the principles and procedures of academic freedom (tenure, judgment by peers, and academic due process) that protect the faculty member from infringements and violations of academic freedom at the hands of trustees and administrators have been almost universally acknowledged and accepted. This aspect of academic freedom is the reality involved in the more specific question of Catholic higher education's acceptance of academic freedom. The remaining chapters of this book will deal with the question of academic freedom in Catholic higher education.

NOTES

1. These statements can be found in American Association of University Professors, *Policy Documents and Reports*, 1984 ed. (Washington, DC: American Association of University Professors, 1984), pp. 3–13.
2. For a description of the history and work of the American Association of University Professors (AAUP), see Louis Joughin, ed., *Academic Freedom and Tenure: A Handbook of the American Association of University Professors* (Madison, WI: University of Wisconsin Press, 1967).
3. AAUP, *Policy Documents and Reports*, pp. 21–30.
4. 1958 Statement, in *Policy Documents and Reports*, p. 11.
5. 1940 Statement, in *Policy Documents and Reports*, p. 3.
6. Ibid.
7. Ibid., p. 4.
8. 1958 Statement, in *Policy Documents and Reports*, pp. 10–13.
9. Ibid., p. 11.
10. For the history of academic freedom in the United States, see Richard Hofstadter and Walter P. Metzger, *The Development of Academic Freedom in the United States* (New York: Columbia University Press, 1955). Hofstadter wrote the first part of the history, and Metzger the second. Further references will cite the particular author.

11. Hofstadter, *Development of Academic Freedom*, pp. 3–40. See also H. Wieruszowski, *The Medieval University* (New York: Van Nostrand Reinhold Co., 1966).

12. Metzger, *Development of Academic Freedom*, pp. 278ff.

13. Ibid., pp. 363–366.

14. Ibid., pp. 413–467.

15. Walter P. Metzger, "Profession and Constitution: Two Definitions of Academic Freedom in America," *Texas Law Review* 66 (June 1988): 1269–1271.

16. Steven G. Oswang and Barbara A. Lee, *Faculty Freedoms and Institutional Accountability: Interactions and Conflicts*, ASHE-ERIC Higher Education Report no. 5 (Washington DC: Association for the Study of Higher Education, 1984), pp. 6, 7.

17. Metzger, *Development of Academic Freedom*, pp. 468–480.

18. Ibid., pp. 476–477.

19. Joughin, *Academic Freedom and Tenure*, pp. 155–157.

20. 1915 Declaration of Principles, in Joughin, *Academic Freedom and Tenure*, pp. 155–176.

21. Metzger, *Texas Law Review* 66 (June 1988): 1276–1277.

22. 1915 Declaration of Principles, in Joughin, *Academic Freedom and Tenure*, p. 169.

23. Metzger, *Texas Law Review* 66 (June 1988): 1274–1275.

24. Metzger, *Development of Academic Freedom*, pp. 482–485.

25. Joughin, *Academic Freedom and Tenure*, p. 157.

26. Ibid., pp. 3–9 and throughout the book.

27. AAUP, *Policy Documents and Reports*, pp. x–xii.

28. Joughin, *Academic Freedom and Tenure*, pp. 11–29.

29. Julius G. Getman and Jacqueline W. Mintz, "Foreword: Academic Freedom in a Changing Society," *Texas Law Review* 66 (June 1988): 1248.

30. Ralph F. Fuchs, "Academic Freedom—Its Basic Philosophy, Function, and History," in Joughin, *Academic Freedom and Tenure*, p. 255.

31. E.g., Milton Fisk, "Academic Freedom in Class Society," in Edmund L. Pincoffs, ed., *The Concept of Academic Freedom* (Austin, TX: University of Texas Press, 1975), pp. 5–26.; Bertell Ollman, "Academic Freedom in America Today," in Craig Kaplan and Ellen Schrecker, eds., *Regulating the Intellectuals: Perspectives on Academic Freedom in the 1980s* (New York: Praeger, 1983), pp. 45–59.

32. Sheila Slaughter, "The Danger Zone: Academic Freedom and Civil Liberties," *The Annals of the American Academy of Political and Social Sciences* 448 (March 1980): 46–61.

33. Ellen W. Schrecker, *No Ivory Tower: McCarthyism and the Universities* (New York: Oxford University Press, 1986); Schrecker, "Academic Freedom: The Historical View," in Kaplan and Schrecker, *Regulating the Intellectuals*, pp. 25–43.

34. For a criticism of this umbrella argument see Rolf Sartorius, "Tenure and Academic Freedom," in Pincoffs, *Concept of Academic Freedom*, pp. 144ff.

35. See Sartorius and the responses to his essay in Pincoffs, *Concept of Academic Freedom*, pp. 133–188.

36. For the classical defense of tenure see Clark Byse and Louis Joughin, *Tenure in American Higher Education* (Ithaca, NY: Cornell University Press, 1959).

37. Fritz Machlup, "In Defense of Academic Tenure," in Joughin, *Academic Freedom and Tenure*, pp. 306–338; Graham Hughes, "Tenure and Academic Freedom," and Amelie Oksenberg Rorty, "Some Comments on Sartorius's Paper on Tenure," in Pincoffs, *Concept of Academic Freedom*, pp. 170–183.

38. Schrecker, in Kaplan and Schrecker, *Regulating the Intellectuals*, p. 40.

39. Rorty, in Pincoffs, *Concept of Academic Freedom*, p. 104.

40. Schrecker, in Kaplan and Schrecker, *Regulating the Intellectuals*, p. 40.

41. William Van Alstyne, "The Specific Theory of Academic Freedom and the General Issue of Civil Liberty," in Pincoffs, *Concept of Academic Freedom*, pp. 59–85.

42. AAUP, *Policy Documents and Reports*, pp. 141ff.

43. John A. Scanlan, "Aliens in the Marketplace of Ideas: The Government, the Academy and the McCarran-Walter Act," *Texas Law Review* 66 (June 1988): 1481–1546.

44. Schrecker, *No Ivory Tower*.

45. Sidney Hook, *Heresy, Yes—Conspiracy, No* (New York: John Day Co., 1953).

46. AAUP, *Policy Documents and Reports*, pp. 158–160; Rebecca S. Eisenberg, "Academic Freedom and Academic Values in Sponsored Research," *Texas Law Review* 66 (June 1988): 1363–1404.

47. David M. Rabban, "Does Academic Freedom Limit Faculty Autonomy?" *Texas Law Review* 66 (June 1988): 1405–1430.

48. Metzger, *Texas Law Review* 66 (June 1988): 1280.

49. Fisk, in Pincoffs, *Concept of Academic Freedom*, pp. 5–26.

50. Bertram H. Davis, "Academic Freedom, Academic Neutrality, and the Social System," in Pincoffs, *Concept of Academic Freedom*, pp. 27–36.

51. Machlup, in Joughin, *Academic Freedom and Tenure*, p. 181.

52. T. M. Scanlon, "Academic Freedom and the Control of Research," in Pincoffs, *Concept of Academic Freedom*, pp. 237–254.

53. Metzger, *Texas Law Review* 66 (June 1988): 1310.

54. Rabban, *Texas Law Review* 66 (June 1988): 1405–1430.

55. Metzger, *Texas Law Review* 66 (June 1988): 1285–1319.

56. Van Alstyne, in Pincoffs, *Concept of Academic Freedom*, pp. 59–85.

2. Catholic Attitudes toward Academic Freedom before the Mid-1960s

Before the mid-1960s, Catholic higher education and its leaders in the United States were strongly opposed to the concept of academic freedom. Catholic educators either objected to the very notion of academic freedom as found in non-Catholic institutions or emphasized the "true concept of academic freedom" existing in Catholic colleges and universities as distinguished from the absolute or liberalistic academic freedom existing elsewhere. This chapter will discuss Catholic attitudes toward academic freedom by considering the general context of Catholic higher education, the various approaches to academic freedom in the sixty-year period from 1900 to 1960, and the reasons proposed for Catholic opposition to academic freedom.

Catholic Higher Education in General

Perhaps the one concern that Catholic colleges and universities have always shared with other American institutions of higher learning is the problem of determining exactly when the institutions were founded. Charters had to be issued, land had to be acquired, plans had to be made and approved, and finally students had to be admitted. Some Georgetown University chroniclers claim 1789 as the founding date of that institution, for that was when the land was acquired. Others, perhaps with more reason, claim 1786, because in that year John Carroll and his closest associates developed their plan for an academy and a college. From 1786 to 1849, forty-two Catholic colleges were founded, but only twelve of them have survived. One hundred fifty-two Catholic colleges for men started between 1850 and 1900, while another seventy-two began between 1900 and 1955.[1]

26

The first Catholic women's college was Notre Dame of Maryland, founded in 1896. Eighteen other Catholic colleges for women began before 1905, and by 1955 one hundred sixteen were operating.[2] However, the early men's colleges were a far cry from our contemporary understanding of a college. From their beginnings these colleges contained both secondary and collegiate students with a seven-year curriculum. Only in the early 1920s did the preparatory departments separate totally from the colleges, which then followed the ordinary American four-year pattern.[3]

Graduate school and full university education in the United States began with the founding of Johns Hopkins in 1876. Systematic graduate work at the masters level began in some Catholic institutions in the 1920s, and some Catholic colleges expanded into graduate work through the incorporation of professional schools. A few institutions awarded the Ph.D. degree, but before 1945 the Catholic University of America, which had been founded as a university in 1887, was the only Catholic-sponsored university in the United States.[4] Most American Catholic institutions never really became true universities until after World War II.

Catholic higher education did not really constitute a system as such. The colleges were generally founded and administered by a religious community of men or women. These independent institutions formed in 1899 the Association of Catholic Colleges, which in 1904 merged with representatives of the parochial schools and seminaries to form the Catholic Educational Association. This voluntary association had no real authority over individual institutions, but it served as a forum and clearing house so that some greater standardization began to appear in Catholic higher education.[5] The association, now called the Association of Catholic Colleges and Universities (ACCU), continues to function with a comparatively small office in Washington, DC.

For our purposes the most distinctive characteristics of Catholic higher education before the mid-1960s were its aloofness from and opposition to American higher education in general. Edward J. Power, who has written the only history of Catholic higher education in the United States, points out that during this time Catholic institutions did not look to other American colleges and universities as models.[6] Andrew M. Greeley, who has written more and better than anyone else on the sociological aspects of Catholic higher education in the

United States, entitled his 1969 study on Catholic higher education, which was sponsored by the Carnegie Commission on Higher Education, *From Backwater to Mainstream*.[7] Only in the late 1960s did Catholic institutions enter fully into the life of the American academy. One factor working toward assimilation was the formation and growth of accrediting associations in the twentieth century, but their influence was not significant before the Second World War. For example, one Catholic college in 1933 petitioned the North Central Association of Colleges and Secondary Schools to recognize priestly ordination as equivalent to a Ph.D.[8] As the first half of the twentieth century progressed there were occasional tendencies toward a very limited assimilation of Catholic higher education to other American colleges and universities, but for the most part Catholic higher education held on to its identity as different from and even opposed to American higher education in general.

Why did Catholic universities and colleges adopt such an attitude toward American higher education? A number of factors help to explain their approach.

First, the broader relationship between being Catholic and being American influenced the Catholic attitude toward American higher education. The Catholic church in the United States worked out its identity in terms of the problem of trying to be both Catholic and American. On the one hand, Catholics formed an immigrant church and were suspect in the eyes of many other Americans. In addition, Catholic leadership could not really accept the American notion of religious freedom and the separation of church and state. Many Americans feared that Catholics owed allegiance to a foreign ruler living in Rome. On the other hand, Rome was suspicious that the American Catholic church would become too American and thus lose its Catholic identity and faith. In 1899 Pope Leo XIII condemned the heresy of Americanism. Nevertheless, the mainstream of the hierarchical leadership of the American Catholic church in the nineteenth and early twentieth century opted for the Americanization of the immigrants. According to this approach the American Catholic church had nothing to fear from a wholehearted participation in American culture and experience. There is no doubt that after the Second World War, United States Catholics were culturally, politically, and economically assimilated into the American way of life. But because of many different circumstances, Catholic leaders adopted a different approach to education. An entire Catholic school system was established and supported by Catholics primarily because the public school system was looked upon as Protestant and inimical to the faith of Catholics. Catholic teaching had always insisted that education belonged to the family and to the church rather than to the state; the role of the state was supplementary and subsidiary. Only through a Catholic education could the faith of Catholics be preserved and strengthened. Non-Catholic education at all levels was viewed as harmful for Catholics. Thus the sociological context influenced the negative attitude of Catholic higher education to its American counterpart.

Second, the very aims and goals of Catholic higher education differed sharply from the approach of other American colleges and universities. On the first page of his history, Edward J. Power sets out the primary purpose of all Catholic education: "from the outset, all schools from primary through college grades were preoccupied with preserving tenets of faith and with teaching policies ensuring the allegiance of Catholic people to their Church. A good end could shape its own means."[9] Catholic higher education was shaped to achieve a primarily religious end. The college was intimately joined to the pastoral arm of the church. Intellectual formation was subordinated to the preservation of the faith and moral formation. Such a distinctive purpose made the Catholic college quite different from and even opposed to the non-Catholic college. Many non-Catholic institutions had started out as denominational colleges, but in the twentieth century the colleges became more and more secularized. The Catholic approach strongly opposed such a secularized worldview, which either ignored or actively opposed the religious and faith dimensions of human existence. Throughout the first half of the twentieth century Catholic thought frequently and strongly opposed secularism in all its forms, including its educational aspect.[10]

The Catholic purposes and goals of higher education, together with the neoscholastic philosophy that Pope Leo XIII endorsed in 1879 as *the* Catholic philosophy, developed an ideology and corresponding curriculum for Catholic higher education that clashed strongly with the educational philosophy of the mainstream of American higher education. Philip Gleason, professor of history at the University of Notre Dame, who has written much on the history of

Catholic culture and education, aptly sums up this Catholic thinking and its practical curricular consequences at Jesuit schools.

> To an age whose education was secular, scientific, and technical in spirit, particularized in vision, flexible in approach, vocational in aim, and democratic in social orientation, the Jesuits thus opposed a system that was religious, literary, and humanistic in spirit, synthetic in vision, rigid in approach, liberal in aim, and elitist in social orientation. There was no place in it for interchangeable parts, electivism or vocationalism. These were simply the educational heresies that sprang from the radical defect, the loss of a unified view of reality.[11]

The religious order of the Jesuits was the leading teaching order in the United States, and they continued to structure their educational curriculum on the basis of the *Ratio Studiorum* identified with the order from its inception. The Catholic colleges thus insisted on a classical liberal arts curriculum, which handed down traditional wisdom to a new generation.

Third, the structure and organization of Catholic higher education before the Second World War strongly influenced its distinctiveness. Most Catholic colleges and universities were run by religious communities of men or women for whom the educational apostolate formed a significant part of their religious ministry and service. The faith and the moral formation of the students committed by their parents to the care of the religious community were primary concerns. The administration and most of the professors were members of the sponsoring religious community. The academic enterprise was thus subordinated to the religious purpose. The educational development and growth of the faculty received little or no consideration. Research and publication were not important and were not rewarded. Catholic institutions badly lagged behind American higher education in general with respect to the professional status of the college or university professor.

In 1942 Wilfred M. Mallon, S.J., did a study on faculty rank and tenure comparing the status of faculty members in Catholic institutions with those in non-Catholic institutions. This study documents the lack of educational professionalization in Catholic institutions when compared not just to the elite but to all non-Catholic colleges and universities. Forty-four percent of the Catholic institutions gave all faculty one year contracts while only ten percent of the non-Catholic institutions did so. Thirty-four percent of Catholic institutions, compared to ten percent of non-Catholic institutions, had no definite faculty rank policies. Whereas only eight percent of the non-Catholic institutions had no definite tenure for faculty, sixty-five percent of Catholic institutions did not grant tenure to their faculty.[12]

The heavy and significant role of religious communities in the administration and faculty contributed to the lack of academic professionalization and marginalized the voice and role of the institution's lay faculty. A constant refrain in the literature in the 1940s and 1950s concerns the role or lack of it given to lay faculty in Catholic institutions. In 1951 a lay professor wrote an article in the Jesuit weekly *America* on the plight of the lay professor who was overworked, underpaid, and without any real say in running the institution. The subject matter was so sensitive that the author used a pseudonym but was described as having had twelve years of experience teaching in Catholic institutions of higher learning.[13] These and other interconnected factors explain why Catholic education was aloof from and even hostile to American higher education.

A few illustrations will suffice to show the aloofness and suspicion that Catholic higher education exhibited toward non-Catholic American colleges and universities. Catholic aloofness accounts for the small number of faculty from Catholic institutions who belonged to the American Association of University Professors (AAUP), the professional association of university and college professors. In a 1956 article a Catholic priest and professor who was the head of a local AAUP chapter at his institution urged his fellow professors in Catholic colleges and universities to a fuller and more active participation in the association. In 1940 only three hundred of the fifteen thousand members of AAUP came from Catholic institutions.[14] Ewald B. Nyquist, a distinguished non-Catholic educator and administrator, refers in an introduction to a book on Catholic higher education written in 1963 to the diffidence of Catholic educators in inviting their non-Catholic brethren into their halls of learning and their reluctance to participate in regional and national educational activities open to all. However, Nyquist also recognizes a tendency on the part of those "separated brethren" to dismiss Catholic higher education as monolithic and nonintellectual.[15]

Not only suspicion and aloofness but also hostility and opposition marked the Catholic relationship to the higher education community in the United States. Catholics were frequently reminded by church leaders of the obligation to send their children to Catholic colleges and universities. Non-Catholic institutions were looked upon as a threat to the Catholic faith of their students.[16] Some religious orders specializing in college and university teaching strongly opposed the existence of Newman clubs or college campus ministry on non-Catholic campuses.[17] As the century progressed, such opposition to Catholic ministry on secular and non-Catholic campuses became less common and frequent, but clashes between Catholic and secular education still continued to erupt.

Perhaps the most publicized episode in the late 1950s took place at Princeton University. Father Thomas Halton, O.P., the Catholic chaplain at Princeton, complained strongly about the atheism and secularism that were being taught at Princeton; in particular, he singled out professors Walter T. Stace and George W. Elderkin. Father Halton was also upset about Joseph Fletcher's book on medical ethics, which Princeton University Press had published and which Professor Paul Ramsey in the religion department used in class and praised. The university took action against Halton and denied him any university standing or recognition. The distinguished Catholic Thomist Jacques Maritain, then at Princeton, firmly sided with the administration. Halton had earlier turned down Maritain's request to give two lectures under the auspices of the Catholic Newman Center. Halton received strong support in the Catholic press.[18]

Catholic educators before 1950 often pointed out the superiority of Catholic higher education and expressed strong opposition to American non-Catholic colleges and universities. In 1938, in a rather extreme example, George Bull, S.J., the dean of the graduate school at Fordham University, strongly opposed the assumption of American higher education that the function of graduate school is research; any Catholic institution that accepts research as the primary objective is basically anti-Catholic in culture, he thought. The differences over what a graduate school should be stem from a fundamental clash between Catholic culture and the culture of the world around us. Bull believed there is a Catholic way of doing everything—including graduate education. The sense of totality and the sense of tradition distinguish the Catholic approach. God is the perfect truth which is absolute, eternal, and, above all, satisfying for the human mind. There are no further realities to explain, no more boundaries of knowledge to broaden. Not only in revelation but also in reason the ultimate truths have been revealed. Contemplation and not research constitutes the intellectual activity that Catholics most cherish. Education involves a deeper and deeper penetration into the velvety manifold of reality as Catholics already possess it. Modern American education wants to discover more and more facts, but such a frantic search only underscores the disintegration and dehumanization of such an approach. Philosophers today know facts, but they do not philosophize.[19] Some Catholic educators sharply disagreed with Bull,[20] but the Fordham dean was merely applying the prevailing Catholic worldview and self-understanding, albeit in a rather rigid and inflexible manner.

Father Hunter Guthrie, S.J., in his inaugural address as the thirty-fifth president of Georgetown University in the spring of 1949, also illustrates the firm Catholic opposition to American secular higher education.[21] The arrogant tone of the speech, on an occasion when representatives from many secular and non-Catholic institutions were present, only heightens the hostility of the remarks. The newly inaugurated president of Georgetown paints a very negative picture of human beings at the midway point of the twentieth century. The contemporary human being is a finer piece of machinery, but much less a person that his horse-and-buggy prototype. Humanity is floundering today because it has lost its ultimate orientations. The blame falls on the contemporary American university, which has persuaded modern humanity to live without God and convinced us that all design, purpose, and meaning "are to be found in the squirrel cage of his [sic] own Ego." In this land of the free many schools by policy, others by law, are not permitted to disclose all aspects of reality. Without revelation we cannot know what is important and cannot attain certain knowledge. Opinion and not truth becomes the final product of American university education. Academic freedom is really license run wild, and all different and contradictory voices are heard. But truth is one, simple, and integral. All these contradictory opinions are so much philosophical balderdash for one who has seen the promised land of total reality.

The tone of Guthrie's address is antiintellectual, and the rhetoric is biting. A charwoman of the thirteenth century knew more about the meaning of life than Plato. "The lowliest child who has completed his penny catechism knows more about the full meaning of this. . . universe than the assembled faculty of some of our universities." The child knows the first or ultimate causes of things; the faculty has a confused and at best inadequate grasp of secondary causes. Without revelation, many of our universities "resort to a fatuous liberalism, which ranges all the way from polite skepticism to the shoddy 'science' of statistics." Today the human person must make a decision, but the "university often does little more than prepare him to side-step it—gracefully. The Kremlin could ask for nothing more." This address abounds in cold war, antiliberal rhetoric. Father Guthrie's antidote to the problem of modern humanity that the secular university brought on emphasizes the religious, moral, and intellectual virtues by which human beings can achieve their full moral stature within the limits of their nature. Such an approach is totally opposed to the monism of unregenerated but self-sufficient nature that characterizes the American non-Catholic university scene.

Nowadays, a Catholic educator can only be embarrassed at reading such an address. Even some of Hunter Guthrie's contemporaries would have disagreed with his all-or-nothing approach and his incendiary rhetoric. But there was nothing but agreement at Georgetown on that spring day in 1949 when Guthrie became the university's president. The students' short greeting, given by the president of the Yard, was obviously written with some outside help; he maintained that the students of Georgetown are taught "to strive for that *eloquentia perfecta* which is described in that priceless document, the *Ratio Studiorum.*" In this materialistic age the students of Georgetown appreciate "the lasting value of life that is at once impregnated with all that is best in classical humanism and all the glories of the Catholic tradition."[22]

These preceding illustrations are extreme and defensive, but all Catholic educators saw their colleges and universities as different from and even opposed to the mainstream of American higher education at the time. This section has attempted to explain the reasons for such a self-understanding on the part of Catholic higher education.

Academic Freedom in Catholic Institutions of Higher Learning

In the period before the 1960s there was unanimous agreement among Catholic and non-Catholic educators alike: Catholic institutions of higher learning did not and could not accept the principles of academic freedom as found at non-Catholic American colleges and universities. Such a position is not surprising in the light of the general context developed in the preceding section.

In 1936 the National Catholic Educational Association expounded its position on academic freedom. Academic freedom is freedom to teach what is true and to receive instruction in what is true; it is not academic license. Human beings are social and called to live together in society, and there are truths that underlie the proper and just association of human beings in human communities. To these truths we have a sacred obligation. When it comes to defining what is true, Catholic education seeks the guidance of the supernatural revelation that has come to us from God through Jesus Christ and is interpreted by the church. In addition, things cannot be taught in the name of academic freedom that violate the natural moral law.[23]

Before 1960 I have found no Catholic educator or author who proposed publicly that Catholic colleges and universities should accept the general American understanding of academic freedom. Non-Catholic higher education also unanimously recognized that Catholic institutions of higher learning could not and did not have academic freedom. Some merely quoted the Shavian dictum that a Catholic university is a contradition in terms.

The 1915 AAUP Declaration of Principles points out the historical reality that in the early period of university development in America the chief opposition to academic freedom was ecclesiastical.[24] The statement does not mention that the opposition came primarily from the Protestant denominations rather than from the Roman Catholic church. The small immigrant Catholic church had neither the influence on American educational institutions nor the concern about what was going on in American higher education outside its own denomination.

The 1915 Declaration of Principles recognizes the existence of proprietary schools or colleges founded for the purpose of propagandizing specific doctrines. One example is the religious or denominational college that is an instrument of propaganda in the interest of the religious faith professed by the church or denomination that runs the college. Such denominational institutions at least cannot accept the principles of freedom of inquiry in religious matters. The committee makes no judgment about the desirability of having such institutions, but they should not be permitted to sail under false colors. However, such institutions are becoming more rare; there are still some denominational colleges and universities, but more and more they have the same freedom as our other untrammeled institutions of learning and are differentiated only by their particular historical antecedents and traditions.[25] As far as the 1915 Declaration is concerned, Catholic institutions are not mentioned as such, but they would certainly lack academic freedom.

In 1925 the American Council on Education called a conference of representatives of its constitutive members, including the AAUP, to formulate a short statement of principles on academic freedom and tenure. The AAUP endorsed the statement in 1929, but it was not widely received because it was conceived as a rigid norm to be accepted by institutions verbatim. However, the 1925 Conference Statement does admit and accept limitations upon the academic freedom of professors "in the case of institutions of a denominational or partisan character" provided "specific stipulations in advance, fully understood and accepted by both parties, limit the scope and character of instruction."[26] The 1925 Conference Statement thus makes room for religious and denominational colleges but recognizes that they have a restricted academic freedom. Notice the difference from the 1915 Declaration: denominational institutions are now accepted as part of the academy. The 1925 statement comes from national and voluntary associations that apparently did not want to ostracize a large number of institutions from the American academy.

The Association of American Colleges and the AAUP drew up what is called the 1940 Statement of Principles on Academic Freedom and Tenure. The Statement proposed a guideline that has generally been accepted throughout the academy and has been endorsed by many professional academic associations. This 1940 document again contains an exception clause for religious institutions: "limitations of academic freedom because of religious or other aims of the institution should be clearly stated in writing at the time of the appointment."[27] Since the 1940 Statement recognized exceptions for religious colleges and proposed no philosophical basis for academic freedom but only procedural norms and safeguards, one might expect that Catholic institutions and commentators would be willing to accept such a statement. In the midst of the general climate of aloofness and opposition, however, Catholic institutions and educators were not willing to endorse it.

As already mentioned, participation of professors at Catholic institutions in the AAUP was comparatively meager. No Catholic professional academic association endorsed the 1940 Statement before 1966! In that year the American Catholic Historical Association and the American Catholic Philosophical Association endorsed it, and many other Catholic associations publicly subscribed to it later.[28]

One of the chief means used by the AAUP to promote and defend academic freedom involves the investigation and censuring of institutions that violate the principles and procedures of academic freedom. Between 1930 and 1967 sixty-two institutions were censured, but only three were Catholic. Only one Catholic institution— St. Louis University—was censured before 1960. St. Louis University was actually censured twice—in 1939 and 1956—and both times the problem arose in the medical school. In the period from 1917 to 1966, the AAUP investigated, reported on, but did not censure fifty-seven other institutions, none of them Catholic.[29]

In 1939 St. Louis University did have a local AAUP chapter. The local chapter specifically stated that its commitment to the Catholic faith was always paramount, and if there were to be a conflict, such a faith commitment would take precedence over anything else. The investigating committee of the AAUP pointed out that an individual local chapter cannot modify the Association's principles. The particular case concerned Dr. Moyer S. Fleisher, a professor of bacteriology in the school of medicine since 1915, who was a sponsor for a lecture held under the auspices of a Spanish loyalist group and given by a man who turned out to be a defrocked priest. Some Catholics in the community objected to Fleisher's sponsorship, since he had been informed that the speaker was a defrocked priest. Under pressure from the local archbishop, the president of St. Louis dismissed Professor Fleisher.[30] The second case, in 1956, concerned Dr. Philip A. Tumulty, who was dismissed from the medical school by the president without a hearing because his administration had caused problems, especially with the religious sisters who ran the hospital.[31] Both censures were later removed;[32] significantly, both occurred in the medical school, which traditionally is somewhat distant from the rest of the university, and at St. Louis

University the majority of the faculty in the medical school was not Catholic.

Thus it is evident that Catholic professors did not appeal to the AAUP to adjudicate any questions of academic freedom. John D. Donovan, who intensively studied Catholic college and university professors in 1960, concluded that real problems of academic freedom did not come up in Catholic institutions because the faculty were generally safe and orthodox in their theological and philosophical orientation.[33] Catholic higher education either lived in its own world where academic freedom was not a problem, or else openly opposed the principles of academic freedom.

Although the AAUP explicitly made room for religious colleges and universities, Catholic institutions before 1960 stayed aloof from the principles and practices of this organization. A few Catholic authors actually discussed the AAUP principles, but apparently no Catholic author was willing to accept the AAUP principles even with the limitations clause. Wilfred Mallon's 1942 study strongly supports the need for Catholic institutions to provide better care and services for their faculty. He urges Catholic institutions to accept faculty rank and tenure processes, but he has problems with the AAUP's understanding of academic freedom. In reality Catholics have even less undue restraint than other institutions since they are bound only by objective truth and not by any political or economic ties. Academic freedom properly understood is no problem at all for the intelligent Catholic and the intelligently administered Catholic college. Can Catholic colleges conscientiously accept the principles proposed by the Association of American Colleges and the American Association of University Professors in the 1940 Statement? Mallon believes they cannot and proposes four reasons. First, there is no indication that the teacher is free to teach the truth; the emphasis on truth is missing in the 1940 Statement. Second, for Mallon, the Catholic has to recognize that revelation, church dogma, and natural law constitute the truth and guide all else. Third, the limitations for religious aims in the Statement apply only to what is taught and not to the personal lives of the faculty members, while Catholic faculty members must bear witness in their lives to their faith commitment. Finally, the judge of violations of Catholic doctrine, moral principles, or the essential properties of the Catholic life cannot be the faculty but the authorized ecclesiastical superior. Mallon's 1942 article is sober, supportive of a creative professionalization in Catholic higher education, and devoid of any rhetorical condemnations of academic freedom; he concludes nevertheless that Catholic colleges in conscience cannot accept the 1940 Statement.[34]

In a 1958 doctoral dissertation at the Catholic University of America, "A Critical Study of North American Views on Academic Freedom," Aldo Tos also criticizes the 1940 Statement: "The Statement as a whole breathes that spirit of untrammeled inquiry, which in turn is based on the 'search for the truth' rather than on the acknowledgement of the fact that the truth can be had."[35] The 1940 Statement declared that institutions of higher learning exist for the common good which depends on the free search for truth and its free expression. However, the common good suffers when each individual relying on her or his own judgment seeks to interpret the meaning of free expression. The first principle in the Statement maintains that the teacher is entitled to full freedom, which obviously means unlimited freedom. But there are limits to freedom, especially for the teacher doing research. It is never acceptable to act immorally no matter what the purpose of the experiment or the good that might accrue to society or an individual. Recall the revulsion of humankind to the Nazi experiments. The second principle of the 1940 Statement is concerned with the function of the teacher in the classroom, but here again the implied emphasis is on unlimited freedom, since the only caveat mentioned is the need for the teacher to avoid controversial issues which have no relation to the subject matter.

How does Tos respond to the 1940 Statement's suggestion that "limitations of academic freedom because of religious or other aims" can be accepted if they are clearly spelled out in writing at the time of the contract? Tos in no way sees acceptance of a limitation clause as a bridge between the AAUP's understanding and the Catholic approach. Religious aims are not restrictive and limiting elements on the freedom of teaching. Only an unlimited freedom sees religion as a hindrance. The Catholic institution claims to teach the sole truth in matters of religion. In keeping with his basic thesis, Tos again insists that academic freedom is limited by the truth.[36]

There were a few reactions more open to the 1940 Statement, but even these recognized differences between the Catholic understanding of academic freedom and the concept of academic freedom proposed by the AAUP. Writing in *America* in 1940, Ruth Byrns of Fordham University defended a Catholic understanding of academic freedom but wanted Catholic institutions to follow AAUP guidelines and spell out their limitations in writing.[37] In 1956 Henry Browne urged professors from Catholic institutions to become involved in the AAUP, and he decried the ignorance and lack of contact between Catholic and non-Catholic educators. Too often Catholics are simply supposed to have no interest in academic freedom or to consider it a "sacred fetish" of "academic libertarians." But he admits that Catholics will have to disagree with some aspects of academic freedom or else counteract in practice some things they oppose in theory.[38]

The AAC and the AAUP in their 1940 Statement, like most national and voluntary associations, were willing to acknowledge and even to accept religious institutions that put some limits on academic freedom, but Catholic institutions either remained totally aloof from the AAUP and its Statement or were openly opposed. Academic freedom was not a problem or even a question at Catholic institutions, and Catholic educators disagreed, often quite vehemently, with the academic freedom found at non-Catholic institutions. Some professors from Catholic institutions joined the AAUP and had local chapters at Catholic institutions, but Catholic involvement was comparatively small.

The major theoreticians of academic freedom in the 1950s saw Catholics as opposed to academic freedom and Catholic institutions as lacking academic freedom. The discussions of the 1950s were very much colored by the controversy over Communists teaching in colleges and universities. The effort by state legislatures, government investigating committees, and others to remove Communists from their teaching posts caused a great stir. The role of Communists in higher education was the primary issue of academic freedom in the 1950s and dominated the theoretical discussions.

Sidney Hook addressed academic freedom and the role of teachers who were members of the Communist party in his 1953 book, *Heresy, Yes—Conspiracy, No.* Hook defines himself as a liberal who believes in the free flow of ideas. The free expression and circulation of ideas may be checked only when their likely effects constitute a clear and present danger to public peace or the security of the country. Competition in the free market of ideas must be honestly and openly conducted. A free society, and above all the academy, must defend the right to profess publicly a heresy of any character. A conspiracy is a secret or underground movement that attempts to achieve its end by playing outside the rules of the game of open competition; the Communist party is a conspiracy that uses secret means to accomplish its end, the destruction of liberal society. The party and its members are conspiratorial, and party members as part of the conspiracy have no place in a liberal society or the academy.[39]

In the light of such an approach, one is not surprised by Hook's statement that there is no academic freedom in Catholic colleges because church dogma is decisive. The Catholic institution cannot protect the rights of heretics, at least not in the domain of religion. Hook also brings up another aspect of the question which was frequently debated at the time: if Communist party members cannot be admitted in the academy, the ban should also include members of many other organizations such as the Catholic church. Hook, however, denies the parallel. Catholics in non-Catholic institutions are expected to fulfill honorably their academic duties and not to take advantage of their positions in order to proselytize for the church. There has never been any evidence of the operation at non-Catholic universities of Catholic cells that require following a party line in the arts and sciences under the pain of excommunication.[40]

Robert M. MacIver, director of the American Academic Freedom Project of Columbia University, distinguishes in his *Academic Freedom in Our Time* (1955) three established lines of attack on academic freedom—the economic line, the religious line, and the line of social tradition. He uses Hunter Guthrie's attack on academic freedom to illustrate the religious line of attack. MacIver does not use an empiricist philosophy to discredit the very existence of religious truth, but he insists on the pluralism of religions and the existence of nonreligious people in our society. Whose authority would be enforced by society and by whom? The church and the university have two unique and distinct missions, and the church cannot dictate to the university. To make the university the center of the propagation of any creed or system of values that a particular church proposes destroys the very nature of the university as a center for the free pursuit of knowledge wherever it may lead.[41]

MacIver devotes a special appendix (A) to "Academic Freedom in the Denominational University."[42] Denominational institutions by their nature restrict the academic freedom of their members, but do so in different ways. The major factors determining the limits on academic freedom come from the degree to which the particular faith makes binding pronouncements about the moral and social relationships of human beings and about other areas of history and science.

MacIver would be willing to recognize that denominational institutions have a double function—the one common to all universities of higher learning, and the other particular to themselves (which for them is paramount). The Columbia University professor strenuously objects, however, to the contention by some Catholics that Catholic institutions have a greater intellectual freedom than nondenominational institutions because they place no restrictions on truth but are able to point out errors for what they are. No one who does not adhere to that particular aspect of Catholic faith can accept such claims; each and every religious body could make the same assertion about conflicting claims to truth. MacIver recognizes that a scholar can and must have value commitments and can also have a personal faith commitment which in no way constitutes a limit on free academic inquiry. The question in denominational colleges results, rather, from the institution's commitment. Thus like other leading philosophers of academic freedom in the 1950s, MacIver recognized that academic freedom does not and apparently cannot fully exist in Catholic institutions of higher learning.

How did the Catholic community view academic freedom in the first six decades of the twentieth century? No Catholic thinker called for full academic freedom in Catholic colleges and universities, and Catholics generally and often vehemently disagreed with the very concept of academic freedom as it was found in the broader American higher academic community. Catholic periodicals and journals were coming out of a context of Catholic commitment which at that time was strongly supportive of Catholic higher education and aloof from or even hostile to non-Catholic higher education. However, there were differences of approaches within the Catholic community and different responses to historical events in this period. The following section will analyze the Catholic approaches to academic freedom by describing three general types of approaches: strong opposition based on a hostility to non-Catholic higher education; opposition to academic freedom based on philosophical grounds; and opposition to full academic freedom in Catholic circles but appreciation for some aspects of academic freedom itself. As might be expected, the position of modified opposition emerged later than the others. These three models or types are found in reality, but often in combination with different models and types.

Strong opposition to academic freedom based on a hostility to non-Catholic higher education often came from Catholic educators themselves. Such people were obviously defensive about their own institutions and firmly believed in the obligation of Catholics to send their children to Catholic colleges and universities. Hunter Guthrie's inauguration address as president of Georgetown in 1949 has already been cited as an example of Catholic approaches to American non-Catholic higher education. In the same speech Guthrie excoriates academic freedom. The modern university believes that the human being's supreme prerogative as a citizen of a democracy is the right to do anything in accord with one's own opinion. Liberty is today's major plague and is undistinguished from license. Guthrie describes academic freedom as a ''protean pulpit whereon may mount atheist and Catholic, fellow traveler and capitalist, agnostic, liberal, dogmatist, and even an occasional teacher.'' The untrained nostril of the student is expected to ''unfailingly detect the sweet odor of truth from this miasma of conflicting opinions'' proposed by instructors. Such a position with all the good faith, tolerance, and civility in the world, is impossible. Contradictory parts can never add up to a whole, for truth is one, simple, and integral. Such a contradictory approach is ''highballing toward self-destruction.''[43]

Father Guthrie's address at Georgetown's 1950 commencment was entitled ''The Sacred Fetish of Academic Freedom.'' ''Freedom must be limited by belief in God, by faith in the omnipotence of truth, and the beneficence of justice. Freedom springs from truth but still truth is rarely freedom's offspring.'' Academic freedom is ''the soft underbelly of our American way of life and the sooner it is armour plated by some sensible limitations, the sooner will the future of this nation be secured from fatal consequences.''[44]

As might be expected, such rhetorical denunciations of academic freedom are often found in addresses of Catholic educators especially when talking to their own. Two presidential addresses to the College and University Department of the National Catholic Educational Association in the late 1930s illustrate this hostile rhetoric. Father Aloysius J. Hogan's presidential address of 1937 maintained that the real enemies of human liberty are found in the secular colleges. A false philosophy that denies free choice has flourished for years on our secular college and university campuses. Catholic education is the only defense of true human liberty. For this reason Catholics should not attend non-Catholic institutions of higher learning.[45] A year later Francis L. Meade, C.M., maintained that Catholic education glories that its freedom is guided by faith, protected by truth, and limited by fact. Academic freedom is wrong because it rests on the libertarian assumption that freedom should be unfettered and absolute. Such absolute freedom is license. One university chancellor traveled over the country defending academic freedom while back home his education, psychology, and philosophy schools and departments taught that human beings have no freedom.[46]

A second type of approach found in the literature opposes academic freedom on philosophical grounds but avoids the rhetorical hostility of the first approach. As might be expected, the philosophers' rejection of academic freedom is less defensive and rhetorical than the Catholic educators'. Andrew C. Smith, S.J., who was dean of the Jesuit College at Spring Hill in Alabama, begins his 1941 article on academic freedom in a philosophical journal by calling attention to the need for a quiet and more balanced approach to academic freedom in the light of recent Catholic rhetoric. He emphasizes the limits on freedom in teaching and defends an epistemology according to which truth is one and unchangeable in opposition to the narrow positivism, vague relativism, and distorted subjectivism that were so prevalent then. The teacher is also limited by the fact that the profession makes him or her an agent of society. Even this explicitly scholarly and philosophical analysis, however, cannot avoid some incendiary rhetoric: the "heritage of the race in religion and organized society is something too precious to be bartered away for the dubious blessing of permitting every crackpot teacher to have his say *ad libitum*."[47]

Bernard Mullahy's 1942 article in *The Proceedings of the American Catholic Philosophical Association* is moderate in its reasoning and in its tone, and any polemical and inflammatory rhetoric is eschewed. Mullahy reasonably and calmly develops his position and calls for some limits on academic freedom, while he opposes the liberalistic notion of unlimited freedom. Mullahy, who taught at the University of Notre Dame, ended his article by insisting that teachers and students must be granted a large measure of liberty if the schools in a democratic society are to achieve their essential purposes. Such liberty will constitute a danger, but this is the splendid risk involved in every great human undertaking. Opposed to the concept of academic freedom found in American secular education, Mullahy's position is nevertheless very moderate and recognizes some important roles for freedom in education.[48]

The third type or model of approach to academic freedom is more conciliatory. While recognizing the necessary limits on academic freedom in Catholic institutions, this approach acknowledges the important contributions of academic freedom in non-Catholic institutions and also calls for a more vital intellectual discussion in Catholic institutions. The best example of this more dialogic and conciliatory model is Journet Kahn's 1956 article in the *Proceedings of the American Catholic Philosophical Association*. The Catholic philosopher Kahn, from the University of Notre Dame, is responding from a Thomistic perspective and implicitly from a liberal political outlook to the contemporary reality that academic freedom is threatened on secular campuses and that many champions of academic freedom see no academic freedom whatsoever on the Catholic campus. In response to the threats to academic freedom on the secular campus, Kahn strongly disagrees with Sidney Hook about the role of Communist party members in higher education. Each case should be judged on its own merits and not by the government or outside authorities; no absolute prohibition should keep Communist party members away from the academy. Kahn faulted Hook for arguing from the universal to the particular and thereby conceiving ethics as involving no more than the subalternation of particulars to the universal. (There is something ironic about a Thomist accusing an American liberal of a deductive methodology!) According to Kahn, human beings are not always consistent; nor is our political commitment so total that it dictates all that we do. Recent investigations and firings of Communists have created a very bad climate for the search for the truth.

Kahn also objects to Hook's and MacIver's claim that there is no academic freedom on Catholic campuses. MacIver had proposed as an example that no Catholic could propose the use of artificial contraception as a solution to the population problem. Kahn counters that MacIver cannot propose killing old people as a solution to the same problem. Kahn does recognize the role of revelation and church teaching in Catholic institutions, but their intellectual life must become much more vital. Contemporary Catholic education needs to foster more disputations such as those that took place in the Middle Ages. Although the liberating power of certitude is the foundation for academic freedom, Catholic institutions must be willing to tolerate some error. There is a heritage of error because we can and do learn from error.[49]

Before 1960 no Catholic proposed that Catholic institutions accept full academic freedom, and most Catholics energetically opposed the very concept of academic freedom. However, these three types of approaches illustrate significant strands of differences within the Catholic community. Historical circumstances and personal perspectives influence these differences. The first significant historical dimension is the factor of time. It is primarily toward the end of the period in the 1950s that the more conciliatory and moderate approaches begin to appear. Looking back from our perspective, it is now easy to see that these developments prepared the way for the very substantial change that ultimately took place in the mid-1960s.

A second very significant historical factor that affected approaches to academic freedom was the role of Communists in higher education. The question arose in the 1930s but reached its height in the 1950s. The threats of the Communist menace and the government investigating committees left their scars on higher education. Communist party members and people who pled the fifth amendment before government investigating committees (often because they refused to name other people) were faced with the loss of their teaching positions. Even some former party members or radical non-Communists faced possible dismissal. The AAUP at this crucial time, especially under the influence of its general secretary Ralph Himstead, failed to take any concrete action against the universities that violated academic freedom by dismissing faculty members. Only in the spring of 1956 were some colleges and universities censured by the AAUP for irregular or unfair dismissals. The McCarthy era created a climate of insecurity and fear in the American academy. Few were the voices who stood up to say that membership in the Communist party should not be a reason for dismissal from a teaching position at an institution of higher learning. The Communist scare, the tactics of McCarthyism, and the theoretical question of Communists in higher education raised serious questions and divisions in the American academy.[50]

As one would readily suspect, no professed Communists or former Communists taught on Catholic campuses; Catholic faculties were safe in every respect. Catholics reacted in different ways to the Communist scare and the investigating committees. In general, they were staunch anti-Communists and opposed to Communists teaching in the schools, but many Catholics objected to McCarthy's tactics.[51] Catholics reacted in two different ways to the Communist presence in higher education.

The more common approach, one frequently taken in the editorials and articles of the weekly Jesuit magazine *America*, held that members of the Communist party should not be allowed to teach in American higher education and that Communists' potential impact proved the dangers of unlimited academic freedom. As early as 1948 an *America* editorial maintained that an institution should be able to take measures to ensure that the political opinions identified with it would be American. Does the college itself not have some corporate academic freedom?[52] This approach remained the editorial position of *America* throughout the decade. In addition, the editorials in *America* raised the question, in the light of the Communist issue, why so few American educators realize that much of what is taught in American colleges, including our law schools, is more dangerous to American liberties than the encouragement of the violent overthrow of the government. Thus, the *America* editorials used the popular concept that Communists should not be allowed to teach in American institutions of higher learning to argue for a more limited concept of academic freedom. Communism is not the only position that should not be taught in American colleges.[53] Articles and editorials in *America* that dealt with issues of academic freedom in the 1930s and early 1940s had taken the same approach.[54]

Robert C. Hartnett, S.J., in two articles in *America* from the spring of 1953 used the presence of Communists in American higher education to attack very vehemently the unfettered concept of academic freedom that was operative in colleges and universities. These educators never did anything on their own to rid their campuses of Communism. Hartnett condemns with invective bite so-called searchers for truth who traipsed to Washington only to wrap themselves in the Constitutional protection of the fifth amendment. All that

American higher education stands for is a policy of noninterference or complete laissez-faire in the search for what its leaders call "truth." The only type of truth admitted by American colleges is scientific truth. The experimental sciences cannot determine if the self-evident truths of the Declaration of Independence are true or not. The American university has no way of knowing if Marxism is true or not. Hartnett agrees with a then recent Association of American Universities (AAU) report that Communist party members cannot teach in colleges and universities, but he strongly disagrees with the rationalistic, individualistic, and subjectivistic assumptions that permeate the report. The American concept of academic freedom exists in a philosophical vacuum. Freedom must always be limited by the truth.

According to Hartnett, the American academic profession is committed to no values. Academicians resent the existence of truths held with a certitude that excludes reasonable doubt; pure liberals do not like Catholicism and stand for nothing. Higher education should have taken the leadership in ferreting out Communists from its own campuses, but it did not. Such a failure forfeits intellectual and moral leadership in scandalous proportions.[55]

Catholic educators were happy to see that liberals and even followers of Dewey such as Sidney Hook had to set limits to academic freedom. Roy J. Deferrari, an administrator at the Catholic University of America, maintained as late as 1963 that as a result of Communist infiltration in the schools, Catholic and non-Catholic educators alike now agree on this basic principle of academic freedom: members of the faculty may speak freely on subjects within their field of competency, providing they say nothing contrary to the professed philosophy and theology of the institution and nothing subversive on the political level.[56] Deferrari's assumptions are inaccurate, but it indicates how Catholic educators used the Communist issue to support their notion of limited academic freedom.

A minority of Catholics viewed the means used to ferret out communists on campus as ultimately creating a climate of fear that would necessarily limit the creative role of the academy. Journet Kahn illustrates this approach; he even opposed the general rule among Catholics that Communist party members should automatically be excluded from the academy.[57] Two Catholic lay persons involved in non-Catholic higher education—George N. Schuster (president of

Hunter College) and Jerome G. Kerwin (a professor at the University of Chicago)—agreed that Communist party members should not teach. Both nevertheless disapproved of the tactics used by government investigating committees and feared that such tactics threatened academic freedom and would ultimately harm the academy's role in American life. Kerwin maintained that the investigating committee itself had become a worthy subject for investigation.[58]

Not only historical factors but also personal perspectives influenced the Catholic community's different approaches to academic freedom. Those involved in Catholic higher education tended to be much more defensive about Catholic higher education and more hostile to academic freedom as found in non-Catholic American schools. On the other hand, Catholics involved in non-Catholic higher education (Schuster and Kerwin, for example) were more supportive of academic freedom, even though they did not call for it to be extended fully on Catholic campuses.

The Jesuits as a community were heavily involved in Catholic higher education, and this explains why the articles in *America* were more hostile to academic freedom than those that appeared in the liberal lay journal *Commonweal*. In 1936, *Commonweal* editorialized against Yale's dismissing Jerome Davis from the divinity school because of his socialist and Marxist tendencies.[59] *Commonweal* also chided Notre Dame for firing Professor Francis E. McMahon in 1943 because of his advanced social positions. (Everyone involved, including the authorities at Notre Dame, admitted that McMahon did not oppose Catholic faith or morals.[60]) Such actions, according to the *Commonweal* editorial, are bad for academic freedom in Catholic universities.

The position of Charles Donahue, S.J., of Fordham University, deserves more intensive study because he is an important transitional figure who wrote more about academic freedom than any other Catholic in the 1950s. He shares many of the negative criticisms of American academic freedom that were traditionally espoused by Catholics. He is, however, more conciliatory towards American higher education, insists that Catholics are and want to be an integral part of the American academic scene, proposes a modified academic freedom for Catholic institutions, and appeals to the American concepts of pluralism and freedom in order to justify the legitimacy of his approach.

Donahue agrees with many Catholics in opposing some theories and educational practices associated with John Dewey, but he also recognizes the educator's contributions. Specifically, Donahue rejects the liberalism, secularism, and reductionism of educational Deweyism. The Fordham professor objects above all to the assertion that Dewey has proposed the one and only truly American way— that whoever disagrees with Dewey cannot be a real lover of liberty, a respecter of science, or a full sharer in the American vision. The real problem comes from the exclusive and sacral approach taken by Dewey and by secularists who assume that whatever is, at least insofar as it is knowable and hence of practical importance to human beings, is entirely contained in the spatiotemporal order. This monistic secularist approach denies the existence of transcendental truth and transcendental value, but many people in our society believe in such realities. In a true sense, secularists must realize that they form a religious body. Unfortunately, the state's use of noncommitment as a strategy to protect the freedom of the sacral has become a metaphysical principle that denies the sacral, the transcendental, and the absolute.[61]

Donahue maintains that absolute academic freedom is a Cartesian chimera that exists—can exist—nowhere. He grants that restrictions on academic freedom exist on Catholic campuses that are not found at noncommitted colleges. Restrictions on human freedom, however, can be justified if they are necessary to assure greater human freedoms.

There is a growing feeling, he thinks, that our university programs are lacking in the theory and science of values. The supreme science of value is theology, the keystone of an academic arch, of a coordinated structure of disciplines in which a rational consideration of moral values will have a part. The freedom to present a rational ordering of human knowledge in the light of theology is an important freedom won by the Catholic college's commitment to religious orthodoxy.

But Catholic colleges can provide an even more important freedom. Donahue contrasts, somewhat simplistically and pejoratively in my opinion, the Catholic personalist view of education with the view of the impersonalists. Impersonalists, like the followers of John Dewey, see truth primarily as a matter of freedom that is found only in the universities; the student brings with him or her nothing that will be of help to the universities. Personalists, whose view Donahue associates with Thomism, give great importance to a lived experience and knowledge available to all people that is distinguished from the more theoretical knowledge of the university. Accordingly, the function of the liberal arts college is to provide a setting where the student, who comes as an already formed person, a religious and ethical being, can obtain the intellectual insights that bring to higher levels of consciousness and vision the implications of her or his own formation: higher education begins with the informed person and not with an abstractly rational animal. The intellectual program and tone appropriate for one person in a pluralistic society are not necessarily appropriate for another. Persons differ; formations differ; and therefore colleges should differ. This is the primary reason for the existence of the Catholic college. Catholic institutions' restrictions on academic freedom assure two important freedoms: the freedom of the student to receive an education suited to his or her own personal formation and needs; the freedom of the scholar to work where her or his totality of experiences will count.[62] Notice how Donahue appeals to the distinctive American ideas of pluralism and freedom to justify a different sort of academic freedom at Catholic institutions of higher learning.

Donahue insists that a proper approach to academic freedom must avoid too individualistic an understanding as well as any over-philosophizing. The academician not only makes a commitment to the general academic life of the university but also to a particular discipline. One belongs to a corporate body of truth seekers within a particular discipline, whether it be English, physics, or biology. Academic freedom consequently is more restricted than free speech in general. The physicist, for example, cannot question the value of physics or disregard the findings of the academy of physicists, but free speech permits ordinary citizens to do both. Thus the academic is limited by a prior commitment to a particular discipline and to the corporate study of that discipline. Most academicians are not conscious of this limiting prior commitment; but it does exist, and it exerts a significant influence.

In any pluralistic society there exist many different disciplines and a variety of philosophies. In the light of this twofold pluralism, philosophizing about academic freedom in a way that proposes a categorical definition that should apply to all different disciplines and philosophies is best avoided. Some suggest that all scholars must follow the scientific method, but it is generally understood that the method applies only to the empirical sciences and not to literary or humanistic studies. Donahue proposes the fundamental question in a practical way that avoids overphilosophizing and recognizes the pluralism of disciplines and the different corporate communities of scholars. Are the various arts and sciences handled by Catholics and Catholic universities in a way that meets the approval of the truth-seeking societies devoted to these arts and sciences? Truth seekers, including theologians and philosophers, should always be able to find an academic home, but theology and philosophy are academic disciplines of a special kind. A scholar in a theology department in a Catholic school has in addition to the prior commitment to the specific discipline another prior commitment: a sacral commitment. Protestant, Jewish, and Catholic theological faculties have a right to exist and such disciplines require this dual sacral and professional commitment. Such a dual commitment based on the very nature of the particular discipline no more violates academic freedom than the physicist's prior commitment to his or her discipline.

Similarly, Donahue insists that philosophy is also a special discipline. Philosophy has traditionally been based on reason alone. In the course of academic development the other sciences were cut off from philosophy, which now deals only with questions of ultimate meaning and ultimate value amid a great deal of pluralism and diversity on these same questions; no one philosophy unites our pluralistic society. However, philosophy as a science resembles theology because it too deals with matters of the highest importance about which great disagreement exists. The principle of dual prior commitment thus also functions for Catholic philosophy departments in Catholic institutions of higher learning. For the Catholic, philosophy as the study of ultimate meaning is Janus-faced. The discipline aims at human wisdom by taking the pieces of knowledge from the other arts and sciences and coordinating them with the data of common sense and common living so that a reasonable understanding of human existence and meaning emerges. But for the Catholic there is not only human wisdom but also revealed wisdom, and the two cannot be incompatible. Catholicism avoids both a secularism that denies the religious aspect of reality and a religious antiintellectualism or fundamentalism that rejects human wisdom and reason. Philosophy in a Catholic institution thus has a dual commitment just as theology does. A pluralistic society must allow for a pluralism of higher education and a pluralist understanding of academic freedom.[63]

Donahue not only developed his own approach to academic freedom, but he also responded to the leading theoreticians of academic freedom in the 1950s. He agrees with Sidney Hook's conclusions that members of the Communist party should not be in the academy because they do not use the methods and means of the academy. Donahue disagrees, however, with much of Hook's liberal theory (illustrated, for example, in his Deweyan fantasy of "Man the Unknowing and Developing Doer"). The liberal wants to discard too much. Donahue is a realistic, not ritualistic, conservative; he is aware of the limits of human intelligence, and he understands the human person as living in history, in society, and in scientific, ethical, artistic, and religious traditions. No fanatic, the realistic conservative believes that principles must always be applied with prudence. Dewey and Hook, too narrow in their approach to reality, reduce all to the hypnotizing values of experimental science and democratic group action. These values are excellent in themselves, but they are insufficient to meet the complex needs of historical and concrete human beings. The religious traditions of our pluralistic society have no place whatsoever in Hook's educational program, while the metaphysical, the artistic, and the ethical have only a very small place. An exclusive liberalism or Deweyism such as proposed by Hook leaves out elements that need to be considered.[64]

In reviewing Robert M. MacIver's *Academic Freedom in Our Time*, Charles Donahue recognizes the need to defend the organized academic life against popular and exaggerated antiintellectual attacks. But he finds MacIver's book in the long run quite disappointing. The Columbia University professor is not a dogmatic secularist, but his concept of academic freedom can be enthusiastically accepted only by dogmatic secularists. MacIver leaves no room for religious faith in the American university; denominational colleges do not and cannot have full academic freedom. In addition, MacIver claims that the Communist party member and the Catholic both subscribe to a creed proposed by an authority that treats all deviation as heresy. According to Donahue, MacIver thus disagrees with Hook and fails to deal with the empirical evidences that Hook proposed in order to show the great difference between Catholic believers and Communist party members in the academy.[65]

Russell Kirk in his treatise on academic freedom comes to basically the same conclusion as Hook in opposing Communists in the American academy, but academic freedom for him is based on a metaphysical and even religious conviction. Donahue agrees with Kirk in seeing academic freedom in the light of our tradition of wisdom. But Kirk makes too many seemingly rash personal judgments and, more importantly, fails to see the role of communities in keeping the tradition of wisdom alive. Wisdom is not merely private just because it does not belong to the state. Donahue thus criticizes Kirk's failure to recognize what was so important an element in Donahue's own defense of pluralistic academic freedom in our pluralistic society.[66]

Donahue stands chronologically at the end of the period examined in this chapter. His approach to academic freedom would certainly have been acceptable to the AAUP, which at the time allowed for exceptions to academic freedom for denominational institutions; but he never refers to the AAUP documents. Donahue's acceptance of a restriction or limit from outside the academic world renders his position unacceptable to defenders of academic freedom on the American scene. The tendencies toward assimilation to American higher education are, however, quite evident in his position.

Reasons for Catholic Opposition to Academic Freedom

Before 1960 Catholics opposed academic freedom both in general and especially in Catholic colleges and universities for many different reasons. This final section takes up in a systematic and synthetic way the manifold reasons for Catholic hostility to academic freedom.

Theological and faith-derived perspectives were important reasons for the Catholic rejection of academic freedom.[67] Catholics believe that God reveals God's self to human beings in many different ways but especially through Jesus and through the church which he founded to carry on his word and work in time and space. Faith is the believer's response to God's revelation, and the assent of faith is certain and absolute because God can neither deceive nor be deceived. A privileged place of revelation is accorded sacred Scripture which has, through the gift of the Spirit, been interpreted by the church throughout the tradition. God has given the church a special hierarchical teaching office by which pope and bishops can interpret and teach faith and morals. Although some church teaching is said to be infallible, most church teaching falls into the noninfallible category; but here the pope and bishops teach authoritatively, and Catholics must give an allegiance of intellect and will to such teaching. Thus in the supernatural realm the Catholic believer has certitude about the truths of faith and has authoritative Church teaching on other matters.

Catholic higher education saw its primary purpose as inculcating Catholic truth and the Catholic understanding of human existence to its students. The colleges and universities constituted an extension of the pastoral mission of the church. No Catholic academician could call into question the authoritative teachings of the Catholic Church; no one even proposed the possible legitimacy of dissent from noninfallible teaching. For Catholics the very title of Hook's book was both provocative and prophetic: *Heresy, Yes—Conspiracy, No.* The title is provocative because it points out very clearly that Catholic institutions could not have academic freedom, but it is also prophetic insofar as it indicates that Catholic institutions did not even want to have academic freedom.

In the first half of the twentieth century, American Catholicism strongly criticized on the basis of its faith the secularism that was becoming more and more manifest in American life and society. Secularism was more than secularity. Secularism maintained that there is no room for God in our society, and it firmly opposed the relevance of any aspect of faith to daily life. In many ways secularism itself was looked upon as a faith that was hostile to Catholicism and all other religions. Not only did God and faith play no role in secular education, but there was hostility against them. Cooler heads pointed out that secularism in education arose not from an antifaith or anti-God stance but from the need in our pluralistic society not to embrace any one particular faith.[68] No matter what its origin, many Catholics pointed out the dangers of this secularism or godlessness that permeated so much of American education. Academic freedom via claiming the right to question all apparent certitudes and not accepting things on faith was seen as another support for the secularism of the schools and of society at large.

Although American colleges and universities came into existence originally as denominational institutions, more and more of these institutions largely gave up their religious character and identity in the twentieth century. This change in the denominational status of American colleges and universities illustrated the secularizing trend of twentieth-century American life. The strong support for academic freedom among academics only began in a concerted way near the turn of the century, in 1915 when the AAUP was founded with the aim of protecting and defending academic freedom. In the nineteenth century, religion had been the primary opponent of academic freedom, and the struggle between religion and science was the first major confrontation involving academic freedom in the United States. Early defenders of academic freedom thus saw religion as opposed to academic freedom. Academic freedom was both a product of and a contributor to the continuing secularization of American higher education.

One would expect that Catholic opposition to academic freedom depended primarily on these religious and theological considerations, but that was not the case. The literature dealing with academic freedom stresses the philosophical much more than the theological. Two reasons explain this emphasis. First, the Catholic tradition has always given a great significance to human reason and philosophy. Philosophy has been intimately connected with theology and was called the handmaid of theology, for philosophy supplied the foundation for Catholic theology. In addition, Catholic opposition to the understanding of academic freedom as it existed in private and public American institutions of higher learning would receive a better hearing from others if it did not appeal only to Catholic presuppositions.

In 1879 Pope Leo XIII had declared that Catholic theology and philosophy were to be taught according to the approach, the principles, and the teaching of St. Thomas Aquinas. Subsequent church legislation confirmed this ruling. Neoscholasticism or Thomism, unfortunately in an inferior understanding typical of handbooks, became identified as *the* Catholic philosophy. For Catholics this was the perennial philosophy. It insisted on the real ability of the intellect to know truth and to grasp objective truth, which was understood as the "adequation" or conformity of the mind to reality. This ability to know objective truth was the basis for the religious, moral, and intellectual life of humankind. Reason itself is able to prove the existence of God. Human reason can also know the first principles of the natural law and deduce from these principles the norms governing human life. The human intellect is capable of knowing human truth. Revelation surpasses the power of human reason, but in faith the created intellect with God's grace can affirm the truth of God's revelation. Catholic educators hold that truth is unchangeable, demonstration reliable, and certitude possible. Error is opposed to the very nature of the intellect.[69]

Catholic philosophy strenuously opposed modern philosophies that attack the assumption that the human intellect can know objective truth. Even the most irenic of Catholics writing on academic freedom during this period finds a fundamental hostility between Catholic philosophy and modern philosophy. Bernard Mullahy— whose philosophical approach to academic freedom stands out for its objectivity, lack of partisan rhetoric, and willingness to challenge the dangers of authoritarianism—recognizes a basic incompatibility between Catholic philosophy and the modern mind. The modern mind is the product of three great revolutions: the Renaissance revolution emancipated the mind from theology and divine authority, thereby opening the door to naturalism; the Cartesian revolution freed the human mind from human authority and tradition and left the mind committed only to individualism; the Kantian revolution liberated the intellect from objective reality and committed the modern mind to subjectivism.[70] Even in the late 1950s John Courtney Murray, who was then doing pioneering work proving the fundamental compatibility between Roman Catholicism and religious freedom, saw a total opposition between Catholic philosophy and the modern American university. Murray claimed that not only can Catholics accept the American proposition that all are created equal and endowed by the Creator with certain inalienable rights, but Catholics are the only ones who can philosophically defend this fundamental proposition. Unfortunately, American secular universities have abandoned the natural law tradition with its realistic philosophy that provides the only real philosophical defense of these fundamental human rights.[71]

The philosophical differences between the Catholic approach and the modern American mind appeared in almost every article and editorial written on academic freedom in the first six decades of the twentieth century. Subjectivism, relativism, pragmatism, and positivism were regularly attacked by Catholic spokespersons. Academic freedom was the child of these intellectual errors. Catholic authors often associated academic freedom with empiricism, which recognizes no truth other than that which is empirically verifiable. The scientific method, rooted in this empiricism, was intimately associated with the proponents of academic freedom. Recall the strong and bitter criticism of John Dewey, one of the leading figures in the American defense of academic freedom. Aldo Tos, for example, in his 1958 doctoral dissertation on academic freedom from a Catholic perspective, traces the background of academic freedom through these philosophical developments and notes the Catholic reaction to these developments in the nineteenth century, especially as embodied in the Syllabus of Errors promulgated by Pope Pius IX in 1864.[72]

Catholic philosophy also strongly opposed the one-sided view of freedom that was so prevalent in the modern world and that supported the concept of academic freedom as understood in the American academy. Catholic thought has generally been fearful of freedom and constantly cautioned against the dangers of too much freedom. In theology it has generally been accepted that before the Second Vatican Council, Catholics stressed order whereas Protestants stressed freedom. In ethics, Catholics emphasized that human beings can know the natural law and hence have a sure guide for their moral conduct. Yes, human beings have freedom, but it is a freedom to respond to the true and to do the good. There is no freedom to reject the true and the good, for these are the ends or purposes of the two most distinctive human faculties—the intellect and the will. Freedom by its very nature cannot be absolutized and is always subordinate to the claim of the true and the good. Official Catholic teaching has recognized its failure to give sufficient importance to freedom. As late as 1961, Pope John XXIII in his encyclical letter *Mater et Magistra* explained the ideal social order in terms of truth, justice, and charity. Only two years later in *Pacem in Terris* did Pope John add the concept of freedom to this triad. John's later correction of the omission of freedom as an important element in the social order illustrates how little importance Catholic thought gave to freedom.[73] Recall that the strong Catholic opposition to religious freedom was only changed at the Second Vatican Council in 1965.

In the nineteenth century Catholicism strongly opposed individualistic liberalism. This liberalism so stressed the individual and the individual's freedom that it basically forgot the individual's relationship to God, to other human beings, and to human communities. Catholic authors often pointed out the origins of nineteenth-century individualistic liberalism. The Protestant Reformation (usually called the Protestant Revolt in Catholic literature) emphasized the freedom of individual conscience in religious matters and cut people off from the authority of the church. Eighteenth- and nineteenth-century philosophers severed the human being's relationship to God and made the individual the measure of all things.

Catholicism opposed not only religious liberalism but also political liberalism. Majority rule could not make something right or wrong. In this context, Pope Leo XIII at the end of the nineteenth century condemned the modern liberties. It is ironic but true that the two great opponents of liberalism were Karl Marx and Pope Leo XIII, although there were significant differences between them. Catholic thought strongly condemned laissez-faire capitalism as a form of economic liberalism. Owners were not free to do whatever they pleased, for workers had rights that had to be respected, including the right to a living wage and to decent working conditions.[74]

Catholics saw academic freedom as another illustration of liberalism. For example, Catholic thinkers in the 1930s brought together their negative criticisms of both academic freedom and capitalism since both exemplified individualistic liberalism.[75] Catholic approaches to liberalism form a firm foundation for the Catholic opposition to academic freedom. Freedom in the Catholic tradition was never an end in itself and always had to be limited by the objective demands of the true and the good, and by the individual's relationship to God, church, neighbor, and the world.

The Catholic understanding of the nature of the academy and of teaching formed another reason for its opposition to academic freedom. Here again the Catholic position was proposed as a middle position avoiding the extremes of liberalism on the one hand and totalitarianism on the other. The academy is the meeting place between two different orders—the speculative order of contemplation and the practical order of human action. The speculative order, which is proper to the intellect, has the true as its only good. There are no ends to be achieved, no purposes to be pursued, for the object of the intellect is not an end-object but purely and simply an object—the truth. The intellect in the presence of evident truth cannot withhold its assent, and therefore there can be no question of liberty of choice. Where no such liberty exists, there also can be no role for authority.

The practical order is the order of achieving goods and ends. In the pragmatic order, liberty becomes restricted, for necessary ends demand a necessary direction for those who have to obtain them. The problem of academic freedom arises precisely because the academy exists in both orders. The academy is the place where the mind devotes itself to the discovery and contemplation of truth—an act of the purely speculative order. But the academy is also the place where knowledge is communicated from concrete human persons to other concrete human persons, all of whom have definite ends that they must achieve and human values that they must cherish. The academy thus involves activities of the practical order where authority has a role to play.

Although authority has no role in the speculative order considered in its abstract nature, it does have a function in that order considered in its concrete existential state. The intellect in its concrete existence is not always fortunate enough to be in the presence of the fullness of intrinsic evidence. There is an imperfection inherent in the human intellect because it is both finite and created. The role of authority in these cases is substitutional, and the intellect must have intrinsic evidence of the legitimacy of the authority to which it is submitting itself. Divine authority (revelation) may enter in precisely because the human intellect is created and cannot of itself know the infinite God and God's self-revelation. Human authority may enter in because the mind is finite and arrives at truth only after a long, laborious search, or it may sometimes find itself impeded by error. The liberty to make a mistake is a defect of our finite rational nature and not a human privilege. Thus there is room for both divine and human authority in the speculative order, but the role of authority is strictly substitutional. Authority obviously has a broader scope on the lower levels of education in dealing with younger people. Authority in the speculative order should always be exercised in such a way that the mind will be brought as quickly as possible to the intrinsic evidence itself. The hierarchical structure of the sciences places another limitation on intellectual liberty. A superior science may judge and in some manner govern an inferior science. For example, true academic freedom demands that theology govern philosophy but in an intrinsic and negative way that only limits philosophy's potential to err.

The problem with authority and academic freedom in the practical order is more complex and less amenable to philosophical analysis precisely because of all the complexity and circumstances involved. Since the practical order deals with human beings who have ends to attain, there is a necessary place for authority in directing human beings to their ends. Prudential judgments must play a great role in mediating conflicts in the practical order.

The primary principle in the practical order, however, is clear—all the rights and duties of teachers and students are governed by the essential purpose of education—that is, to promote the true good of the students. Teachers have a right to teach what students have a right to learn. Students have the right not to learn error and not to have their religious, moral, and social life undermined or rendered insecure.

What is the competency of authority in the practical order? There are three societies that have some authority over students' education—the family, the church, and the state. The rights of parents are most fundamental and teachers exist in *loco parentis* for students who have not reached the age of maturity. Since the spiritual is primary, the church takes precedence over the state. The church has the right to demand of Catholic schools a positive teaching of supernatural truths. Of public schools, she has the right to demand that at least nothing be taught that proves prejudicial to the faith and morals of her children. The state in a democratic society should sponsor a democratic, and not an authoritarian, education. To accomplish such an education the schools need a large measure of freedom, including the ability to criticize the existing cultural, social, political, and economic orders. The teachers and the schools cannot, however, have the freedom to undermine the very democratic ethos itself. Teachers and students must be granted a large measure of freedom if the schools are to obtain their essential purpose.

The position sketched above, according to Bernard Mullahy, thus finds a middle way between the extreme dangers of totalitarianism and liberalism. Totalitarianism rightly understands the need for some authority in the practical order but fails to appreciate the

freedom of the speculative order. Liberalism rightly recognizes freedom existing in the speculative order, but it fails to recognize the
limitations of the concrete intellect in that order and the need for
substitutional authority because of such imperfection. Also, liberalism errs by carrying over into the practical order the freedom that
belongs to the speculative order. The Catholic approach tries to give
due weight to the proper role of both freedom and authority.[76]

These were the principal arguments employed by Catholics in
their opposition in the first six decades of the twentieth century to
the concept of academic freedom found in American higher education. As we shall see in the next chapter, Catholic attitudes were
to undergo a striking change by the end of the 1960s.

NOTES

1. Edward J. Power, *Catholic Higher Education in America: A History*
(New York: Appleton-Century-Crofts, 1972), pp. 36–45.

2. Ibid., pp. 302–304.

3. Philip Gleason, "American Catholic Higher Education: A Historical Perspective," in Robert Hassenger, ed., *The Shape of Catholic Higher
Education* (Chicago: University of Chicago Press, 1967), pp. 35–38.

4. Power, *Catholic Higher Education in America*, pp. 327–378.

5. Gleason, in Hassenger, *Shape of Catholic Higher Education*, p.
37.

6. Power, *Catholic Higher Education in America*, pp. 334–368.

7. Andrew M. Greeley, *From Backwater to Mainstream: A Profile of
Catholic Higher Education*, Carnegie Commission Studies (New York:
McGraw-Hill, 1969). In this volume and in an earlier work Greeley gives
a short history of Catholic higher education based heavily on both Power
and Gleason. See Andrew M. Greeley, *The Changing Catholic College*
(Chicago: Aldine Publishing Co., 1967).

8. Power, *Catholic Higher Education in America*, p. 370.

9. Ibid., p. 3.

10. Burton Confrey, *Secularism in American Education* (Washington,
DC: Catholic University of America Press, 1931).

11. Gleason, in Hassenger, *Shape of Catholic Higher Education*, p.
46.

12. Wilfred M. Mallon, "Faculty Rank, Tenure, and Academic Freedom," *National Catholic Educational Association Bulletin* 38 (1942–43):
177–194.

13. Charles Rice, "The Plight of the Professor," *America* 85 (September
8, 1951): 543–544, 548.

14. Henry J. Browne, "Catholics and the AAUP," *Commonweal* 65 (Octoer 5, 1956): 10–12.

15. Ewald B. Nyquist, "Foreword," in Roy J. Deferrari, *Some Problems of Catholic Higher Education in the United States* (Boston: St. Paul Editions, 1963), p. 10.

16. Editorial, "More Academic Freedom," *America* 55 (May 30, 1936): 171; John A. Hardon, "Prophets of Error," *Catholic World* 163 (1946): 527–531.

17. John Whitney Evans, *The Newman Movement: Roman Catholics in American Higher Education, 1833–1971* (Notre Dame, IN: University of Notre Dame Press, 1980), pp. 15–55.

18. Aidan M. Carr, "Princeton Versus Father Halton," *Homiletic and Pastoral Review* 53 (January 1958): 353–366.

19. George Bull, "The Function of the Catholic Graduate School," *Thought* 13 (1938): 364–380.

20. Martin R. P. McGuire, "Catholic Education and the Graduate School," in Roy J. Deferrari, ed., *Vital Problems in Catholic Education in the United States* (Washington, DC: Catholic University of America Press, 1939).

21. Very Reverend Hunter Guthrie, "Presidential Address," in *Tradition and Prospect: The Inauguration of the Very Rev. Hunter Guthrie, S.J., as Thirty-Fifth President of Georgetown University, April 30 and May 1, 1949* (Washington, DC: Georgetown University Press, 1949): 70–74.

22. Robert Edmund Hogan, Jr., "Greetings from the Students," in *Tradition and Prospect*, p. 65.

23. "Resolutions," *National Catholic Educational Association Bulletin* 33 (1936): 73–74.

24. 1915 Declaration of Principles, in Louis Joughin, ed., *Academic Freedom and Tenure: A Handbook of the American Association of University Professors* (Madison, WI: University of Wisconsin Press, 1967), p. 166.

25. Ibid., p. 159.

26. "1925 Conference Statement," *AAUP Bulletin* 40 (1954–55): 85.

27. 1940 Statement of Principles, in Joughin, *Academic Freedom and Tenure*, p. 36.

28. *AAUP Bulletin* 54 (1968): 24.

29. Joughin, *Academic Freedom and Tenure*, pp. 143–146.

30. "Academic Freedom and Tenure: St. Louis University," *AAUP Bulletin* 25 (1939): 514–535. However, subsequent historical research indicates that John Glennon, the Catholic archbishop of St. Louis, insisted that the university dismiss Dr. Fleisher. See José M. Sanchez. "Cardinal Glennon and Academic Freedom at St. Louis University," *Gateway Heritage* (Winter 1987–88): 2–11.

31. "Academic Freedom and Tenure: St. Louis University," *AAUP Bulletin* 42 (1956): 108–129.

32. *AAUP Bulletin* 33 (1947): 7; 43 (1957): 360.

33. John D. Donovan, *The Academic Man in the Catholic College* (New York: Sheed and Ward, 1964), p. 182.

34. Wilfred M. Mallon, *National Catholic Educational Association Bulletin* 38 (1942–43): 177–194.

35. Aldo J. Tos, "A Critical Study of the Modern American Views on Academic Freedom" (Ph.D. diss., The Catholic University of America, 1958), p. 92.

36. Ibid., pp. 89–97.

37. Ruth Byrns, "Academic Freedom Is not a Reckless Grant," *America* 64 (November 23, 1940): 172–173.

38. Henry J. Browne, "Catholics and the AAUP," *Commonweal* 65 (October 5, 1956): 10–12.

39. Sidney Hook, *Heresy, Yes—Conspiracy, No* (New York: John Day Co., 1953).

40. Ibid., pp. 219–220.

41. Robert M. MacIver, *Academic Freedom in Our Time* (New York: Columbia University Press, 1955), pp. 134–146.

42. Ibid., pp. 285–289.

43. Guthrie, in *Tradition and Prospect*, pp. 70–74.

44. Very Rev. Hunter Guthrie, "The Sacred Fetish of Academic Freedom," *Vital Speeches of the Day* 16 (1949–50): 632–633.

45. Aloysius J. Hogan, "Liberty and the Colleges," *National Catholic Educational Association Bulletin* 34 (1937–38): 82–87.

46. Francis L. Meade, "Academic Freedom in Catholic Education," *National Catholic Educational Association Bulletin* 35 (1938–39): 109–114.

47. Andrew C. Smith, "Academic Freedom," *The Modern Schoolman* 18 (1941): 73–76.

48. Bernard I. Mullahy, "Teaching the Truth: The Philosophy of Academic Freedom," *Proceedings of the American Catholic Philosophical Association* 18 (1942): 66–95.

49. Journet Kahn, "The Threat to Academic Freedom," *Proceedings of the Catholic Philosophical Association* 30 (1956): 160–170.

50. Ellen W. Schrecker, *No Ivory Tower: McCarthyism and the Universities* (New York: Oxford University Press, 1986).

51. Donald F. Crosby, *God, Church, and Flag: Senator Joseph R. McCarthy and the Catholic Church, 1950–1957* (Chapel Hill, NC: University of North Carolina Press, 1978).

52. Editorial, "Academic Freedom," *America* 80 (November 6, 1948): 118–119.

53. Editorial, "The Right to Teach," *America* 80 (February 12, 1949): 506–507; "Current Comment," *America* 81 (June 1, 1949): 331.

54. Editorial, "More Academic Freedom," *America* 55 (May 30, 1936): 171; John P. Delaney, "Russell is a Creature of a Clique of Dictators," *America* 62 (April 6, 1940): 708–709; Paul L. Blakely, "The Teacher and Caesar's Wife," *America* 63 (April 13, 1940): 6–7; editorial, "Clouds over Chicago," *America* 71 (June 3, 1944): 226.

55. Robert C. Hartnett, "Commies and 'Academic Freedom,'" *America* 89 (April 18, 1953): 77–78; (May 16, 1953): 186–190.

56. Deferrari, *Some Problems of Catholic Higher Education*, p. 122.

57. Kahn, *Proceedings of the American Catholic Philosophical Association* 30 (1956): 160–170.

58. George N. Shuster, "Academic Freedom," *Commonweal* 58 (April 10, 1953): 11–13; Jerome G. Kirwin, "Fear and Freedom," *Commonweal* 58 (July 3, 1953): 315–317.

59. Editorial, "The Case of Jerome Davis," *Commonweal* 25 (November 27, 1936): 115.

60. Editorial, "Dr. F. E. McMahon Severed at Notre Dame," *Commonweal* 39 (November 19, 1943): 108.

61. Charles Donahue, "Freedom and Education: The Sacral Problem," *Thought* 28 (1953–54): 209–233.

62. Charles Donahue, "Freedom on the Campus," *America* 97 (April 27, 1957): 104–108.

63. Charles Donahue, "Freedom and Education, III: Catholicism and Academic Freedom," *Thought* 29 (1954–55): 555–573.

64. Charles Donahue, "Heresy and Conspiracy," *Thought* 28 (1953–54): 528–546.

65. Charles Donahue, "The Academic Freedom of Professor MacIver," *America* 94 (February 11, 1954): 526–528.

66. Charles Donahue, Review of Russell Kirk, *Academic Freedom: An Essay in Definition*, *Thought* 30 (1955–56): 273–283.

67. This section will briefly summarize the arguments found in the literature already mentioned.

68. Confrey, *Secularism in American Education*.

69. Rudolph P. Bierberg, "Basis of Academic Freedom in Catholic Education," *Catholic Educational Review* 54 (1956): 400–403.

70. Mullahy, *Proceedings of the American Catholic Philosophical Association* 18 (1942): 78.

71. John Courtney Murray, *We Hold These Truths* (New York: Sheed and Ward, 1960), pp. 39–43; 290–294.

72. Tos, "Critical Study," pp. 1–70.

73. Pope John XXIII, *Mater et Magistra*, par. 212, in Joseph Gremillion, ed., *The Gospel of Peace and Justice: Catholic Social Teaching since Pope John* (Maryknoll, NY: Orbis Books, 1976), p. 188; Pope John XXIII, *Pacem in Terris*, par. 35, in Gremillion, p. 208.

74. Charles E. Curran, *American Catholic Social Ethics* (Notre Dame, IN: University of Notre Dame Press, 1982), pp. 103ff.

75. Edmund A. Walsh, "Education and Freedom Under Democracy," *National Catholic Educational Association Bulletin* 33 (1936–37): 88–94; also, Hogan, *National Catholic Educational Association Bulletin* 34 (1937–38): 82–87.

76. Mullahy, *Proceedings of the American Catholic Philosophical Association* 18 (1942): 66–95.

3. Acceptance of Academic Freedom by the Mainstream of Catholic Higher Education in the 1960s

The 1960s saw a dramatic change in Catholic higher education's attitude toward academic freedom. Even in the early years of the decade there was universal recognition that Catholic institutions of higher learning could not accept a total and complete academic freedom such as that which existed in most non-Catholic institutions. In addition, even within the mainstream of Catholic higher education strong opposition to academic freedom in American secular education still flourished. But by the end of this tumultuous decade that affected many ideas and institutions, the mainstream of Catholic higher education strongly supported academic freedom and the need for it in Catholic colleges and universities. This chapter will describe and try to explain how and why such a complete about-face occurred during this short length of time.

Documenting the Change

The change in academic freedom occurred both in the realm of practice and in the realm of ideas. Before the 1960s, problems involving academic freedom did not exist for all practical purposes in Catholic institutions of higher learning. The general consensus of Catholic and non-Catholic educators alike was that full academic freedom did not and could not exist at Catholic colleges and universities.

Practical Developments

From the practical perspective, a number of significant controversies about academic freedom flared up in Catholic schools in the 1960s. Recall that before 1962 the American Association of University Professors (AAUP) had investigated and condemned only one Catholic institution: St. Louis University was censured twice for violations of academic freedom and tenure in its medical school, but medical schools are somewhat removed and distanced from the heart of the university. As the 1960s progressed, however, the AAUP became increasingly involved in issues touching on academic freedom in Catholic institutions. Faculty members with a growing consciousness of their professional identity as academics were now willing and eager to bring their grievances to the AAUP, and the AAUP was more than willing to investigate.

In 1962, the AAUP censured Mercy College, a small liberal arts college in Detroit that was founded in 1941 by the Sisters of Mercy and that had 550 full-time students in 1961–62.[1] Dr. Austin Jesse Shelton, Jr., had begun teaching as an instructor at Mercy College in 1954, was promoted to full professor in 1959, and in September of 1960 began the third year of a five-year contract. On October 3 he received a letter from the president informing him that he would be terminated as of June 1961 because he was the occasion of negative criticism of the college and the college's constituency had complained about him. A telegram of October 23 from the president informed Shelton that he would be terminated as of Monday, October 24, 1960.

Professor Shelton appealed to the Washington office of the AAUP, which tried unsuccessfully to obtain academic due process for him. The AAUP finally appointed an investigative committee; but Mercy's president refused to talk with the committee, and the administration never gave its reason for the dismissal. The committee concluded that the problem probably arose from a text that Shelton used in class but especially from his first novel; apparently constituents of the college were offended by the novel's sexual content and theme. Also, a newspaper article about his second novel described him as a Hemingwayesque character. The committee report and ultimately the AAUP censured the college for not having provided academic due process to Professor Shelton. The college in its governing documents had basically accepted the procedures contained in the 1940 Statement of Principles but was unwilling to use them in this case. Note here the general propensity of the AAUP to emphasize procedure. The committee report, however, did point out that a college or university has the duty to withstand negative criticism and to defend itself when the criticism is aimed at the responsible exercise of academic freedom by faculty members.

The censure was officially passed at the annual AAUP meeting in 1964. A new administration at Mercy College made an amicable settlement with Professor Shelton and committed itself to follow the accepted principles of academic freedom and tenure. The censure was officially removed by the AAUP in 1968.[2]

On March 24, 1960, Richard T. Tench, a professor of law at Gonzaga University in Spokane, Washington, received a formal notice stating that his contract would not be renewed for the 1960-61 school year.[3] The efforts of the AAUP's Washington office to resolve the problem were unsuccessful. The AAUP then appointed its investigative committee.

The Tench case illustrates well the state of Catholic higher education in the early 1960s and the sweeping transformation that had begun to occur. Gonzaga University, founded by the Society of Jesus in 1887, was under the authority of the religious superior of the Oregon province of the Jesuits. At the time of this case, Gonzaga's president was appointed by the superior of the order upon the recommendation of the provincial and his board. The legal governing body of the university consisted of a self-perpetuating group of five or more Jesuits in residence at the university who had been appointed by the provincial. A board of regents served in an advisory capacity.

In 1960 the university had no written policy on tenure, although there was a widespread understanding on campus that tenure did exist. Tench was hired as a part-time professor for the 1954-55 academic year. Suffering from a war-related illness and disability that continued to require medical treatment, he was originally recommended to the university either by a Jesuit priest who had become acquainted with him at a Veterans Administration hospital, or by the Jesuit provincial, or by both. (The investigative committee was not able to determine exactly how his hiring came about, and the very informal and nonacademic nature of the process stands out.) Tench, offered a full-time position as an instructor in the department of political science for the 1955-56 academic year, entered into a faculty employment agreement with the university that was renewed for the next two years. He accepted an invitation to become a faculty member of the school of law for the 1958-59 year with a substantial increase in salary, but no faculty agreement or contract was signed. In law school documents Tench was referred to as "Professor," but the administration later claimed that the title was honorary and Tench was not really a professor. The faculty contract allowed the administration to dismiss a faculty member, sometimes without even a hearing. In addition, if the appointee was guilty of a grave offense against Catholic doctrine or morality, or was involved in a public crime or scandal, or belonged to an organization declared to be subversive, the university could dismiss him or her summarily, without notice and without penalty or salary obligation beyond the date of dismissal.

The university's president and administration cooperated with the AAUP's investigating committee, but the committee could not determine the reasons for the university's action. Professor Tench claimed that the action was taken because he had become a fallen-away Catholic. Even during the course of the investigation the university made improvements in its policies and regulations, but the investigating committee judged them still to be deficient by AAUP standards. The investigating committee also concluded that Professor Tench had tenure and had been wrongly deprived of his rights to due process in a hearing by peers. The university subsequently worked with the AAUP Washington office to reconcile the difficulties, and a satisfactory settlement was negotiated between the university and Tench. In addition, the university adopted formally and without qualification the 1940 Statement of Principles and the AAUP's 1958 Statement on Procedural Standards, and it willingly and quickly abandoned its very informal and paternalistic policies and practices. Committee A of the AAUP welcomed these changes and recommended no censure against Gonzaga.[4] For its part, Gonzaga obviously wanted to be a part of the American higher education community.

At its 1968 convention, the AAUP censured St. Mary's College in Winona, Minnesota, for Richard Caldwell's dismissal, which had involved a violation of academic freedom and academic due process.[5] Again the record shows the informal and casual, not necessarily autocratic, way in which the institution was run. An appendix to the faculty handbook, for example, explicitly recognized that the college administration does not adhere strictly to all the material in the handbook! Caldwell, in his first year as an instructor at the college, had received a contract for the following 1966-67 school year, but after his civil marriage outside the Catholic church to a sophomore from a neighboring Catholic women's college, the president of St. Mary's summarily dismissed him. After the AAUP intervened, the president of the college agreed to rescind the action, and dismissal procedures were instituted according to the 1958 Statement on Procedural Standards in Faculty Dismissal Proceedings. The faculty committee hearing the case twice voted narrowly not to dismiss Mr. Caldwell, but the trustees sent the report back to the committee each time. Finally the committee voted to dismiss, and the trustees concurred. The investigating committee noted serious procedural mistakes but recognized that they were probably not malicious. From a substantive perspective, the investigating committee concluded that dismissal because of scandal was not justified under any existing academic standard. Scandal is a very vague claim, and Mr. Caldwell had not been granted the freedom to be what he is and to live as he believes.[6]

The censure of St. Mary's was removed one year later at the 1969 meeting of the AAUP.[7] The board of trustees and the administration at St. Mary's College agreed to accept new regulations that protected academic freedom and academic due process in accordance with AAUP standards, and they also reached an amicable settlement with Caldwell.[8]

The Shelton, Tench, and Caldwell cases illustrate well the dynamics of change in Catholic higher education in the '60s. Paternalistic and informal institutional governance was giving way to the reception of regulations for institutional governance that had already been accepted by the American academy in general and especially as they were proposed by the AAUP. Catholic institutions were very willing to accept the AAUP norms on academic freedom and academic due process. The three institutions that were involved in the disputes worked quickly to have the censures removed and to be perceived as belonging to the mainstream of higher education. Each of the three cases involved a small institution, one faculty member, and an administration that was generally willing in the end to accept the principles and norms of academic freedom and tenure that had been proposed by the AAUP.

Without a doubt the most dramatic development in Catholic higher education in the 1960s occurred at St. John's University in Queens, New York,[9] a large institution where many faculty members were involved in a dispute with an intransigent administration. The primary issue at St. John's was not directly academic freedom as such, but rather the firing and dismissal of faculty members. The controversy was widely publicized, and its reverberations were felt throughout Catholic higher education.

Throughout the 1960s tensions, frustrations, and grievances accumulated in the faculty's relationship with the administration of St. John's University. There was little or no faculty participation in the governance of the institution. In 1963 university administrators refused to recognize a recently organized local chapter of the AAUP and would not permit the group to use university facilities for holding meetings or distributing notices. At this time a local union was organized by the United Federation of College Teachers, an affiliate of the AFL-CIO. The administration then recognized the local AAUP chapter, but not the union. Tensions continued to grow between the faculty and administration and also within the faculty itself. On December 16, 1965, the university informed thirty-three members of the faculty (including six who should have had tenure) that they would be terminated when their contracts expired. Twenty-two of them were notified that they were relieved of all duties, effective immediately. No cause or reason was given. Among those terminated were the leaders of the union local. The union called for a strike to begin when classes resumed on January 4, 1966. Because it opposed such means to settle faculty grievances, the Executive Committee of the AAUP did not endorse the strike. The AAUP statement defended the right of the faculty to refuse to cross picket lines but also emphasized the need to honor the positions of those who saw a moral obligation in continuing to meet their classes.

The administration and trustees of the university remained adamant. The strike was unsuccessful; the fired faculty, with two exceptions, were not rehired. Although the AAUP did not endorse the strike, the association quickly formed an investigating team on January 2, 1966, and ultimately censured St. John's University for one of the most flagrant violations of the principles of academic freedom and tenure to have been committed by an unresponsive and intractable administration. St. John's reputation suffered in the view of the academic community at large, but the institution never lost its accreditation with the Middle States Association.

Catholic education's reaction, as exemplified by articles in journals of opinion such as *America* and *Catholic World*,[10] was quite negative to St. John's University. However, the incident served in a negative way as a catalyst and a warning for other Catholic institutions of higher learning to accept the standard principles and procedures of American higher education. Most Catholic institutions did not want to have a similar problem. The issue at St. John's centered on dismissing faculty, but such dismissals are intimately connected with academic freedom.

In the 1960s a number of minor controversies flared between faculty and administration at Catholic institutions such as the College of St. Thomas in St. Paul, Duquesne University in Pittsburgh, and the San Diego College for Women.[11] However, the issue of academic freedom in Catholic higher education became prominent not only in the Catholic press but also in the national media because of incidents that involved the theology departments at the University of Dayton and, especially, at the Catholic University of America. The incidents involved the direct confrontation of faculty and universities with the hierarchical teaching office of the church.

The imbroglio at the University of Dayton began in earnest in the fall of 1966 when Assistant Professor Dennis Bonnette (philsophy) sent a letter to Karl J. Alter, Archbishop of Cincinnati (in whose jurisdiction Dayton lies), and to the apostolic delegate (the pope's representative) in Washington; Bonnette charged four members of the university's philosophy and theology departments with publicly disagreeing with Catholic teachings.[12] The Reverend Raymond A. Roesch, a priest from the Marianist order which runs the university and the president of the university, investigated and concluded on December 3, 1966, that the accused faculty members were innocent of the charges of teaching and advocating doctrines contrary to the magisterium of the church. According to Roesch, Archbishop Alter accepted the decision.

On December 8 eight faculty members from the department of philosophy called the president's report a whitewash. The university's faculty forum censured the eight faculty members. The controversy raged again when it was announced on January 9, 1967, that Archibishop Alter had appointed a fact-finding committee of his own to investigate the situation at Dayton. The local AAUP chapter and the university's student council opposed the existence and purpose of the archbishop's committee, but the president defended the archbishops' action. The fact-finding commission reported to Archbishop Alter on February 13, 1967. Its report ended with this enigmatic sentence: "In view of certain presuppositions it is to be noted that the Commission has made no suggestions with respect to the dismissal of any professors involved in the investigation."

Roesch addressed the faculty on March 1, 1967. He assured his audience that genuine academic freedom must exist at Dayton but defended the action of Archbishop Alter. The president also accepted the report of an ad hoc committee that he had formed to ensure academic freedom at Dayton. The committee reported that a Catholic university cannot accept any direct relationship to the magisterium in academic matters; only its Catholic members as individuals are related to magisterial authority. After further consultation, the university's board of trustees eventually asserted that Dayton would accept the validity of revealed as well as reasoned truth and is committed to genuine and responsible academic freedom supported by proper respect for the church's magisterium. The leader and two other professors who had made the original charges resigned from the university in the spring term of 1967.

Two widely publicized incidents involving academic freedom occurred at The Catholic University of America in 1967 and in the following years. Occupying a unique position and role in American Catholic higher education, Catholic University had earlier made the news in 1963 when the administration banned four well-known liberal Catholic theologians from speaking at the university.[13] I was centrally involved in the incidents in 1967 and 1968.

On April 17, 1967, the rector (president) of Catholic University, Bishop William J. McDonald, informed me that the board of trustees had decided not to renew my contract as an assistant professor of theology. No reasons were ever given for the decision, but the common knowledge of the time and the pertinent documentation revealed later indicated that the trustees, the vast majority of whom were bishops, were troubled by my position on issues of moral theology, especially on artificial contraception and masturbation.[14] The department of theology and the academic senate of the university had unanimously voted for my promotion to associate professor, but the trustees went against that judgment and decided not to renew my contract. Word of my dismissal spread on campus the next day, and the student body and others scheduled various meetings and rallies. On April 19 my colleagues in the school of theology unanimously concluded: "We cannot and will not function unless and until Father Curran is reinstated." The next day the entire faculty of the university voted by an overwhelming majority to join the strike. The students' and faculty's effort closed down the university. After a considerable amount of behind-the-scenes negotiating, the chancellor of the university, Archbishop Patrick A. O'Boyle, met with the faculty on April 24, and that evening he announced that the action of the trustees was rescinded. I was then offered a three-year contract as an associate professor. (In accord with AAUP norms that contract actually gave me a tenured appointment.) The strike at Catholic University shows in a very graphic way that changes were occurring in Catholic higher education.[15] Everyone realized that this case hinged on an issue of academic freedom: bishops had tried to dismiss a nontenured faculty member for taking positions in opposition to church teachings.

The year 1968 brought a new and even more explosive case concerning academic freedom to the Catholic University of America.[16] On July 29, 1968, Pope Paul VI released an encyclical letter entitled *Humanae Vitae,* which renewed the Catholic condemnation of artificial contraception for married couples. On July 30 I acted as a spokesperson for eighty-seven Catholic theologians who issued a statement concluding that Catholic spouses might responsibly decide according to their own consciences that artificial contraception in some instances is permissible and even necessary to preserve and foster the values and sacredness of marriage. Over six hundred Catholic scholars in the sacred disciplines finally signed the statement affirming the legitimacy of Catholic dissent from this noninfallible official church teaching. The issue did not involve just one theologian or only one book; rather it involved a large number of Catholic theologians who in a public and organized way made a statement of dissent from an official church teaching.

A majority of the statement's original drafters were members of the faculty of the Catholic University of America, and twenty faculty members from the university signed it. After a number of meetings between bishops and theologians and among university officials, trustees, and theologians, the board of trustees held a special meeting on September 5. In its statement to the press, the board reaffirmed the commitment of the Catholic University to accept the norms of academic freedom in the work of theologians and to affirm the due process protective of such freedom. The dissenters' declaration and actions, however, had raised serious questions, and the trustees instructed the acting rector to convene an inquiry in accord with academic due process to determine if the dissenters had violated their responsibilities to the university under its existing charter and under their commitments and obligations to the university, especially as teachers of theology and/or other sacred sciences. After extensive hearings, the faculty board of inquiry concluded in March of 1969 that the dissenting theologians had acted responsibly in their capacity as scholars; the academic senate of the university unanimously approved the report. The trustees accepted the report of the faculty board of inquiry insofar as it pertained to the academic propriety of the faculty members involved. But the trustees did say that their acceptance of the report did not represent approval of the theological position taken by the dissenters.[17]

The events at Catholic University were very significant. No institution of Catholic higher education in the United States is more Catholic than the national Catholic University, which the Vatican chartered and the American bishops founded and supported. It has often been called the bishops' own university. Such an institution nevertheless accepted the principles and due process of academic freedom even in the face of dissent from official, noninfallible church teaching. There could be no greater practical proof that American Catholic higher education had accepted by the end of the 1960s the principles and practices of academic freedom.

Theoretical Developments

One would expect that such a sudden and total about-face in Catholic attitudes to academic freedom had been brought about by a detailed and convincing theoretical defense for academic freedom in Catholic higher education, but such was not the case. In fact, comparatively little in-depth theoretical justification of academic freedom for Catholic higher education prepared the way for the dramatic turnabout.

In a short article in *Commonweal* in 1964, Leslie Dewart, a systematic theologian teaching at St. Michael's College in Toronto, proposed the need for academic freedom at Catholic institutions of higher learning. The teachings of theology are not something fixed and immutable. Newer understandings, changes, and developments can be brought about through dissent. The church is constantly trying to possess the truths of faith but never possesses them perfectly; accordingly, the church must engage the freedom of professors and not just their service. Some Catholic liberals say that a professor may dissent from official church teaching as an individual, but not as one who belongs to the Catholic academy. But the dissent of Catholic academicians is needed precisely for the good of the church itself. The pursuit of truth by the whole church requires the risking of error. Yes, errors will be made; but the risk of error must be taken for the sake of the pursuit of truths of faith. Dewart did not discuss the principles and processes of academic freedom as found in the American academy.[18]

Gerald F. Kreyche, the chair of the department of philosophy at DePaul University in Chicago, defended academic freedom for Catholic institutions in 1964 and again before the annual convention of the National Catholic Educational Association in 1965. Both of his contributions are comparatively short and impressionistic in their approach; they are personal statements rather than in-depth scholarly studies. Academic freedom is treated as the freedom of conscience and is not discussed or developed in any detail. Reality, he suggests, is in part historical, in part evolutionary, and in part dynamic. Yes, the truth will make us free, but it is not readily or easily attained, for it is not static but dynamic, and the winning of it must be an unending process. The dangers of error might attend accepting academic freedom, but error impels or stimulates truth more often than ignorance. In addition, more dangers to the church arise from the lack of academic freedom. Writing as a Catholic intellectual and academic no longer willing to accept the mediocrities and limitations characteristic of the American Catholic academy, Kreyche appealed to the tradition of the medieval universities, lamented the lack of American Catholic intellectuals, and called for the abolition of the

Index and of anything else that limits the Catholic scholar's free inquiry.[19]

A symposium was held at the University of Notre Dame in April of 1966 to discuss academic freedom in Catholic institutions of higher learning. The very existence of such a symposium illustrates the radical transformation that had taken place in Catholic higher education. "From anathema to dialogue" summarizes well what had occurred. Many different viewpoints were represented at the symposium. Although no basic agreement emerged among all the participants, most of them seemed to favor a greater role for academic freedom in Catholic higher education.[20] However, the papers that were subsequently published do not furnish a strong theoretical foundation for the role and importance of academic freedom at Catholic schools. Father John E. Walsh of Notre Dame proposed a novel justification of academic freedom: a Catholic university is not a part of the teaching function of the church, rather the university can best be described as the church learning. The relation between the teaching church and the university or learning church should be governed by processes proper to learning, and these require an atmosphere of free and open inquiry; all the demands of learning can and must be present in a Catholic university. Walsh's sketch does not address how this idea would work in practice. He correctly senses the need to distinguish the role of the church and the role of the university, but his distinction between the church teaching and the church learning still includes the university as a part of the church. In addition, such a distinction means that theologians and scholars have no role in the teaching function of the church, which would be contrary to the whole Catholic tradition.[21]

The other paper at the symposium that directly dealt with academic freedom was given by Frederick Crosson of Notre Dame. Crosson maintained that all scholarship is based on a commitment, whether the scholar be a physicist, an historian, or a theologian. The practitioners of a particular discipline do not and perhaps cannot demonstrate the validity or the existence of what they deal with, e.g., the mathematician with numbers or the historian with historical facts. The committed university is not a contradiction in terms; in a religious university there is also a religious commitment. Again, the idea here is suggestive and not systematically developed and worked out. Without explicitly saying so Crosson correctly points out the limitations of an empirical and positivistic worldview. However, his principle of commitment seems to call for some limit on the academic freedom of the committed believer and the religious university. The editors of the volume in which his essay was published express a similar misgiving about his ideas.[22]

Much ferment in and discussion about Catholic higher education took place in the mid-1960s.[23] Academic freedom was a part of that discussion. Reactions to the strikes at St. John's in 1966 and at Catholic University in 1967 raised the question of academic freedom. In the symposium in *Commonweal* after the Catholic University incident a number of participants strongly supported the need for academic freedom in Catholic institutions, but their short contributions could not develop the point at any great length.[24] Reports were published about possible violations of academic freedom involving two academics who were not theologians—Francis E. Kearns at Georgetown[25] and Paul M. Michaud at Boston College.[26] One gets the impression that many Catholic educators were willing to accept and embrace academic freedom in Catholic institutions, but they were still groping and searching for a satisfying theory and explanation.

The now famous Land O'Lakes Statement, issued in the summer of 1967, marked the decisive change in Catholic higher education's reaction to academic freedom and proved that academic freedom for Catholic higher education was a reality to be embraced, even though a systematic rationale in support of it was still lacking. The meeting at Land O'Lakes, Wisconsin, of twenty-six leaders of Catholic higher education in North America occurred under the auspices of the North American Region of the International Federation of Catholic Universities. The leaders who attended the meeting represented the major Catholic universities in the United States and Canada. In the course of their deliberations they reached a consensus on the nature of the contemporary Catholic university. The opening paragraph of their Statement makes the case for academic freedom very pointedly:

> The Catholic university today must be a university in the full modern sense of the word, with a strong commitment to and concern for academic excellence. To perform its teaching and research functions effectively the Catholic university must have a true autonomy and academic freedom in the face of authority of whatever kind, lay or

clerical, external to the academic community itself. To say this is simply to assert that institutional autonomy and academic freedom are essential conditions of life and growth and indeed of survival for Catholic universities as for all universities.[27]

The Land O'Lakes Statement brought about a swift and sweeping change in the self-understanding of Catholic higher education in the United States. The mainstream leaders of Catholic colleges and universities now wholeheartedly accepted what had been anathema less than a decade before.

The dominant figure at the Land O'Lakes meeting was Father Theodore M. Hesburgh, then the president of the University of Notre Dame and the president of the International Federation of Catholic Universities. Father Hesburgh has been the leading figure in Catholic higher education in the United States for the past few decades, and under his leadership the University of Notre Dame has developed and prospered as an academic university.[28]

In his speeches and writings, Hesburgh continued to stress the need for academic freedom in Catholic colleges and universities after the Land O'Lakes Statement was issued.[29] He and other mainstream leaders of Catholic higher education in the United States were now committed to the fact that their institutions had to be universities in the full American sense of the term. Being Catholic added something distinctive and characteristic, but it cannot erase or be a substitute for what is required of a university. Hesburgh and his colleagues were well aware of both the history of American higher education and of some contemporary trends. Many of America's most prestigious colleges and universities began as Protestant institutions, but they gradually lost any connection to their sponsoring church; in the past academic freedom was often intimately connected with the secularization of American higher education. The authors of the Land O'Lakes Statement, Father Hesburgh, and other leaders of Catholic higher education insisted that their institutions could be both Catholic and universities at the same time.

Hesburgh, for example, dealt with the frequent charge that was then even on the lips of some Catholic critics in the 1960s that a Catholic university is a contradiction in terms. For example, Dr. Rosemary Lauer, who had been involved in the St. John's debacle, had concluded that the church should get out of higher education.

Jacqueline Grennan, president of Webster College, announced that she was leaving her religious community which sponsored the college and that the college itself was going to be secularized; she did not think that a Catholic university or college could exist. In response to these claims, Hesburgh and others insisted on the identity of their institutions as universities and as Catholic. Hesburgh realized that the real crisis of academic freedom and autonomy in Catholic institutions of higher learning does not ultimately lie in political science or literature or chemistry, but in theology. The Notre Dame president makes his thesis very clear: "Theology in the Catholic university must enjoy the same freedom and autonomy as any other university subject because, otherwise, it will not be accepted as a university discipline and without its vital presence, in free dialogue with all other university disciplines, the university will never really be Catholic."[30] The Holy Cross priest was willing to admit that a difference exists between teaching undergraduates and doing graduate research. In the latter endeavor a conflict might arise between the hypothesis of a proven university theologian and the church's magisterium. Bishops can express their judgment that the theologian is not being faithful to accepted Catholic teaching, but they may not jeopardize the theologian's honest efforts within the realm of university research.

This mainstream approach of trying both to be American universities with academic freedom and institutional autonomy and to be truly Catholic was attacked from the right wing of the Catholic church. Some still strongly opposed the concept of academic freedom and saw it as inimical to truly Catholic institutions. (The next chapter will discuss this position in greater detail.)

The Land O'Lakes Statement not only made a radical change in American Catholic self-understanding, but it also set the agenda for the immediate future of the mainstream of Catholic higher education—how in practice can an institution be both a university and Catholic? Land O'Lakes had insisted on the need for academic freedom but also tried to spell out ways to ensure a Catholic presence. From that time on Catholic higher education has been trying to articulate and live out a Catholic presence that is compatible with autonomy and academic freedom. Shortly after the Land O'Lakes Statement, a number of Catholic authors tried to work out a rationale and justification of academic freedom for Catholic higher education.[31]

Reacation of the American Academic Community

Before the decade of the 1960s ended, the mainstream of Catholic higher education had accepted the principle of academic freedom and institutional autonomy as essential for Catholic colleges and universities. What was the attitude of American higher education in general to this issue? The higher academic community consisted of a number of voluntary associations (e.g., accrediting associations and others), including all the institutions involved in the enterprise. Even in the early 1960s church-related colleges and universities constituted more than one-third of all the colleges and universities in the country with more than one-sixth of the students.[32] Forty-two percent of these institutions were Catholic.[33] Since church-related higher education was such a significant part of American higher education, these institutions had to be accepted as part of the reality. It is fair to say, however, that they were probably accepted as second-class citizens precisely because of the problem of academic freedom, as the relationship of the AAUP to church-related institutions shows. Although the AAUP is not comprised of institutions but of individual professors, it still did not want to put church-related colleges and universities outside the parameters of American higher education. Recall that the AAUP 1940 Statement of Principles simply states: "Limitations of academic freedom because of religious or other aims of the institution should be clearly stated in writing at the time of the appointment." Although many questioned whether these institutions could be truly colleges and universities, most national and voluntary groups were willing to tolerate their existence, but many in American higher education were still not totally satisfied with this tolerance.

In June of 1962 trustees of the Danforth Foundation authorized the study of church-related higher education. Nine persons formed the commission that guided the project, and they consulted broadly and at length with all concerned. The commission's report, published in 1966, included a set of conclusions and recommendations. It succinctly summarized the fundamental dilemma: "How can a college do justice to its avowed purpose as a Christian institution, a purpose which carries with it a commitment to a set of beliefs, and at the same time maintain the freedom of inquiry which most academic people think is necessary for good education?"[34] In general the report insists that neither commitment nor freedom should be treated as an absolute. The conclusion recommends four steps to reconcile commitment and freedom:

1. A substantial number of those appointed to the faculty should be practicing religionists and sympathetic to the aims of the institution;
2. Freedom of inquiry should exist for all faculty and students;
3. The philosophy of the institution should be reasonably and persuasively presented in different ways without pressing for acceptance;
4. Faculty and students should be encouraged to explore the relationship between religion and modern life.[35]

In an earlier section the report insisted that the principle of faculty and student freedom must be made unmistakably clear, and the administration and the trustees must be willing to tolerate heresy. An institution with a strongly affirmative climate in support of its philosophy can afford to have some members of the faculty hold conflicting views. One way of creating a supporting climate is by the type of appointments made in the first place, but once appointed, the faculty members should enjoy full academic freedom.[36] This report not only reflected some changes already taking place in Catholic higher education but also had an influence on bringing about further changes, such as the Land O'Lakes Statement.

Developments within the AAUP's approach to church-related institutions in the '60s illustrate the changes that had occurred in Catholic higher education and the attempts that were made to nudge church-related institutions to go further. In 1965 Committee A of the AAUP recognized the need for a more definitive statement of policy on the limitations of academic freedom in church-related institutions. A number of factors contributed to their request at this time—two AAUP investigations involving church-related (Catholic) institutions; the current ecumenical movement (Vatican Council II); the study of church-related schools then being conducted by the Danforth Foundation.[37] An earlier report of the self-survey committee of the AAUP had pointed out that the limitation clause for church-related institutions was one of three inadequacies in the 1940 Statement.[38]

A special committee on academic freedom in church-realted colleges and universities was appointed at the 1965 meeting, and the committee made its report in 1967. The committee argued that its charge from the 1965 meeting did not include the question of removing the limitations clause. In issuing its report, however, the committee did not intend to endorse practices that restrict academic freedom. The committee in fact commends to the attention of the academic community the ongoing tendency of church-related colleges and universities to waive or drastically restrict the use of the limitations clause. The committee recommended that any limitation invoked be essential to the religious aims of the institution, be thoroughly discussed by the faculty, and be clearly stated in writing. A faculty member should respect the stated aims of the institution, but academic freedom protects the right to express, clarify, and interpret positions—including those identified as one's own—which are divergent from those of the institution and of the church that supports it.[39] In retrospect one can see, in the light of the change that was occurring very rapidly in Catholic institutions, that this more restrictive interpretation of the limitations clause would quickly be seen to be too weak. In 1968 Committee A thought it would be desirable to appoint a subcommittee to study and report on theological criticism and academic freedom in church-related colleges and universities.[40] The committee was obviously referring to theological dissent from *Humanae Vitae* and to the faculty inquiry at Catholic University.

In May 1969, Committee A called the report of the faculty board of inquiry at Catholic University a significant development in the general area of academic freedom at church-related institutions. The faculty report, which Committee A recommended be published in the *AAUP Bulletin*, exonerated the professors involved and concluded that Catholic University should adopt the 1940 Statement of Principles without the special limitation clause for church-related institutions. This report from the faculty committee at Catholic University provided an added reason for Committee A to expedite its previously planned study of the limitation clause.[41]

In 1970 Committee A completed its study and released its statement on the limitations clause in the 1940 Statement of Principles. The report summarized previous developments in this area and ended with the Catholic University board of inquiry report which

urged, ''as other Catholic universities already have done, the acceptance of the 1940 Statement without reservation and without the
limitation clause. It is the conclusion of Committee A that most
church-related institutions no longer need nor desire the departure
from the principle of academic freedom implied in the 1940 Statement, and it does not endorse such a departure.'' This interpretive
comment was subsequently adopted by the AAUP.[42]

At the same time at its annual meeting in April 1970, the
AAUP conferred the Alexander Meiklejohn Award for outstanding
contribution to academic freedom on Father Hesburgh. The citation
praised Hesburgh for his sustained and stalwart efforts to shape a
role for Catholic higher education that places Catholic universities
squarely in the tradition of academic freedom and uninhibited intellectual inquiry. In the forefront of leadership in the remarkable
changes that have occurred in church-related higher education (as
illustrated especially in the Land O'Lakes Statement), Hesburgh also
staunchly supported academic freedom at Notre Dame, especially
those faculty members who dissented from the papal encyclical
Humanae Vitae in its condemnation of artificial contraception. In
his acceptance speech Hesburgh reiterated the fundamental importance of academic freedom for higher education in general and
especially for Catholic higher education.[43]

The American higher education community had tolerated limitations on academic freedom in church-related institutions. While
tolerating such limitations, efforts were made to nudge church-related
institutions fully into the mainstream of American higher education
with its commitment to academic freedom. American higher education warmly welcomed and institutionally embraced with enthu-
siasm and haste Catholic higher education's acceptance of academic
freedom in the late 1960s.

By the end of the 1960s Catholic higher education had made
a complete turnabout in its approach to academic freedom. The
mainstream of Catholic higher education insisted that Catholic institutions above all had to be colleges or universities in the accepted
American understanding of the terms, and had to have a true
commitment to academic freedom and institutional autonomy. Such
autonomy and academic freedom did not oppose the Catholic sponsorship of such institutions. Catholic universities can be and should
be universities and Catholic. However, this dramatic reversal occurred

without strong agreement on any theoretical foundation for it. Thus the questions naturally arise, why and how could such a dramatic turnabout occur in such a short span of time?

Why the Change on Academic Freedom?

The 1960s were a turbulent period in the life of Catholic education, higher education in general, society at large, and in the self-understanding and life of the Roman Catholic church. The ground for a dramatic shift in Catholic attitudes toward academic freedom was prepared by the coming together of many factors, including changes in Catholic self-understanding, in Catholic relationships to American culture, in Catholic education, and in American education in general.

Changes in Catholic Self-understanding

The Second Vatican Council (1962–65) produced significant and profound changes in Catholic theory and practice. Bernard Lonergan, perhaps the most respected scholar among English-speaking theologians in the last few decades, has claimed that underlying the change brought about at Vatican II was the shift from classicism to historical consciousness.[44] The church still had the same scriptures, the same tradition, the same history, but pervasive change resulted from the perspective in which all these things were considered. Classicism stresses the eternal, the immutable, and the unchanging. Historical consciousness gives more significance to the particular, the individual, the changing, and the historical. A classicist perspective by its very nature adopts a deductive methodology, whereas the historically conscious approach tends to be more inductive.

Catholic philosophy and theology before the Second Vatican Council definitely employed a classicist perspective and a deductive methodology. The syllogism was the logical instrument that was most often employed in Catholic philosophy and theology. In syllogistic reasoning the conclusions are deduced from the major and the minor premises, and the conclusion is just as certain as the premises. In a deductive and classicist perspective the goal of science in general is certitude. One strives to arrive at such certitude by knowing the ultimate causes of reality. Thus, for example, Thomas Aquinas defined *science* as the certain knowledge of things in their causes. The more historically conscious and inductive approach by its very nature does not aim at certitude. Contemporary science, as distinguished from the medieval notion of science, does not aim at certitude but at a hypothesis or the best possible explanation, with the recognition that such an hypothesis must constantly be tested and criticized in order to arrive at more adequate explanations. This more historically conscious approach affected both Catholic philosophy and theology in the period after the Second Vatican Council.

Catholic philosophy had claimed to be the perennial philosophy based on Aristotle and especially Thomas Aquinas. However, the reality of historical consciousness called into question the very existence of a perennial philosophy. Even in the 1960s it was clear that there could be no one Catholic philosophy valid for all times, all cultures, and all situations. (Recall that in American Catholicism the opposition to academic freedom came not only from theology but also from philosophy.) But the very concept of a perennial philosophy was called into question.

An historically conscious theology could likewise not be a perennial theology. Historical consciousness recognizes that each age and time must try to understand God and God's self-revelation in the light of contemporary realities. The theology of the present cannot merely repeat what has been said in different times and cultures. An historically conscious theology must recognize both continuity and discontinuity and can never neglect the past. The faith and theology of the church must always be in continuity with the work and word of Jesus. However, the past cannot be canonized in an ahistorical manner. Historical consciousness first came to the fore in recent Catholic theology in the area of biblical studies. The scriptures themselves are historically and culturally conditioned. In 1943 Pope Pius XII opened the door to the use of an historical-critical method in biblical studies. The historically conscious perspective so prominent at Vatican II called for theology to seek to understand God, God's revelation, and God's ways in the light of changing historical and cultural situations.[45] However, such particular and contemporary understandings must always be in continuity with the Christian tradition and with the church universal. Thus the acceptance of historical consciousness avoids a total relativity or sheer existentialism.

The very reality of Vatican II with its call for dialogue with the modern world was living proof of historical consciousness at work.

The council also illustrated the role and importance of theology in bringing about change in the church. In an historically conscious perspective, theology will constantly try to understand and appropriate the word and work of Jesus in light of ongoing historical and cultural realities. The Second Vatican Council proved in practice the importance of this theological role. Theologians had no vote at the Second Vatican Council (in earlier church councils theologians sometimes did have voting rights), but they nevertheless played a primary role in bringing about change at Vatican II. Ironically the very theologians who had been silenced or under suspicion in the 1950s— Yves Congar, Karl Rahner, Henri de Lubac, John Courtney Murray, Bernard Häring—were instrumental in bringing about the changes of the council. Theologians, like the whole church, are called to a creative fidelity that constantly strives to find a better understanding of God's self-revelation. Theology thus constantly searches for the truth and can never claim that it possesses and has attained the truth perfectly. Such an understanding sees theology as analogous to other academic disciplines which are similarly striving for the truth. Like their colleagues in, say, music history, theologians will make some mistakes, but theology needs freedom in order to carry out its essential mission and purpose. The abuses involved in curtailing the freedom of some of the theologians who most influenced Vatican II underscored the need for a greater freedom among Catholic theologians.

A second theological development associated with the Second Vatican Council was a greater appreciation of freedom in the church and the acceptance of a greater role for freedom in society in general. There can be no doubt that in its understanding of the church, society, and the world at large in the pre-Vatican II period, the Catholic approach was fearful of the role of freedom. In terms of the church itself, the popular mentality accurately expressed the reality by saying that whereas Protestantism stressed freedom, Roman Catholicism emphasized order, structure, and authority.

In my judgment and in the opinion of most Catholic theologians, the Roman Catholic church in the twentieth century before the Vatican Council was more centralized and authoritarian than it had ever been before.[46] Historical circumstances, especially modern transportation and communication, had spurred this development. For most of the church's life the individual churches enjoyed a great deal of local autonomy. Modern communication made it much easier for Rome to know what was happening throughout the world and to give minute regulations governing all the particular problems that arose. Only in the last hundred years, for example, did the policy develop whereby the pope appointed all the bishops in the church. Before then bishops were elected in many different ways, but they always had to be received into communion by the bishop of Rome. The authority of the pope in naming bishops is something quite new in the history of the Roman Catholic church.

Vatican II did not deny the hierarchical role in the church, but this role was put into a broader perspective. The church is not primarily the institutional hierarchy but the people of God, all of whom are called to Christian holiness. In addition to hierarchical teachers there are also prophets and other teachers in the church. The Vatican Council especially stressed the role of the individual bishops and the college of bishops so that the bishop could no longer be considered a delegate or a vicar of the pope in a particular area. Bishops on their own govern a particular church and together with the pope have a solicitude and care for the whole church. The emphasis on the collegiality of all bishops thus affects the notion of papal primacy as an office seen completely apart from the college of bishops. The pope is the head of the college of bishops, but he is not an absolute monarch. The Petrine office in the church must be seen in its relationship to the college of bishops, and both structures serve the people of God.

Vatican II also addressed the teaching authority of pope and bishops. Such authority must always be subject to the word of God and to truth. The philosophy of Thomas Aquinas, which the church claimed to be following, had always insisted that truth and goodness are intrinsic, not extrinsic. Something is commanded because it is good and not the other way around. Authority must always conform itself to the true and the good. Such an understanding makes authority the servant of the true and the good and not their master. The experience of the council, change, and the acceptance of historical consciousness all contributed to a greater Catholic appreciation of the importance of freedom and rights within the church. The Second Vatican Council thus was critical of an overly juridical, authoritarian, and institutional understanding of the church.[47]

The council even addressed the question of freedom of inquiry and thought in its discussion of the harmony between culture and Christian formation in the Pastoral Constitution on the Church in the Modern World (par. 62): "But for the proper exercise of this role, the faithful, both clerical and lay, should be accorded a lawful freedom of inquiry, of thought, and of expression, tempered by humility and courage in whatever branch of study they have specialized."[48] Yes, freedom is and should be qualified, but nonetheless something new is in the air.

Throughout the twentieth century, Catholic teaching and self-understanding came to a greater appreciation of the importance of freedom in society and in the world.[49] Catholic teaching throughout the nineteenth century had been strongly opposed to what was called individualistic liberalism with its great stress on the freedom of the individual. In the eyes of many Catholic thinkers this liberalism and excessive freedom started in religious matters with the teaching of Luther. Subsequent philosophy freed human beings from God and God's law. In the political order, democracy with its notion that the majority makes something right illustrated such freedom run amok. In Catholic understanding such freedom was license because God's truth and law are supreme and must be embraced by human beings.

However, as the twentieth century progressed, Catholicism was no longer in opposition to individualistic liberalism but to totalitarianism. Catholic social teaching condemned Marxism, Fascism, and Communism,[50] but Catholics were often more willing to tolerate totalitarianism on the right than on the left. In opposing totalitarianism Catholics came to defend the freedom and dignity of the individual. The papal encyclical *Pacem in Terris,* issued by Pope John XXIII in 1963, illustrates this change and development. This encyclical for the first time in official Catholic social teaching proposed a sustained discussion and development of human rights.[51] Previously the Catholic tradition had been very heavy on duties but light on human rights because of the fear of individualism that was connected with the very concept of rights. But now Catholic teaching became a firm defender of human rights. Such a teaching, to its credit, insisted not only on civil or political rights that had often been stressed in the individualistic traditions of the past, but also economic rights that recognize the communitarian aspect of human persons. In 1961 in *Mater et Magistra* Pope John XXIII had devoted the last chapter of the encyclical to the reconstruction of social relationships in truth, justice, and love.[52] Only two years later, in *Pacem in Terris,* the pope added a fourth element to the triad of truth, justice, love: freedom.[53] The difference between the two documents points out the growing importance of freedom in Catholic social teaching. One Catholic teaching seemed incompatible with this newly developing emphasis on freedom in society, namely, the official Catholic rejection of religious freedom.

The discussion of the question of religious liberty took place at the Second Vatican Council and was finally resolved in 1965.[54] The older Catholic teaching called for the union of church and state and denied religious freedom as the right of all to practice any religion publicly. Only the true religion could be practiced publicly. However, in practice Catholic teaching was willing to tolerate religious freedom if trying to deny it would involve a greater evil. In practice it seemed as if Catholics wanted religious freedom whenever they were in the minority, but insisted on no religious freedom in Catholic countries. After much discussion, Vatican II promulgated its teaching on religious freedom. It should be noted that religious freedom is not based on the fact that all religions are of equal value. Religious freedom according to the Declaration on Religious Liberty (par. 2) means that every person is immune from external coercion that either forces one to act against one's conscience in religious matters or prevents one from acting in accord with one's conscience.[55] The state cannot interfere in religious matters as such. The full and complete acceptance of religious freedom by Vatican II together with the growing Catholic recognition of the importance of freedom in the church and in society at large made it much easier for Catholics to be open to the concept of academic freedom. Vatican II's emphasis on historical consciousness and on freedom, together with their broader ramifications, laid the groundwork among Catholics for a greater openness to academic freedom.

The teaching endorsed by Vatican II that stressed the autonomy of earthly affairs and culture had to have an impact on Catholic acceptance of academic freedom. According to the Pastoral Constitution on the Church in the Modern World (par. 36) "the autonomy of earthly affairs" means that created things and societies themselves enjoy their own laws and values which must be gradually deciphered, put to use, and regulated by human beings. In this context one can and should speak of the rightful independence of science. However, the independence and autonomy of temporal affairs cannot mean that created things do not depend on God and that human beings can use them without any reference to their creator.[56] The document highlights the church's interest in promoting and influencing human and civil culture, but such a relationship does not mean that the church absorbs culture. Just as the church understands faith and reason to be true sources of knowledge, without faith absorbing or challenging a proper autonomy of reason, so too the church affirms a legitimate autonomy of human culture and especially of the sciences.[57] "Culture...has continual need of rightful freedom of development and a legitimate possibility of autonomy according to its own principles."[58] By accepting the autonomy of earthly affairs, institutions and culture, Vatican II opened the door for the acceptance of the American college and university as it exists within this culture. That academic freedom is intimately connected with the autonomy of the university is not mere coincidence.

The change at Vatican II in Catholic teaching on religious liberty also recognized the autonomy of the state or the temporal governing authority.[59] The older approach to religious freedom recognized the state as supreme in its own sphere, or end, of the temporal welfare of its citizens. In the Catholic attempt at synthesis the temporal, while supreme in its own sphere, must, however, always be in the service of the spiritual. Consequently, the state as an institution that deals with the temporal must in some way be subordinated to the church that deals with the spiritual. The characteristic Catholic approach to human questions has been inclusive, synthetic, and orderly. The word *catholic* means universal, and the Catholic church has stressed universality both in its understanding of a universal church that should embrace all and in its insistence that faith should animate all that we are and all that we do. Since faith is all-pervasive, it must touch everything, and a synthesis is called for between faith and reason, faith and daily life, faith and human realities. In putting together such a synthetic and inclusive approach it is necessary to order things according to their relationship to one another. The Catholic tradition recognizes the principle of hierarchical ordering in which the lower is subordinated to the higher. This vision stands behind the older Catholic approach to the union of church and state. Synthesis requires that all be brought into a unity, but unity requires subordination. The state is supreme in the temporal realm, but the state and the temporal realm are subordinated to the spiritual realm and to the church. The state thus does not have full autonomy, for that would deny the synthetic whole of reality by making the state independent of the spiritual realm.

The newer teaching recognizes that precisely by being autonomous and independent of the church, the state can truly accomplish its own purpose and be of help to the church by guaranteeing its freedom. The church does not have to subordinate other institutions or cultural realities but can accept them as they are, operating in accord with their own finalities and functions. They best serve the church by being true to their own functions and purposes. For example, art is good art in accordance with principles of art and not because of its relationship to faith and the church. The autonomous state best serves both its own purposes and ultimately the good of the church.

Before 1960, Catholic thought in the United States did not respect the autonomy of the university or the college. These institutions of higher learning were seen as part of the pastoral function of the church itself. The Catholic emphasis on hierarchical ordering was definitely at work in this understanding: the university served the church and was subordinated to it. To accept the autonomy of the university means that the university must function in accord with its own proper purposes. In American culture, the university must be a free and autonomous center of study; institutions of higher learning must retain their own characteristics and not lose them by being subordinated to the church. A Catholic university must first and always be a university.

Cultural and Sociological Change

As pointed out in the second chapter the American Catholic church faced from its very beginning a twofold aspect of its own identity—could it be both Catholic and American at one and the same time?[60] On the one hand, Rome was constantly worried that the American Catholic church would become too American and thereby lose its Catholic character. The condemnation of Americanism in 1899 by Pope Leo XIII underscored this position. Many felt that the American ethos with its stress on freedom was not compatible with the Catholic understanding. Catholic schools evolved to protect and nurture the faith and identity of Roman Catholics. Catholics tended to remain aloof and did not become a part of the mainstream of American life.

On the other hand, some Americans remained suspicious of American Catholics. In the nineteenth and early twentieth centuries American Catholics were primarily immigrants. So-called native Americans (the *real* natives had been thrown off the land) looked down on the immigrants. Waves of anti-Catholicism and less overt forms of discrimination continued well into the twentieth century. Above all, Americans were suspicious of Catholics in the political order; they owed obedience to a foreign ruler in Rome. For their part, Catholics could not accept the American political experiment with its emphasis on freedom, particularly on religious freedom. The leaders of American Catholicism in general tried to downplay the tensions of being both Catholic and American, but many aspects of the tensions remained.

Great changes occurred in the wake of World War II. Ever since the First World War Catholics were self-consciously patriotic, proving they were loyal Americans. The waves of European immigration were over as the twentieth century unfolded. Catholics entered into the mainstream of American life and achieved economic prosperity. Many Catholics were able to buy homes and cars for the first time after the Second World War. The move to the suburbs broke up many of the Catholic ghettos that had existed in the larger cities. On the international scene the cold war emphasized the opposition between the United States and atheistic Communism. One of the strongest allies in opposition to atheistic Communism was the Vatican and the Catholic Church, so Catholic interest and American interest were closely associated. Catholics were not giving up their Catholicism in the post–World War II period, but there was a greater existential recognition that being Catholic and being American were not incompatible.

The early 1960s witnessed two events that symbolized the reality that no fundamental incompatibility existed between being Catholic and being American. Before the election of John F. Kennedy as president in 1960, the accepted political wisdom claimed that a Catholic could never be elected president of the United States. Kennedy's election, more than any other single event, illustrated the compatibility between being Catholic and being American. In the intellectual sphere John Courtney Murray, the American Jesuit, proved the same compatibility. Other Americans were fearful that Catholics could not accept the fundamental principle of American government with its emphasis on God-given freedom. Murray claimed that Catholics could wholeheartedly accept the American proposition that all human beings are created equal and endowed by their Creator with certain inalienable rights, among these life, liberty, and the pursuit of happiness. Not only can Catholics accept this, but Catholic philosophy as expressed in natural law is singularly able to defend and ground the proposition. Unfortunately, most contemporary American philosophers no longer can provide such a philosophical foundation. Murray made the seemingly incredible claim that *only* the Catholic philosophical tradition could adequately explain and defend the American proposition.[61] Above all Murray proved to the Catholic Church that the American system of religious freedom and separation of church and state was totally acceptable to Catholic thought. Murray's work on religious freedom was finally accepted by the Second Vatican Council in 1965.[62]

For the sake of completeness one should note the danger that may arise from stressing the compatibility between being Catholic and being American. Catholicism could accept too readily whatever is American and lose the prophetic and critical role that the Christian gospel must always provide. In many ways the rise of a more radical Catholicism in the later 1960s that opposed government policies in Vietnam was a reaction against an uncritical acceptance of everything American.[63] From my perspective of Catholic moral theology, the relationship between the gospel and culture must avoid the two extremes of simple identification or total opposition. Sometimes the church learns from the culture, as in the case of the American emphasis on the dignity, freedom, and rights of the person; sometimes the church should criticize the culture, as in the recent statements by the American Catholic bishops of the United States' policies on nuclear deterrence and the economy.[64] But in the historical context of the stress on the compatibility between being Catholic and being American in the early 1960s, Catholics were more prone to see that their colleges and universities could both be truly American institutions of higher learning and be Catholic.

Changes in Catholic Higher Education

The Carnegie Commission on Higher Education sponsored a series of profiles on higher education in the 1960s. Andrew M. Greeley, a sociologist and program director of the National Opinion Research Center in Chicago, contributed the work on Catholic higher education. The title of his book, published in 1969, exemplifies the remarkable change that had taken place by the late '60s in Catholic colleges and universities—*From Backwater to Mainstream: A Profile of Catholic Higher Education.*[65] Under the general perspective supplied by Greeley's title, this section will briefly discuss the changes that occurred in the Catholic colleges and universities that culminated in their entrance into the mainstream of American higher education.

Catholic higher education grew and expanded greatly after World War II and throughout the 1950s. Some critical voices, however, began to speak up in the mid-1950s. The existence of such criticism indicates that Catholic higher education had already attained enough maturity to raise questions. The rapid developments that followed this criticism and responded to other social changes illustrated the willingness of Catholic higher education to change. In the 1950s criticism began with some Catholic intellectuals, including lay people, who were associated with Catholic higher education. The Catholic Commission on Intellectual and Cultural Affairs, a small group of Catholic intellectuals, became the institutional embodiment of criticism.[66] To this group Monsignor John Tracy Ellis gave his now-famous address on the failure of American Catholics to contribute to the intellectual life.[67]

Then (1955) professor of church history at the Catholic University of America, Ellis devotes most of his essay to the historical reasons for the lack of Catholic intellectuals in the United States. He quotes statistics of various kinds to show that the contribution of Catholics to the sciences and humanities in the United States was proportionately much less than their percentage of the population. Anti-Catholic attitudes have played some part, but the real blame must fall squarely on the shoulders of the Catholic community itself. The Catholic community in the United States until 1920 was primarily composed of immigrants, and all of its energies and resources were geared to help the immigrant retain Catholic faith and succeed on the American scene. No true intellectural tradition and respect for the search for knowledge existed among American Catholics. Converts to Catholicism have done much more for the intellectual life than have the vast majority of those who were born Catholic. The Catholic leaders in the United States for the most part have not experienced the life of the university and have been engaged primarily in the fundamental work of building the church as an institution.

Ellis's judgment about Catholic higher education was severe. He refers to a study by Robert H. Knapp and Joseph J. Greenbaum published in 1953 that determined from the undergraduate backgrounds of students who had won distinction in graduate schools during the years 1946–52 what colleges had provided the largest number of promising scholars. In all seven categories of their investigation Catholic institutions consistently ranked the lowest compared to nondenominational and Protestant schools. In agreement with the criticism leveled against Catholic higher education by Robert M. Hutchins in 1937, Ellis also believed that Catholic higher education had imitated the worst of American higher education in the form of athleticism, collegiatism, vocationalism, and antiintellectualism. He thinks the first two areas might have improved somewhat since 1937, but not the latter two. Above all, the academic ideals of research and a lively intellectual life are sorely lacking in Catholic higher education.

The history professor excoriates the proliferation of Catholic graduate schools, "none of which is adequately endowed, and few of which have the trained personnel, the equipment in libraries and laboratories, and the professional wage scales to warrant their ambitious undertakings."[68] He criticizes the senseless duplication of effort that together with wasteful proliferation has prevented the emergence of a top-flight Catholic graduate school in this country.

American Catholics, even a large number of Catholics involved in higher education, lack the love of scholarship for its own sake. Authorities have overemphasized the college as an agent for moral development and have insufficiently stressed the college as an instrument for fostering intellectual excellence and the love of learning.

Ellis's criticism resonated with the ideas of the small Catholic Commission on Intellectual and Cultural Affairs. This group supported the work of Thomas O'Dea, who constructed a theoretical explanation for the phenomenon of Catholic antiintellectualism, and the research of John Donovan, who investigated the lay professoriate in Catholic institutions.[69] A Catholic higher educational system that was beginning to be self-critical could definitely be more open to the ecclesial, societal, and educational changes that converged very dramatically in the 1960s.

The changes that took place in Catholic higher education in the 1960s can aptly be described as a movement toward a greater professionalization of Catholic higher education. The most pervasive change that influenced all others concerned the fundamental purpose and function of Catholic higher education. Before 1960 Catholic higher education understood its role as intimately associated with the church's mission to protect and promote the faith and morals of Catholic young adults. By the end of the 1960s the leadership of the mainstream of Catholic higher education rejected that understanding of its purpose; rather, growth in learning is the immediate goal of the Catholic university while concern for faith and morals is clearly a less direct goal. In sociological terms, according to John D. Donovan, Catholic higher education before the 1960s stressed pattern maintenance and integrative functions for the church and the country. The foundation and growth of these institutions was not inspired by intellectual goals as ends in themselves. Responding to the needs of an immigrant church, Catholic colleges and universities sought to transmit religiously approved cultural values and to integrate all new knowledge with the teachings of the church. The college primarily served the pastoral ministry of the church, or the sponsoring religious community, or both. These religiously derived characteristics of Catholic higher education were reinforced by the defensive posture of an immigrant minority group that marked American Catholicism in general. Such attitudes of pattern maintenance reduced the openness of the leaders of Catholic higher education to the dominant non-Catholic intellectual values and attitudes.[70]

Michael Walsh, who had served as president of both Boston College and Fordham, clearly recognized the complete turnabout that had taken place in Catholic higher education in the 1960s. Father Walsh believed that such a dramatic change should be publicly recognized and admitted despite the fear and hesitation of a few. Academics above all must be willing to face the evidence. In a somewhat defensive way Walsh insists that Catholic higher education can be justly proud of what it is doing. Yes, it has changed the priorities set by the founding fathers and mothers of Catholic colleges and universities, but we need have no qualms of conscience. Other Catholic institutions do not feel called upon to apologize because their aim is to aid the poor, train the blind, help faltering marriages, or send food and clothing to underdeveloped countries. So, too, for colleges and universities, whose aim is to search for the truth in a manner that is in keeping with academic professionalism. The university must be a community of scholars involved in the work of discovering and communicating truth. Just as Catholic marriage counselors and Catholic social service providers need to be professionals in their own field, so too Catholic colleges and universities best serve the church by being good colleges and universities. The concern for faith is mediate and ultimate, but the proper immediate goal of the colleges or universities is to be as fully academic and as professional as possible.[71]

By the end of the 1960s leaders in the mainstream of Catholic higher education were convinced that Catholic colleges and universities had to be colleges and universities in the full American sense of the terms. Being Catholic added something distinctive to these institutions, but being Catholic entailed the acceptance of institutions of higher learning as free and autonomous centers devoted to the study and transmission of truth in all areas. Leo McLaughlin, the president of Fordham, put it very succinctly: "Fordham will pay any price, break any mold, in order to achieve her function as a university."[72] The opening words and first heading of the Land O'Lakes Statement precisely and simply make the point: "The Catholic University: A True University with Distinctive Characteristics."[73] Similarly, Father Hesburgh of Notre Dame often stressed at this time that a great Catholic university must begin by being a great university. Its being Catholic adds something distinctive to its being a university, but its being Catholic cannot deny, substitute for, or subtract or detract from what is necessary and essential to its being a real university with the truly intellectual goal of being a university in the accepted American sense.

The leaders of Catholic higher education still wanted their institutions to remain Catholic, and a rationale was now needed so that the institutions could be American colleges and universities that are simply distinguished by being Catholic. From the late '60s to the present, Catholic higher education has struggled, on the one hand, to understand and to work out the exact meaning of its Catholic identity and how being Catholic makes the institution distinctive, and, on the other hand, to provide a Catholic identity that would build on what was American about a university. At the least, such an understanding requires no direct ecclesiastical control. Further, there seems to be general agreement on the need for a Catholic college or university to have theology and philosophy departments, to take an approach that is broadly human in perspective, to welcome the presence of a worshipping community, to carry out an effective pastoral ministry, to foster dialogue between theology and faith in the modern world, to serve society and church, and to give institutional witness to the importance of an intellectual life that flows from a tradition that maintains that faith and reason cannot contradict one another.[74] We need delve no deeper here into the question of just what specifically constitutes Catholic distinctiveness; it suffices to point out that the leaders of Catholic higher education did not want to abandon their Catholicity but saw it as compatible with their schools' becoming American institutions of higher learning. The most significant change in Catholic higher education in the 1960s thus went to the heart of the matter—the very purpose and function of Catholic colleges and universities.

This radical and fundamental change influenced all other aspects of the structure of Catholic higher education, but this development in the late '60s also resulted from growing changes in other particular aspects of Catholic colleges and universities. The significant areas of change in Catholic higher education in the 1960s began with the faculty, but then went on to include institutional governance and the students. Evolution in these areas began soon after the debate about Catholic intellectualism that John Tracy Ellis sparked in 1955.

The professionalization of the faculty was a significant factor in the changing face of Catholic higher education at this time.[75] The majority of the faculty in Catholic higher education before World War II were clergy and religious who found their identity in their religious roles and not primarily as faculty members or academics. Most of them appointed by their superiors to go on to further studies and were even told which area to study. Academic professionalism was not a high priority. In fairness, many were good teachers and showed an interest in and concern for their students, but the intellectual life was always subordinate to their church role and mission.

After World War II Catholic higher education rapidly expanded. Older institutions grew and many new Catholic colleges came into existence in order to educate both veterans returning from the war with the GI Bill of Rights to pay for their education and the ever-growing number of Catholics who now as members of the middle class wanted to attend college. To meet these needs for expansion, many lay faculty had to be employed, and soon they constituted a majority of the faculty in Catholic higher education. In the 1950s, however, lay faculty had practically no say in how the institution was run and were definitely looked upon as second-class citizens.

For the most part, the faculty, both religious and lay, that came into Catholic higher education in the late '40s and '50s had not earned doctoral degrees at the time of their appointments; a good many of them never obtained a Ph.D. They had little or no contact with the broader American academy. Almost without exception, they were themselves products of Catholic education—often they had studied at the same institution where they now taught. These faculty members saw themselves primarily as teachers who seldom published and were not really involved in research. Catholic college teachers at this time seldom participated in professional societies. They had very heavy teaching loads, and some of them invested much time and energy in extracurricular activities connected with the students.

The lay faculty at this time shared all the above characteristics but had other problems of their own. Most of them willingly accepted their roles as second-class citizens and dutifully bowed to whatever Father or Sister said. In comparison with their counterparts in secular and non-Catholic institutions, these professors were poorly paid and often lacking in basic amenities such as offices and secretarial assistance. Many of the lay faculty had a great loyalty to the religious orders running the college and were very happy to be teaching at such institutions. Without any real commitment to the academic profession or careers, they were not interested in moving on to more prestigious academic institutions even if they did have the prerequisite Ph.D. degree and publications. For many lay people their teaching at a Catholic college was part of their lay apostolate as Catholics and not primarily a matter of academic commitment.

However, by the 1960s, Andew M. Greeley detected and described a new breed of lay professors in Catholic higher education. Catholic colleges and universities continued to grow and needed new faculty. Above all, many colleges expanded into graduate work. The new breed of lay professor was often trained in non-Catholic institutions and brought with him or her all the traditions of the American academy. Such faculty members were well trained, highly professional, and usually had obtained their Ph.D. degrees before they began to teach. Their commitments were primarily professional and academic. They were often interested in research and publishing and saw themselves moving on to better and more prestigious institutions in the future. These academics were no longer content with the passive and subordinate role of the old-time Catholic lay professor. Such faculty were strong supporters of the principles and procedures of the academy found in non-Catholic higher institutions.[76] This growing professionalization also affected theology departments. In the period before 1960, the theology department of a Catholic institution of higher learning was probably the weakest department in the entire institution. Many theology courses were required. Their content could best be described as catechetical rather than academic. The whole Catholic college or university in those days saw itself primarily as a pastoral arm of the church, and theology departments also perceived their function in pastoral terms. The Catholic institution of higher learning was entrusted with the faith of the student and tried to protect and deepen that faith, especially through theology courses. However, the theology professors were generally poorly trained as academics; it was commonly maintained that priests by ordination, and religious by virtue of their vows and training, were capable of teaching theology on a college level. Theology was looked upon as a static discipline that never changed. The student was generally expected to memorize basic truths.[77]

Even in the 1950s a growing awareness emerged on many Catholic campuses that theology needed to be changed and to become more professional. A professional organization—the Society of Catholic College Teachers of Sacred Doctrine—was founded in 1954 to work toward improving the teaching of theology on Catholic campuses.[78] This group later changed its name to the College Theology Society. Universities such as the Catholic University, Fordham, and Marquette developed respectable doctoral programs to train college teachers of theology. The point was beginning to be made that seminary training did not qualify a priest or a religious to teach college theology. Lay people began to enter the profession and professionalization occurred. At its 1966 national meeting the College Theology Society voted not to endorse the 1940 AAUP Statement of Principles on Academic Freedom and Tenure, but the following year's convention did endorse the document.[79] Such an action by this society is indicative of the type of professionalization that it tried to bring to the field of teaching theology. The basic idea was for professors to see themselves as primarily academics, just like their other colleagues.

The growth of lay faculty and the professionalization of faculty were two factors that also influenced the professionalization of the governance and structure of Catholic institutions of higher learning in the 1960s. Catholic colleges and universities were seen before that time primarily as part of the apostolate of the religious community which owned the college. Comparatively few Catholic institutions were run by dioceses. Presidents and administrators as well as clerical and religious faculty were appointed by religious superiors, and the institution was generally run in the same way that religious communities were run. Before the professionalization of the faculty, faculty rarely participated in the governance of the institution. As was noted in some of the AAUP reports in the early 1960s, generally accepted American academic policies and procedures were often nonexistent in Catholic institutions of higher learning. Administrators appointed by the religious community were often chosen because of their qualities as good religious, not because they were good academicians or good academic administrators.

Significant developments also occurred in the internal structure of Catholic higher education in the 1960s. Gradually the procedures for tenure and the recommended policies and procedures of the AAUP were incorporated into Catholic higher education. No longer could the college be run as an extension of the religious community. Competent lay people with experience in the American academy were now appointed more frequently to administrative positions below the level of president. Academic planning and fund raising were two absolute requirements for the continued health of institutions. Soon it was evident that the presidents had to be experienced and competent in order to run professional academic institutions effectively. By the end of the '60s the tide was definitely turning toward seeing Catholic colleges and universities primarily as academic institutions and not as religious apostolates; thus they had to be staffed by competent and trained academic faculty and administrators. The growth, vitality, and even continued existence of Catholic colleges and universities required a truly professional administrator.[80]

Perhaps the most revolutionary change in the institutional governance and the structure of Catholic higher education was the shift to lay boards of trustees. In this new situation a religious order no longer controlled the college or university but merely sponsored it, while the legal ownership and control of the institution passed out of the hands of the religious community. In 1967 St. Louis University and the University of Notre Dame became the first major Catholic institutions to have predominately lay boards of trustees. Subsequently many other Catholic institutions followed this move. Father Hesburgh of Notre Dame recognized the great advantages and need for such an arrangement, but in blunt terms he also described the problems involved in bringing about such a change and the opposition from some members of the religious order that had previously contolled the institution.[81] The shift to lay trustees marked a definitive structural change in Catholic higher education that clearly put Catholic institutions on an even footing with the rest of the American academy. Professionalization and autonomy were now complete.

Students played a very significant role in the changes in higher education in the United States in general in the late 1960s and 1970s. The activity of students in Catholic institutions was not as dramatic or traumatic as in many non-Catholic institutions, but students had an effect on Catholic higher education. Even well into the 1960s most Catholic colleges and universities treated their students according to the traditional attitudes toward human nature that have held sway in religious orders for the past few centuries. Catholic institutions lagged far behind others in recognizing that they did not exist *in loco parentis*. Professionalization in Catholic higher education also brought personnel services onto Catholic campuses in the 1960s. By the end of the 1960s, the tendency was clearly away from the earlier very restrictive and paternalistic approaches.[82]

One of the greatest problems confronting Catholic higher education in the late 1960s was its acute financial distress, and the solution to financial problems also pushed Catholic institutions in the direction of becoming first and foremost good academic institutions. Catholic colleges and universities lived almost exclusively off their tuitions. Endowment was small or nonexistent. The upgrading of lay faculty both in number and in pay raised budgets. Professionalization of other areas, such as libraries, laboratories, and student services, also called for budgetary increases. At the same time the religious faculty was shrinking for various reasons, and what was often called the "living endowment" (religious did not receive full salaries and the difference between what they received and a normal salary often was returned to the institution) became much smaller. If tuition were raised too much, institutions would price themselves out of existence because of stiff competition with other private and, especially, public institutions. Catholic institutions thus saw the need to develop their own endowments and to encourage gifts from their alumni and friends. But even then, Catholic institutions could not survive without corporate grants and above all without state and federal government aid.

The question of state and federal government aid to Catholic institutions was somewhat unclear at the time. Was government aid to such institutions constitutional, both on a federal and a state level? To be sure, throughout the 1960s Catholic institutions received growing amounts of government dollars. The continued existence of Catholic higher education required maintaining and ever increasing funding from government sources. To attract corporate and government support, Catholic schools had to prove their importance and contribution to American society in general. These institutions had to be colleges and universities in the American sense of the term with the recognition of the importance of academic freedom and autonomy.[83] In fact, at this time a legal challenge was raised against government aid to four particular Catholic colleges. Finally in 1971, the Supreme Court decided that aid to these institutions was constitutional because, unlike Catholic grammar and high schools, these colleges were not centers of indoctrination and catechesis. The institutions accepted the princples of academic freedom and autonomy and therefore differed from Catholic high schools and Catholic grammar schools.[84] During this period charges were made that Catholic higher education was selling its soul in order to ensure its survival. However, the mainstream of Catholic higher education firmly proclaimed that such institutions could and should be Catholic institutions as well as American colleges and universities in the accepted understanding, practices, and procedures.

Changes in the American Academy
and in the Defense of Academic Freedom

The 1960s also saw significant changes occurring in the American academy in general and in the arguments supporting academic freedom that affected Catholic attitudes towards academic freedom. Recall that a traditional Catholic argument against American academic freedom came from a philosophical perspective—the rejection of the narrow empiricism that was often used to support academic freedom. In the 1960s questions about values and commitments came to the fore as our nation dealt with the growing problems of poverty, racism, and war. These three issues, especially the war in Vietnam, sharply divided the country but brought to the forefront of consciousness the importance of values and commitment to values. In this context many recognized the limitations of the scientific method with its need for empirical verification. A whole range of human life exists beyond the domain of the empirical scientific method, as aesthetics, ethics, and other branches of philosophy all recognize.

Many scholars became aware that even the empirical sciences could not necessarily prove their own foundations. For example, the mathematician could not prove the existence of numbers, nor could the historian prove the reality of facts. In this context the idea of the sciences being objective, impartial, and value free began to be questioned. Some social scientists recognized the impossibility of attaining absolutely neutral knowledge; the observer always brings his or her values, bias, and perspective to reality. Somewhat later many would realize that history is always written by the victors. If United States history books were written by native Americans, it would not be a generally accepted historical "fact" that Columbus discovered America in 1492. The methods of the academy could no longer be reduced to the empirical method and to value-free approaches.

In this context with its stress on values and commitment, the case could be made that theology, even Catholic theology, had a place within the academy. Above all, within this context academic freedom could not be grounded in a methodology that denied values, spiritual aspects of existence, and human and even scientific commitment. The earlier Catholic opposition to academic freedom was no longer apropos, because the limits of empiricism were being recognized by the academy itself.

The proponents and defendants of academic freedom in the 1960s seldom appealed to empiricism as had some of their predecessors. The AAUP was the group most associated with the defense and promotion of academic freedom. The 1940 Statement of Principles, however, wisely avoided any kind of philosophical grounding or basis and tended to be more pragmatic. The American academy itself thus recognized that the empirical and scientific method was good but limited and that there was a place in the academy for values, ethics, and even some types of commitment. In this context it was much easier for Catholic leaders to accept the pragmatic concept of academic freedom, for some of the earlier Catholic objections to academic freedom no longer loomed as problems. All these circumstances taken together—developments in Roman Catholicism coming from the Second Vatican Council, the newer American Catholic attitude toward American institutions and culture, changes in Catholic higher education, and the developments in the American academy itself—all created the climate in which by the end of the 1960s Catholic higher education radically, and quickly, changed its attitude to academic freedom.

NOTES

1. "Academic Freedom and Tenure: Mercy College," *AAUP Bulletin* 49 (1963): 245–252.

2. "Report of Committee A on Academic Freedom and Tenure, 1967–68," *AAUP Bulletin* 54 (1968): 178.

3. "Academic Freedom and Tenure: Gonzaga University," *AAUP Bulletin* 51 (1965): 8–12.

4. "Report of Committee A, 1964–65," *AAUP Bulletin* 51 (1965): 247.

5. "The Fifty-Fourth Annual Meeting," *AAUP Bulletin* 54 (1968): 243.

6. "Academic Freedom and Tenure: St. Mary's College (Minnesota)," *AAUP Bulletin* 54 (1968): 37–42.

7. "The Fifty-Fifth Annual Meeting," *AAUP Bulletin* 55 (1969): 151.

8. "Report of Committee A, 1968–69," *AAUP Bulletin* 55 (1969): 172.

9. Joseph Scimecca and Roland Damiano, *Crisis at St. John's: Strike and Revolution on the Catholic Campus* (New York: Random House, 1968); John Leo, "Some Problem Areas in Catholic Higher Education," in Robert Hassenger, ed., *The Shape of Catholic Higher Education* (Chicago: University of Chicago Press, 1967), pp. 193–201; William P. Fidler, "From the General Secretary," *AAUP Bulletin* 52 (1966): 5–11; "Academic Freedom and Tenure: St. John's University (N.Y.)," *AAUP Bulletin* 52 (1966): 12–19.

10. E.g., Francis Canavan, "St. John's University: The Issues," *America* 114 (January 22, 1966): 122–124; James Hitchcock, "Reflections on the St. John's Case," *Catholic World* 203 (April 1966): 24–28; Philip A. Grant, "Ferment on the Campus," *Catholic World* 205 (August 1967): 293–297.

11. John Tracy Ellis, "A Tradition of Autonomy?" in Neil G. McCluskey, ed., *The Catholic University: A Modern Appraisal* (Notre Dame, IN: University of Notre Dame Press, 1970), p. 257.

12. Erving E. Beauregard, "An Archbishop, a University, and Academic Freedom," *Records of the American Catholic Historical Society* 93 (1982): 25–39.

13. Editorial, "The Goldfish Bowl," *America* 108 (March 9, 1963): 329; editorial, "Breaking the Silence," *Commonweal* 78 (March 24, 1963): 4; symposium, "Zeroing in on Freedom," *Commonweal* 86 (June 2, 1967): 316–321.

14. Memo from the file of Joseph B. McAllister, Vice Rector of the Catholic University of America, dated May 5, 1967.

15. Albert C. Pierce, *Beyond One Man* (Washington: Anawim Press, 1967); David M. Knight, "What Happened at Catholic U?" *America* 116 (May 13, 1967): 723–725; Charles E. Curran, *Ongoing Revision in Moral Theology* (Notre Dame, IN: Fides Publishers, 1975), pp. 272–278.

16. Charles E. Curran, Robert E. Hunt, et al., *Dissent in and for the Church: Theologians and Humanae Vitae* (New York: Sheed and Ward, 1969); John F. Hunt, Terrence R. Connelly, et al., *The Responsibility of Dissent: The Church and Academic Freedom* (New York: Sheed and Ward, 1969).

17. Hunt, Connelly, et al., *Responsibility of Dissent*, p. 207.

18. Leslie Dewart, "Academic Freedom and Catholic Dissent," *Commonweal* 80 (April 3, 1964): 33–36.

19. Gerald F. Kreyche, "Academic Freedom in Catholic Colleges," *College and University Journal* 3, n. 3 (Summer 1964): 8–12; Kreyche, "American Catholic Higher Learning and Academic Freedom," *National Catholic Educational Association Bulletin* 62 (1965): 221–222.

20. Philip Gleason, "Academic Freedom," *America* 115 (July 16, 1966): 60–62.

21. John E. Walsh, "The University and the Church," in Edward J. Manier and John W. Houck, eds., *Academic Freedom in the Catholic University* (Notre Dame, IN: Fides Publishers, 1967), pp. 103–118.

22. Frederick Crosson, "Personal Commitment as the Basis of Free Inquiry," in Manier and Houck, *Academic Freedom in the Catholic University*, pp. 87–101.

23. E.g., John D. Donovan, *The Academic Man in the Catholic College* (New York: Sheed and Ward, 1964); Hassenger, *Shape of Catholic Higher Education*.

24. "Zeroing in on Freedom," *Commonweal* 86 (June 2, 1967): 316–321.

25. Francis E. Kearns, "Social Consciousness and Academic Freedom in Catholic Higher Education," in Hassenger, *Shape of Catholic Higher Education*, pp. 223–249.

26. Michael J. Bennett, "Incident at Boston College," *Commonweal* 80 (May 29, 1964): 284–285.

27. Land O'Lakes Statement, in McCluskey, *Catholic University*, pp. 336–337.

28. John C. Lungren, *Hesburgh of Notre Dame* (Kansas City, MO: Sheed and Ward, 1987).

29. Theodore M. Hesburgh, *The Hesburgh Papers: Higher Values in Higher Education* (Kansas City, MO: Andrews and McNeel, 1979), pp. 37–38.

30. Ibid., p. 75.

31. Examples of significant articles defending academic freedom for Catholic theologians at Catholic colleges and universities include the following: Ladislas Orsy, "Academic Freedom and the Teaching Church," *Thought* 43 (Winter 1968): 485–498; Robert E. Hunt, "Academic Freedom and the Theologian," *Proceedings of the Catholic Theological Society of America* 23 (1968): 261–267; John Kelley, "Academic Freedom and the Catholic College Theologian," in George Devine, ed., *Theology in Revolution: Proceedings of the College Theology Society, 1969* (Staten Island, NY: Alba House, 1970), pp. 169–183. For more in-depth studies, see Frederick W. Gunti, "Academic Freedom as an Operative Principle for the Catholic Theologian" (S.T.D. dissertation, The Catholic University of America, 1969); Hunt, Connelly, et al., *Responsibility of Dissent*.

32. Manning M. Pattillo and Donald W. MacKenzie, *Church Sponsored Higher Education in the United States: Report of the Danforth Commission* (Washington: American Council on Higher Education, 1966), p. v.

33. Ibid., p. 21.

34. Ibid., p. 204.

35. Ibid.

36. Ibid., pp. 74–75.

37. "Report of Committee A, 1964–65," *AAUP Bulletin* 51 (1965): 241.

38. "Report of the Self-Survey Committee of the AAUP," *AAUP Bulletin* 51 (1965): 148.

39. "Report of the Special Committee on Academic Freedom in Church-Related Colleges and Universities," *AAUP Bulletin* 53 (1967): 369–371.

40. "Record of Council Meeting, Washington, DC, October 25–26, 1968," *AAUP Bulletin* 55 (1969): 96.

41. "Report of Committee A on Academic Freedom and Tenure," *AAUP Bulletin* 55 (1969): 398.

42. "Report of Committee A, 1969–70," *AAUP Bulletin* 56 (1970): 166–167; AAUP, *Policy Documents and Reports*, 1984 ed. (Washington, DC: American Association of University Professors, 1984), p. 5. The AAUP continues to struggle with the limitations clause for church-related institutions. In my judgment logic demands that there should be no exceptions for church-related or any other special types of institutions. If these institutions put limits on academic freedom, they cease to be colleges and universities in the American understanding of the term. I think the limitations clause came into effect in the 1925 Statement because the American Council on Education and others as voluntary organizations did not want to write church-related institutions out of the American academy. Even in 1970 the AAUP stated that it did not endorse the invocation of the limitations clause because church-related institutions themselves no longer want or need the clause. Today many rightly want to assert that academic freedom in principle cannot admit of limitations for religious or any other reasons.

The theoretical problem is compounded by a serious practical problem. The 1940 Statement was originally proposed by the AAUP and the Association of American Colleges and subsequently has been endorsed by over 120 educational and professional organizations. In 1970 the AAUP officially accepted the interpretive comment about not endorsing a departure from the principle of academic freedom as contained in the limitations clause. The Association of American Colleges has not officially adopted this interpretive comment. How can a document that has been subscribed to by so many different groups be amended? The AAUP is now studying this very significant question. See "Report: The 'Limitations' Clause in the 1940 Statement of Principles," *Academe* 74 (September-October 1988): 52–59. In 1989 Committee A of the AAUP declined to accept its subcommittee's recommendation that the invocation of the limitations clause exempts an institution from the world of American higher education, in part because it is not appropriate for the AAUP to decide what is and what is not an authentic institution of higher education. The chair of committee A recognized that the limitations clause and the nature of academic freedom at church-related institutions will continue to be a vexing problem. See "Report of Committee A, 1988–89," *Academe* 75 (September-October 1989): 54.

43. "The Twelfth Alexander Meiklejohn Award," *AAUP Bulletin* 56 (1970): 148–152.

44. Bernard Lonergan, *Collection* (New York: Herder and Herder, 1947), pp. 252–267.

45. Donald Senior, "Dogmatic Constitution on Divine Revelation, *Dei Verbum*," in Timothy E. O'Connell, ed., *Vatican II and Its Documents:*

An American Appraisal (Wilmington, DE: Michael Glazier, 1986), pp. 122–140.

46. J. Robert Dionne, *The Papacy and the Church: A Study of Praxis and Reception in Ecumenical Perspective* (New York: Philosophical Library, 1987); Patrick Granfield, *The Papacy in Transition* (New York: Doubleday, 1980); Granfield, *The Limits of the Papacy: Authority and Autonomy in the Church* (New York: Crossroad, 1987).

47. Avery Dulles, *Models of the Church* (New York: Doubleday, 1974). Dulles has written extensively on the church. His latest book is *The Reshaping of Catholicism: Current Challenges in the Theology of Church* (San Francisco: Harper and Row, 1988).

48. Pastoral Constitution on the Church in the Modern World, par. 62, in Austin Flannery, ed., *Vatican Council II: The Conciliar and Post-Conciliar Documents* (Northport, NY: Costello Publishing Co., 1975), p. 968.

49. For the development of this point at greater length, see Charles E. Curran, *Directions in Catholic Social Ethics* (Notre Dame, IN: University of Notre Dame Press, 1985), pp. 6–15.

50. Terence P. McLaughlin, ed., *The Church and the Reconstruction of the Modern World: The Social Encyclicals of Pope Piux XI* (Garden City, NY: Doubleday Image Books, 1957), pp. 299–402.

51. Pope John XXIII, *Pacem in Terris*, par. 8–34, in David J. O'Brien and Thomas A. Shannon, eds., *Renewing the Earth: Catholic Documents on Peace, Justice, and Liberation* (Garden City, NY: Doubleday Image Books, 1977), pp. 126–132.

52. Pope John XXIII, *Mater et Magistra*, par. 212ff. in O'Brien and Shannon, *Renewing the Earth*, pp. 102ff.

53. Pope John XXIII, *Pacem in Terris*, par. 35, in O'Brien and Shannon, *Renewing the Earth*, p. 132.

54. Richard J. Regan, *Conflict and Consensus: Religious Freedom and the Second Vatican Council* (New York: Macmillan, 1967).

55. Declaration on Religious Liberty, par. 2, in Flannery, *Vatican Council II*, p. 800.

56. Pastoral Constitution on the Church in the Modern World, par. 36, in Flannery, *Vatican Council II*, p. 935.

57. Ibid., par. 53–63, pp. 958–968.

58. Ibid., par. 59, p. 963.

59. John Courtney Murray, *The Problem of Religious Freedom* (Westminster, MD: Newman Press, 1965).

60. For the development of this position in greater detail, see Charles E. Curran, *American Catholic Social Ethics: Twentieth-Century Approaches* (Notre Dame, IN: University of Notre Dame Press, 1982).

61. John Courtney Murray, *We Hold These Truths: Catholic Reflections on the American Proposition* (New York: Sheed and Ward, 1960), especially pp. 290ff.

62. Regan, *Conflict and Consensus*.

63. Charles A. Meconis, *With Clumsy Grace: The American Catholic Left, 1961–1975* (New York: Seabury Press, 1979).

64. National Conference of Catholic Bishops, *The Challenge of Peace: God's Promise and Our Response* (Washington, DC: United States Catholic Conference, 1983); National Conference of Catholic Bishops, *Economic Justice for All: Pastoral Letter on Catholic Social Teaching and the U.S. Economy* (Washington, DC: United States Catholic Conference, 1986).

65. Andrew M. Greeley, *From Backwater to Mainstream: A Profile of Catholic Higher Education*, Carnegie Commission Studies (New York: McGraw-Hill, 1969).

66. Ibid., p. 85.

67. John Tracy Ellis, "American Catholics and the Intellectual Life," *Thought* 30 (1955–56): 351–388.

68. Ibid., p. 375.

69. Thomas F. O'Dea, *American Catholic Dilemma: An Inquiry into the Intellectual Life* (New York: Sheed and Ward, 1958); John D. Donovan, *The Academic Man in the Catholic College* (New York: Sheed and Ward, 1964).

70. Donovan, *Academic Man*, pp. 190–191.

71. Michael P. Walsh, "Nature and Role Today," in McCluskey, *Catholic University*, pp. 53–54.

72. Quoted in William J. Richardson, "Pay Any Price, Break Any Mold," *America* 116 (April 29, 1967): 624.

73. Land O'Lakes Statement, in McCluskey, *Catholic University*, p. 336.

74. College and University Department of the National Catholic Educational Association, "The Relations of Catholic Colleges and Universities with the Church," *Catholic Mind* 74 (October 1976): 51–64.

75. Donovan, *Academic Man*.

76. Andrew M. Greeley, *The Changing Catholic College* (Chicago: Aldine Publishing Co., 1967), pp. 105–134.

77. Ibid., pp. 134–135.

78. Rosemary Rodgers, *A History of the College Theology Society* (Villanova, PA: College Theology Society, 1983).

79. Ibid., pp. 28–30.

80. Greeley, *Changing Catholic College*, pp. 141–175.

81. Hesburgh, *Hesburgh Papers*, p. 70.

82. Greeley, *From Backwater to Mainstream*, pp. 131–137.

83. Ibid., pp. 141–150; Paul C. Reinert, "Development Problems in America: 1968–1975," in McCluskey, *Catholic University*, pp. 197–205.

84. *Tilton v. Richardson*, 430 U.S. 672 (1971). See Charles H. Wilson, Jr., *Tilton v. Richardson: The Search for Sectarianism in Education* (Washington: Association of American Colleges, 1971).

4. Some Continued Opposition to Academic Freedom in Catholic Institutions

By 1970 the mainstream of Catholic higher education in the United States accepted the principle that academic freedom had to exist in Catholic institutions of higher learning in all areas, including philosophy and theology. The challenge faced by Catholic colleges and universities from the 1970s on was how to prosper and survive as colleges and universities that are both American and Catholic. Such institutions had to be American colleges and universities in the accepted sense of the terms, and they had to add the Catholic distinction to this reality.

The financial challenge faced by Catholic colleges and universities in the 1970s was relieved somewhat by Supreme Court rulings that held that under certain conditions government aid to such institutions was constitutional. By the slim margin of five to four the Supreme Court ruled in the *Tilton v. Richardson* case in 1971 that the Higher Education Facilities Act, which provided grants and loans for buildings to colleges and universities (including church-related institutions), did not violate the first amendment in the specific colleges that were being challenged. In making this particular ruling the court proposed three criteria that must be met in order to justify aid to church-sponsored institutions of higher learning: (1) the law must reflect a truly secular legislative purpose; (2) the primary effect of the law cannot be to advance or inhibit religion; (3) the administration of the law cannot involve an excessive entanglement with religion. As a result of the reasoning of this decision, Catholic institutions should have the following characteristics to be eligible for government aid: persons other than Catholics are admitted to the student body and faculty; attendance at religious services is not required; religion courses are not limited to the religion of the sponsoring body; the institutions do not proselytize; the college adheres to the principles of academic freedom. The Supreme Court ruling in this case and in the later Roemer case dealt with only the particular church-related colleges in question, but the principles laid down were now being observed by all Catholic institutions that wanted to obtain federal money. The adherence to the principles of academic freedom was seen as a necessary condition for public aid for Catholic higher education in the United States.[1] The presence of academic freedom and the lack of proselytizing are two primary characteristics that distinguish Catholic higher education from Catholic grammar and high schools. These judicial decisions strongly reinforced the commitment of the mainstream of Catholic higher education to continue on its new course.

Catholic colleges and universities and their voluntary association, the College and University Department of the National Catholic Educational Association (NCEA), took great pains to develop their own understanding of how their institutions could be both American and Catholic and to explain their position to others. A 1976 document from the College and University Department of the NCEA listed these points as necessary to the identity of Catholic universities and colleges: service to society and church, a strong program in theological studies, a leadership role in ecumenical questions, pastoral ministry on campus, theological and ethical reflection on the social disciplines, the existence of a worshipping community on campus, the providing of an important forum for dialogue in the church.[2] The College and University Department actively cooperated with international Catholic groups such as the International Federation of Catholic Universities (IFCU) and the Congregation for Catholic Education (one of the bureaus of the Roman Curia). The NCEA Department encouraged papers and discussions on Catholic identity at its meetings and in its publications and also established permanent committees on Catholic purpose and identity, relations with sponsoring religious bodies, and campus ministry; it also proposed and helped to set up a joint committee of Catholic college presidents and American bishops to discuss the reality and problems of Catholic higher education. Thus the leadership of Catholic higher education tried to defend, develop, and win support, especially from its Catholic constituency, for the idea that Catholic colleges and universities first had to be good American colleges and universities.[3]

Very few Catholic colleges refused to enter the mainstream. By 1973 St. John's University in Queens, New York, had not accepted state aid and still maintained an institutional commitment to the Catholic church's teaching office and magisterium.[4] A few small Catholic colleges have been founded in the past fifteen years for the express purpose of being truly Catholic and institutionally committed to the teachings of the hierarchical magisterium (e.g., Christendom College in Front Royal, Virginia). But even opponents of academic freedom for Catholic higher education and of government funding for such institutions recognize that the vast majority of Catholic institutions have already accepted academic freedom and probably will not change their approach.[5]

Theoretical Opposition to Academic Freedom

From the late 1960s on, a small but vocal number of American Catholic thinkers have strenuously attacked the mainstream of Catholic higher education for accepting academic freedom as it exists in non-Catholic institutions. This opposition comes from people who support positions in Catholic theology and philosophy that in the light of the ongoing Catholic debate after the Second Vatican Council are very conservative. These theoreticians recognize that they constitute a distinct minority among Catholic educators and intellectuals. Many of them joined together in 1977 to form the Fellowship of Catholic Scholars, a group of Catholic intellectuals dedicated to upholding the teachings of the hierarchical magisterium in all matters; they were generally opposed to any deviation from official church teaching, even noninfallible teachings. Msgr. George A. Kelly, one of the Fellowship's founders and a professor at St. John's University, admitted that the group was established in response to a question posed in 1976 by Cardinal Gabriel Garrone, prefect of the Vatican Congregation for Catholic Education in Rome: "Is there no other voice in America for Catholic higher education than Father Theodore Hesburgh and the NCEA?"[6]

In the closing argument in an article from 1967, Germain Grisez, a philosopher and later a member of the Fellowship of

Catholic Scholars, reveals the traits typical of those opposed to the secular concept of academic freedom. He defensively pleads guilty to the charge of having a classicist outlook, a fundamentalist frame of mind, and a preconciliar mentality. A classicist outlook means that not everything is subject to change; Christ is the truth that never varies and that is not discovered by human inquiry, however free. A fundamentalist's mind holds fast to the essential principles and living magisterium of the church and listens to that magisterium as if listening to Christ. Grisez's preconciliar mentality understands Vatican II as a legitimate development of a continuous tradition, not a revolution. In this light Grisez strongly opposes those who would subject the organized structures of Catholic intellectual life to the narrow requirements of academic freedom.[7] Similarly, those opposed to academic freedom in Catholic higher education in the United States in the last two decades have also objected strenuously to many recent theological developments in Roman Catholicism and have strongly supported the teachings of the hierarchical magisterium while arguing against the legitimacy of dissent within the church.

Arguments against academic freedom in Catholic institutions have generally followed the same lines in the last two decades as they did before, but with two exceptions. One new argument attacks the expediency of accepting academic freedom and the characteristics of American higher education in general in order to obtain funding for the survival of Catholic higher education; it would be much better to have only a few truly Catholic institutions than to have a large number that have sold out to secularism.[8] A second new point of opposition maintains that by accepting academic freedom Catholic institutions of higher learning were now adopting the liberal model of the university as the only possible model, but behind the liberal model lies an understanding of an institution with no commitments whatsoever. Already in other educational circles in the 1960s this understanding of the university was being attacked; certainly Catholics do not want to promote such noncommitment, which has its roots ultimately in the secularized ground of the Enlightenment. Catholic institutions must have a commitment and stand for their Catholic approach.[9]

The other reasons for opposition to academic freedom in Catholic higher education generally repeated past arguments. They can be briefly summarized under three types of approaches—theological, ethical, and genetic.

The theological argument is grounded in the very nature of the discipline of theology itself. Theology presupposes faith in God and God's self-revelation to human beings. The Catholic believes that a special teaching role and office have been given to the hierarchical magisterium to teach matters of faith and morals. By definition what the Catholic theologian claims to expound, interpret, and develop is the mind of the church. The magisterium does not violate the intellectual freedom of the theologian, for the theologian deals with revelation and church teaching and not just with reason. Compared to other academics, theologians are in an enviable position. They, like all academics, must obey what their subject matter teaches them. Unlike other academics, however, the theologian has the advantage that his or her subject matter—the mind of the church—is alive, can talk back, and can help, not hinder, her or his knowing the truth.[10]

Germain Grisez, who has published widely in the areas of philosophical ethics and moral theology, has developed the theological argument in a similar way, but he especially contrasts the conditions necessary for the nonbeliever and the believer to obtain truth. For the nonbeliever the primary condition for obtaining truth is freedom, because truth can be found only by human efforts. For the believer, freedom is necessary, but secondary. Since God graciously reveals God's self in truth and divine revelation, the primary conditions for obtaining truth are humility and the obedience of faith. No restriction on intellectual freedom, faith opens the human intellect to the realm of transcendent truth and is not reducible to reason and the ways of knowing of which human beings are naturally capable. Catholic theology, related to the magisterium of the church in a special way, must respond to the magisterium much as a natural science must respond to the facts of nature, or better, to the instruments that record those facts.[11]

Contemporary opponents of academic freedom for Catholic higher education continue to use what might be called moral or the ethical arguments, which revolve around the meaning of freedom and its relation to other values, especially truth. Absolute freedom is connected to an individualism that fails to recognize the community setting and responsibilities of all peoples. Freedom can never be an absolute, precisely because it has a purpose and a content, because other values need to be considered, and because people exist in a web of human relationships with corresponding rights, responsibilities, and duties. Especially in the intellectual sphere, freedom is a means to arrive at the truth. But even as a means, freedom cannot be absolutized, for the end and the primary value is truth: truth, not skepticism, sets us free.[12] Further, absolute freedom can itself be used as an argument against other commitments and responsibilities. As George Kelly remarks: "Absolute commitment to absolute noncommitment is no less a restriction on academic freedom than a faith commitment and indeed may be less honest because the serious observer is hard pressed to discover real life examples of the totally uncommitted man."[13]

The third type of argument, the genetic argument, understands academic freedom as inextricably connected to the Enlightenment. The secular American university and its concept of academic freedom have their roots in the Enlightenment, which absolutized reason from the rest of reality and made it a solitary God. The Enlightenment's rational ideal forgot that truth was embedded in cultural wisdom, in the intellectual tradition of the past, and in faith like that of the Christian Church.[14]

Contemporary opponents of academic freedom in the Catholic colleges still understand academic freedom to be rooted in secularism, which Grisez describes in the following manner. Legitimate religion must be reduced to human experience and reason, and the supernatural has no place. Truth can only be obtained through methodical research that is based especially on research in the physical sciences. Reality contains no unalterable truth that can be known with certitude and no transcendent sense of value. Knowledge furnishes power, and through this power human beings can improve themselves in indefinite progress. Such an ideology is totally at odds with the Catholic faith. Born of the Enlightenment and nurtured by rationalistic agnosticism and empiricism, academic freedom cannot be accepted by Catholic higher education, which can never be seen as an isolated reality narrowly viewed through the prism of secularism. Catholic higher education must be seen as a part of total Catholic education and formation. And the formation of the whole person in faith and reason must be the primary concern of all Catholic education, including Catholic higher education.[15]

A comparatively small but determined group of Catholic thinkers continues to this day to oppose the acceptance of academic freedom for Catholic institutions of higher learning in the United States, especially for the field of theology. The most important and significant relationship for Catholic higher education, however, involves the hierarchical leadership of the Roman Catholic church.

Relationship with the Hierarchical Leadership: In Theory

The Roman Catholic church understands itself as the people of God with a hierarchical structure of bishops as leaders of the local community in union with other bishops and with the bishop of Rome, the pope, who has a universal primacy. The relationship of Catholic colleges and universities to the hierarchical church involves first of all the American bishops and then the authorities in Rome, especially the pope and the congregations of the Roman curia that carry out the administrative tasks of the church universal under the pope. From the Catholic perspective the attitude of the official leaders of the church is most important. This section will discuss in detail the reactions of the official leaders in the Roman Catholic church to the acceptance of academic freedom by the mainstream of Catholic higher education in the United States and by most Catholic thinkers.

The relationship of American Catholic higher education to the American Catholic bishops is complex. Since the bishop is the head of the church in a particular diocese, local Catholic institutions are somehow related to the particular bishop. Since the Second Vatican Council greater importance has been given to the National Conference of Catholic Bishops in setting some policy for the Catholic church as a whole in the United States.

The vast majority of Catholic colleges and universities were founded and run by religious orders of men and women rather than being established directly by the bishops or dioceses. Thus the actual administration of Catholic colleges and universities has not been the work of bishops. Bishops together with religious orders of men and women had much more direct leadership over and involvement with Catholic education on the levels of grammar school and high school. The last twenty-five years have witnessed a great decline in the number of Catholic elementary and high schools, and the bishops are very aware of the acute financial problems that have caused this decline on the local level.[16] In this light most bishops have been supportive of the struggles of Catholic colleges and universities to survive and grow; as prudent administrators the bishops generally do not want to cause problems for Catholic colleges and universities. The bishops in the United States have appeared to accept and allow Catholic colleges and universities to chart their own course and to embrace the standards of the American academy. The two most significant changes in Catholic higher education from the viewpoint of bishops are academic freedom and the independence of the institutions from the founding religious communities. Since the institutions are independently controlled by lay boards of trustees, the local bishop has no authority as such over these institutions. Academic freedom is the most practical illustration of this independence. But institutional independence and academic freedom could create problems, especially in the area of theology, for bishops understand themselves to have the pastoral office of teacher in the church and theological dissent could readily be seen as a threat to the good of the whole church. Before the early 1960s bishops could and did intervene in Catholic institutions of higher learning to remove a faculty member or to do what was deemed necessary for the good of the church. Recall that the dismissal of Professor Fleisher from the medical school of St. Louis University in the late 1930s was the decision of Archbishop John Glennon. Bishops in those days could readily exert their authority through the religious order which ran the institution, but now that the colleges and universities have independent and lay boards of trustees the bishops cannot exercise their influence in this way.

The presidents and leaders of Catholic colleges and universities have attempted to develop a good rapport with the bishops and have carefully explained their position to the bishops. The formation of a joint committee of bishops and Catholic college presidents indicates very concretely the efforts by Catholic higher education to work with the bishops. To be truly Catholic these institutions want to maintain good relations with the local bishops. Generally speaking, these efforts by Catholic higher education have been successful, for until recently there has been support for and no outright opposition to what Catholic colleges and universities are trying to do. In practice, from 1970 to the present, except at the Catholic University of America, bishops have not publicly confronted theologians teaching at

Catholic institutions of higher learning. In theory, the American Catholic bishops in 1980 accepted the concept of academic freedom and institutional autonomy for Catholic higher education. The bishops were more ambivalent in the early 1970s, but their position has evolved.

In 1972 the National Conference of Catholic Bishops issued a pastoral message on Catholic education entitled "To Teach as Jesus Did."[17] Only a small part of this document deals with Catholic colleges and universities. The bishops note that cordial, fruitful, and continuing dialogue on the complex issue of the relationship of the Catholic college or university to the church is going on among leaders of Catholic higher education (par. 76). The bishops admit that Catholic colleges and universities must be institutions of higher learning "according to sound contemporary criteria" and that they must remain "strongly committed to academic excellence and the responsible academic freedom required for effective teaching and research" (par. 74). Note the two adjectives "sound" and "responsible." The bishops maintain that academic freedom for Catholic institutions has a special dimension. The authentic Christian message is committed by Jesus Christ to the church. "Theological research and speculation, which are entirely legitimate and commendable enterprises, deal with divine revelation as their source and material, and the results of such investigation are therefore subject to the judgment of the magisterium" (par. 75). Earlier the document had declared: "While fully maintaining the autonomy concomitant to its being a college or university, the institution will manifest fidelity to the teaching of Jesus Christ as transmitted by His church" (par. 73). Opponents of academic freedom for Catholic institutions of higher learning could well use such ambiguous statements in support of their position. This 1972 statement was not, however, the bishops' last word.

In 1980 the United States Roman Catholic bishops issued a pastoral letter, "Catholic Higher Education and the Pastoral Mission of the Church."[18] Very supportive of and grateful for those who are currently involved in Catholic higher education, the letter makes no negative comment of any kind about the contemporary state of Catholic higher education; the bishops were obviously very well informed. In fact this document closely resembles the position paper published by the College and University Department of the National

Catholic Educational Association in 1976. In developing the Catholic identity of Catholic institutions this earlier position paper stressed service to the church and society, the role of theological studies, the training of Catholic teachers, leadership in ecumenism, pastoral ministry on campus, theological and ethical reflection on secular disciplines, and the existence of a faith and worshipping community.[19] All of these aspects plus a few others (e.g., justice concerns, including minorities and the international perspective) are mentioned by the bishops in their document. The leadership of Catholic higher education could well congratulate themselves on having educated the bishops of the United States about their self-understanding and proper function.

In addition, in their 1980 pastoral letter the American Catholic bishops clearly support academic freedom and institutional autonomy. "Academic freedom and institutional independence in pursuit of the mission of the institution are central components of educational quality and integrity: commitment to the Gospel and the teaching and heritage of the Catholic Church provide the inspiration and enrichment that make a college fully Catholic."[20] In addition, the bishops quote from an earlier position paper issued by delegates at a meeting in Rome in 1972 on the nature of a Catholic university: "We shall all need to recall and to work for that 'delicate balance... between a Catholic university and the responsibilities of the hierarchy.'" The American bishops immediately add: "There should be no conflict between the two."[21]

Nevertheless, episcopal support for academic freedom in American Catholic higher education has eroded somewhat in the last few years. In spring of 1988 the Vatican Congregation for Catholic Education published a summary of all the responses received from around the world to its proposed draft of a document on Catholic higher education.[22] The Association of Catholic Colleges and Universities (formerly the College and University Department of NCEA) strongly opposed this document, which insisted that Catholic institutions have a juridical relationship to the church and limited academic freedom. The bishops' conference in the United States responded in a manner similar to the ACCU, but the congregation's summary indicates that seven individual bishops strongly supported the proposed norms.[23]

In my case at the Catholic University the board of trustees acted in opposition to the American principles and practices of academic freedom. The Congregation for the Doctrine of the Faith declared that I was neither suitable nor eligible to be a professor of Catholic theology. The board of trustees of the university in June of 1988 accepted this declaration as binding upon the university as a matter of canon law and religious conviction. Without any judgment of my incompetency having been made by my peers, I was prohibited from teaching theology at the Catholic University. William J. Byron, the president of the university, has explained that there is an ecclesial limit on academic freedom at Catholic University.[24]

The action by the board of trustees at Catholic University is significant. The trustees include all the active cardinals in the United States as well as many significant archbishops and bishops (the elected board consists of half clergy and half laity). The most visible leaders of the Catholic hierarchy in the United States have thus put themselves on record as setting ecclesial limits on academic freedom, and individual bishops have now begun to speak publicly about the limits of academic freedom. For example, Archbishop Daniel E. Pilarczyk of Cincinnati, who has served as the chair of the Catholic University board and is now president of the National Conference of Catholic bishops, maintains that academic freedom is limited if one accepts that such a thing as revealed truth exists and that the church has the responsibility of maintaining faithfulness to that revealed truth and to its own pastoral task of sanctification.[25] Archbishop Oscar H. Lipscomb of Mobile, Alabama, a board member at CUA and chair of the bishops' committee on doctrine, insists that academic freedom for theology is limited and has its own modality: at times the church must intervene in the academy.[26] Bishop Donald W. Wuerl of Pittsburgh rejects the full academic freedom of theology in Catholic institutions of higher learning.[27]

In 1980 the American Catholic bishops as a whole expressed their support for academic freedom for Catholic institutions of higher learning. The leaders of Catholic higher education had apparently convinced the bishops to accept their position. However, the hierarchy of the Catholic church in the United States has shifted toward a more conservative stance in the decade of the 1980s. In keeping with that change some individual bishops now oppose the American concept of academic freedom for theology in Catholic colleges and universities.

The central governing body of the Catholic church in the Vatican has expressed doubts and disagreements on the matters of academic freedom and institutional autonomy and has suggested procedures different from those admitted by the mainstream of Catholic higher education in the United States. One probably should expect greater tension in American Catholic higher education's relationship with the Vatican than in its relationship with the American Catholic bishops. The American bishops historically have no direct, immediate, juridical control over most of Catholic higher education and have not been directly and immediately concerned with Catholic colleges and universities. In addition, the bishops understand the cultural context of the country's higher educational system, are quite aware of the financial problems facing Catholic higher education, and recognize the need for government support to ensure Catholic institutions' survival. The Vatican is obviously further removed from the context and the practical concerns of United States Catholic colleges and universities. In addition, the curia or central administrative arm of the papacy has a bureau or congregation dealing specifically with Catholic colleges and universities. Until 1968, the congregation was called the Congregation for Seminaries and Universities, but after that the title was changed to the Congregation for Catholic Education. In 1989 it became the Congregation for Seminaries and Educational Institutions. Through this congregation the Vatican claims to have a supervisory role over all Catholic colleges and universities throughout the world. The importance of the growing Catholic university movement throughout the world had already been recognized by the church in 1949 when Pope Pius XII established the International Federation of Catholic Universities (IFCU), which was canonically and juridically subject to the Congregation for Seminaries and Universities.[28]

In its relationship with the Vatican from the 1960s to the present American Catholic higher education has been trying to convince the Vatican that a college or university could be Catholic without having a juridical relationship with Rome or the church and that academic freedom is necessary for truly American institutions of higher learning. These discussions have taken place in the aftermath of the experience of the Second Vatican Council in the life of the church.

In 1963 Father Theodore Hesburgh, then the president of the University of Notre Dame, was elected president of the IFCU. The Vatican congregation ruled, however, that the election was invalid, and the congregation constituted a commission to run the federation for the next three years. Hesburgh brought the whole matter to the attention of his good friend Pope Paul VI, whose reaction was immediate. Hesburgh was confirmed as president of the IFCU and a new constitution was to be drawn up for the organization that would make it independent, without juridical ties to the Congregation for Seminaries and Universities.[29] Hesburth was later influential in leading IFCU to a redefinition of the Catholic university in the modern world.

With Hesburgh as president at the Tokyo meeting of the IFCU in 1965, the delegates chose as the theme for their next triennial meeting (to be held in 1968 at the Lovanium University in Kinshasa, Congo) the nature and the role of contemporary Catholic universities. Preliminary sessions to prepare for the next meeting were scheduled for the IFCU's four geographical regions. The conference at Land O'Lakes, Wisconsin, in July of 1967 prepared the North Americans' contribution to Kinshasa. Twenty-six North American leaders of Catholic higher education arrived at a consensus and published their statement on the nature of the contemporary Catholic university.[30] As discussed in chapter 3, this statement marked the definitive breakthrough for the acceptance of academic freedom for Catholic institutions of higher learning in the United States.

About one hundred delegates arrived in Kinshasa, Republic of the Congo, for the eighth triennial congress of the IFCU in September of 1968. At Kinshasa the differences among the delegates were both theological and cultural. The American group, generally progressive theologically, warmly supported American university culture and experience; but for theological and cultural reasons many other delegates opposed the American approach to academic freedom and university autonomy. The group at Kinshasa also split on the question of what made an institution Catholic. Does such an institution need a juridical bond with church authority?

From the American perspective the final document had to be a disappointment.[31] Academic freedom was not mentioned, nor was the possibility of an institution being Catholic without having a juridical connection to church authority. In addition, the assembly voted against a proposal that juridical relationship with church authority is not necessarily an essential characteristic of a Catholic institution.[32] One section could easily be understood as expressing opposition to academic freedom: "To these special tasks, Catholic universities are dedicated by an institutional commitment which includes a respect for and voluntary acceptance of the church's teaching authority."[33]

Meanwhile, the Congregation for Catholic Education in Rome began to prepare new norms for Catholic institutions of higher learning. As a first step the congregation sent out a detailed questionnaire that was based primarily on the Kinshasa discussions. The congregation also invited Catholic universities to send delegates to a meeting to be held with the congregation. In April of 1969 these delegates from Catholic universities throughout the world met in Rome. At this first congress, an official meeting neither of the Congregation for Catholic Education nor of the IFCU, the elected delegates freely discussed and drafted a final report that became known as "The Rome Statement: The Catholic University and the Aggiornamento."[34]

From the American perspective the document made a great advance by recognizing that an institution could be Catholic without having juridical bonds to the church and church authority. Although at one time most Catholic colleges and universities in the United States had been under the control of a founding religious community, these institutions were now usually governed by an independent board of trustees that was not dominated by religious. The document's acceptance of such institutions as Catholic probably stems from the recognition of the de facto diversity that exists in the world of Catholic universities and that could not be changed. The Americans viewed this recognition as a great step forward.

The issue of academic freedom was much more controversial, and, in the end, the final document remains ambiguous. In a number of different places the wording is such that the American delegates could understand the document as accepting their understanding of academic freedom, whereas their opponents could insist that true academic freedom exists only within the parameters of Catholic faith and morals as taught by the church. For example, the document mentions the need for "a true autonomy and academic freedom"; it also recognizes that "the university will depend upon its social sponsorship and cannot be completely autonomous but remains subject to the legitimate exigencies of the society which sustains it."[35] The university must be able "without restrictions to follow the imperatives which flow from its very nature: pursuit of the truth without restrictions." But the "authentic Christian message is not available to us except with a guarantee of doctrinal authority, which is the magisterium of the Church. . . . The freedom of the theological researcher, at the risk of basic self-destruction, rests on the foundation of revelation."[36] The defenders of American practice won one very important point: in universities without juridical relationships with hierarchical church authorities, the authorities must deal with the theologian as an individual member of the church, and any church intervention in university affairs must be excluded.[37]

A congress of representative delegates from around the world and the Congregation for Catholic Education are two very different realities, however, as far as Catholic church governance is concerned. The congregation met to discuss the delegates' document, and in 1970 its decision was sent with the approval of the pope to all heads of Catholic institutions of higher learning. The congregation maintained that every Catholic university must be related to those who preside over the Catholic community, that is, the Catholic hierarchy. In addition, "the exigencies of scientific freedom are not opposed to the mission of the church's magisterium to announce and safeguard Catholic doctrine with appropriate means. The doctrinal and moral guidance which the church gives in higher studies, both through the faith of the individuals involved and through the intervention of the magisterium, not only does not limit the horizon and activity of such studies, but, as a matter of fact, protects and assists them."[38] The U.S. delegates had some success in convincing their colleagues from other countries about the American understanding of a Catholic institution of higher learning, but the Congregation for Catholic Education adamantly rejected academic freedom and called for all Catholic institutions of higher learning to have a juridical bond with church authority.

Catholic educators in the United States and abroad continued to discuss the nature of a Catholic university. A 1971 report of the North American Region of the IFCU again emphasizes institutional autonomy and academic freedom. "The Catholic university is not simply a pastoral arm of the church. It is an independent organization serving Christian purposes but not subject to ecclesiastical-juridical control, censorship or supervision.'' In a university without a statutory relationship to Rome, the hierarchical magisterium might in an extreme case issue a public warning about the theologizing activity of a particular theologian, but there can be ''no question of juridical intervention in the institutional affairs of the university itself.''[39] Nine American delegates attended the Congregation for Catholic Education's Second World Congress of Catholic Education at Rome in November of 1972. This meeting followed the model of the first congress. It was an independent assembly of elected delegates who produced their own document, ''The Catholic University in the Modern World.'' Participants acknowledged a continuing struggle between progressive and conservative approaches, but the final document was nevertheless approved by the forty delegates without dissent (there were some abstentions).[40]

The document accepts the strongly held American position that institutions could be called Catholic without having juridical bonds or relationships with ecclesiastical authority (par. 15).[41] A compromise was reached in the treatment of academic freedom. On balance, the statement seems to favor the concept of academic freedom as found in American institutions so that Catholic educators in the U.S. could strongly applaud the work.

The 1972 document is not as strong on university autonomy and academic freedom as the Land O'Lakes Statement of 1967. The basic assertion of Land O'Lakes is kept: ''To perform its teaching and research functions effectively, a Catholic university must have true autonomy and academic freedom'' (par. 20). Missing, however, is the next clause: ''in the face of authority of whatever kind, lay or clerical, external to the academic community itself.'' At least the 1972 document asserts that freedom is ''limited by no other factor than the truth which it pursues'' (par. 20). ''Fulfilling their function in the university, theologians must be able to pursue their discipline in the same manner as other research scholars'' (par. 56). Ordinarily the judgment of a theologian's research will be left to one's peers; only in an extreme case may the hierarchical teaching authority declare a theologian's teaching to be incompatible with Catholic doctrine. ''However, unless statutory relationships permit it this will not involve a juridical intervention whether direct or indirect in the institutional affairs of the university'' (par. 59). Where statutory relationships with the ecclesiastical authorities exist, the statutes will spell out the conditions and modalities to be observed in any hierarchical intervention; where there are no statutory relationships, church authorities will deal with the individual theologian only as a member of the church (par. 59). The leadership of American Catholic higher education could thus claim that the document accepts academic freedom for their institutions, although some hierarchical intervention is permitted for institutions that have statutory relationships with the church.

Opponents of academic freedom in the United States could find some support in the document, but in my judgment their position is less convincing. The Roman congress does not quote the full Land O'Lakes Statement, and the recognition that theologians need the same freedom as other research scholars is modified so that the particular nature of each discipline must be kept in mind (par. 56). Freedom is limited only by truth, but according to Jeremiah Newman and others, truth comes to people in the church and to theologians through the magisterium. There is no violation of the freedom of the theologian in accepting the truth proposed by the magisterium.[42] Others (e.g., Germain Grisez) stressed the four essential characteristics proposed by the document for Catholic universities, especially the requirement of fidelity to the Christian message as it comes to us through the church; these writers understand this characteristic as being opposed to the American understanding of academic freedom.[43]

Catholic educators in the United States thus disagreed in their evaluation of the 1972 document. Father Robert Henle, the president of Gerogetown University, saw the statement as totally supportive of the decision of the mainstream of American Catholic higher education, while Father Joseph Cahill, the president of St. John's University in Long Island, understood the document as calling for an institutional commitment of colleges and universities to the church and its hierarchical magisterium.[44] In my judgment, despite some general statements that could be opposed to academic freedom and despite the fact that church authorities can intervene in institutions that have statutory relationships with the church, "The Catholic University in the Modern World" supports the generally accepted American understanding of academic freedom for Catholic higher education as it exists in the United States.[45]

The 1972 statement was studied by the Congregation for Catholic Education, which made an official response in April of 1973.[46] The congregation sees the document's marked progress over against the 1969 report and finds it "valid but needing improvement." To avoid false and damaging interpretations, the congregation insists that the 1972 "document must be considered as a whole so that no single element can be extrapolated from its entirety and used out of context, especially regarding the treatment given to autonomy of teaching and research." Although the document recognizes that Catholic institutions can exist without statutory bonds linking them to ecclesiastical authorities, such institutions are not "removed from those relationships with the ecclesiastical hierarchy which must characterize all Catholic institutions."

Generally speaking, the leaders of Catholic higher education in the United States, such as Robert Henle of Georgetown and Theodore Hesburgh of Notre Dame, were pleased with both the 1972 document and the subsequent Roman letter. Hesburgh called it a "reasonably effective" document that did not fully satisfy either the university world or the congregation.[47] Writing in *America,* John W. Donohue even described the letter from the congregation as a green light for Catholic higher education in the United States.[48] However, the letter itself indicated the hesitancy of the congregation with regard to the whole concept of autonomy and academic freedom. Subsequent history has proved that the congregation and the Roman authorities in general are opposed to the American understanding of university autonomy and academic freedom for Catholic institutions.

In 1976 the Congregation for Catholic Education announced that it was preparing norms for ecclesiastical universities and faculties, that is, for those universities and faculties that have been canonically erected or approved by Rome and that have the right to confer academic degrees accredited by Rome. (Faculty is here used in the European sense and refers to what in this country is called a department or a school.) In the United States there are comparatively few ecclesiastical faculties, e.g., the Jesuit faculties of theology at Berkeley and at Weston, the Dominican faculty of theology in Washington, the faculties of theology, philosphy, and canon law at the Catholic University of America in Washington. The first announcement was somewhat vague, and after anxious inquiries the congregation responded that these norms would deal only with ecclesiastical universities and faculties and not with independent Catholic institutions. Leaders of Catholic higher education in the United States did not want Rome to formulate any norms for Catholic colleges and universities for fear that such norms might cause problems in the United States.[49]

The Second Vatican Council's Declaration on Christian Education called for a revision of the norms and statutes governing ecclesiastical faculties and universities[50] that had been established earlier in Pope Pius XI's Apostolic Constitution *Deus Scientiarum Dominus* (1931).[51] In May 1968, the Congregation for Catholic Education, after consultations and preparatory meetings, issued *Normae Quaedam*, a partial set of norms to be used experimentally by ecclesiastical faculties and universities in preparation for a complete and new apostolic constitution. *Normae Quaedam* recognized the proper freedom for professors in their research and teaching, but this freedom must always be contained and exercised within the limits of the word of God as it is preserved, taught, and explained by the living magisterium of the church. The document insists that teachers do not act as teachers in their own name but in virtue of the mission they have received from the magisterium; a canonical mission is not explicitly required for such teachers.[52] *Deus Scientiarum Dominus* in 1931 had required a canonical mission from church authorities for all professors in such institutions,[53] a necessity not found in the code of canon law that had gone into effect in 1918. A canonical mission for teachers first arose in Germany in the late 1840s when the schools were secularized. To protect the freedom of the church to teach religion in all schools from primary grades through university, the church decreed that only those with a canonical mission from church authority could teach religion in the secularized schools. However, in the 1931 apostolic constitution such a mission was now applied to official Catholic universities themselves.[54]

In 1976 the Congregation for Catholic Education announced that a new and final constitution for ecclesiastical faculties and universities would soon be released. The document, *Sapientia Christiana*, was finally promulgated by Pope John Paul II on April 15, 1979.[55] Both of his predecessors, Pope Paul VI and Pope John Paul I, had died before being able to issue the constitution. All ecclesiastical faculties and universities were to reformulate their statutes in accord with the new norms and have their statutes approved by

Rome. Article 27 of *Sapientia Christiana* requires all those who teach disciplines concerning faith or morals to have a canonical mission from the chancellor (the ecclesiastical ordinary or superior of the institution who represents the Holy See), for they do not teach on their own authority but by virtue of the mission they have received from the church; ecclesiastical authority must approve and can remove approval from all teachers of disciplines involving faith or morals. Likewise, all teachers promoted to the highest rank of professor or to a permanent position must receive a declaration of *nihil obstat* (nothing stands in the way) from the Holy See. Such processes obviously are not compatible with the American notion of university autonomy and academic freedom. The regulations apply only to ecclesiastical faculties or universities, so most American institutions of higher learning were not directly affected. The regulations, however, indicated similar developments that would directly and immediately affect all Catholic colleges and universities in the United States.

When Pope John XXIII proposed the need for an ecumenical council in 1959 he also recognized the need for an updated code of canon law for the church. Work on the code of canon law started even before the Second Vatican Council ended, but the process began in earnest after the council. Preliminary drafts of parts of the new code were submitted to the bishops and other involved persons beginning in 1972. In 1977 the first draft on the teaching office of the church was released. The proposed canon, which created a furor among the leaders of American Catholic higher education, maintained that "those who teach courses in theology or courses related to theology in any kind of institute of higher studies require a canonical mission."[56] This requirement stands in opposition to the principle and procedures of academic freedom, for ecclesiastical authority outside the university can directly affect the hiring and dismissing of faculty. Catholic educators in the United States had been able to convince their colleagues in the IFCU about the legitimacy of academic freedom for colleges and universities in the United States, but now it became evident that they had failed to convince church authorities in Rome.

American Catholics involved in higher education attempted to have the proposed canon changed, and they engaged in a wide-ranging lobbying process to achieve their purpose. The Association of Catholic Colleges and Universities and the bishops' and presidents' committee strongly objected to the proposed canon. Since it was incompatible with academic freedom, the canon was seen as a threat to the continued existence of Catholic higher education in the United States. Again appeals were made to the fact that Catholic higher education was stronger in the United States than anywhere else in the world and that Rome had to recognize the peculiar nature of Catholic colleges and universities on this side of the Atlantic. Delegates from the ACCU even had a special audience with the pope himself in March of 1982 in order to argue for the removal of the proposed canon. All these efforts were to no avail. Canon 812 in the new Code of Canon Law promulgated in 1983 now reads as follows: "It is necessary that those who teach theological disciplines in any institute of higher studies have a mandate from a competent ecclesiastical authority." The final wording involved some changes, but the canon still stands in direct opposition to the principle and procedures of academic freedom. For example, the authorization was changed from a "canonical mission" to a "mandate" because a canonical mission involves the giving of ecclesiastical jurisdiction, which does not happen in this case.[57]

The promulgation of Canon 812 is not, apparently, an isolated act but very much a part of the present overall approach of Roman Catholic church authorities to the role of theologians in the church and to the role of Catholic colleges and universities. Despite the opposition of leaders of American Catholic colleges and universities, the Congregation for Catholic Education continued its preliminary consultations and finally published "A Proposed Schema for a Pontifical Document on Catholic Universities" on April 15, 1985.[58] This document's proposed norms attempt to legislate for all Catholic institutions of higher learning throughout the world. The schema wants all such institutions to have some juridical relationship with church authority, either approval by the Holy See, by episcopal conferences, by relationship with a religious community or other canonical entity, or by a juridical connection with the diocese and bishop (Norms, Articles 11–22).

The schema strongly opposes the American notion of the autonomy and academic freedom of institutions of hgher learning. While recognizing a proper autonomy for Catholic universities, the schema continues that "this autonomy is never absolute but is inspired and disciplined by truth and the common good'' (Norms, Article 10). Article 9 states that episcopal conferences and diocesan bishops have the duty and the right to see that principles of Catholic doctrine are faithfully observed. According to Article 26, which incorporates the provisions of Canon 810, teachers are to be distinguished by doctrinal integrity and uprightness of life; teachers lacking these requirements are to be dismissed in accord with statutory procedures. Article 31 repeats Canon 812: "Those who teach theological subjects in any institute of higher studies must have a mandate from a competent ecclesiastical authority.'

Sharp responses to the document came from the ACCU and from fourteen presidents of major Catholic universities in the United States. In addition, many other responses to the congregation were sent by individual institutions, by the bishops' conference, and by individual bishops.

The ACCU and the university presidents responded in a tone of controlled exasperation. Roman church authorities have not really understood the nature and the reality of Catholic higher education in the United States even after so many years. Catholic colleges and universities are chartered by the individual states, accredited by voluntary associations of accrediting agencies and specialized professional groups, and controlled legally by independent boards of trustees that have no juridical or formal ties to the Catholic church or even to a religious community. More Catholic colleges and universities (235) are found in the United States than in all other parts of the world combined. American Catholic higher education has flourished for many reasons, but especially because of the financial assistance that comes from private sources and public monies. Except in a very few instances, the Catholic church gives no direct support to Catholic higher education.

The proposed norms would put in jeopardy the accreditation of and government funding for Catholic higher education. In the United States no general ruling of the Supreme Court has upheld the right of church-related colleges to be eligible for public funds. Two important legal decisions (Tilton and Roemer) have decided that eight institutions were eligible for public funding. The Supreme Court held that they could receive public funds for a number of different reasons, including the fact that theology courses were academic courses and not indoctrination courses, that prosyletizing did not take place, and that the institutions, unlike Catholic grammar and high schools, accepted the standards for academic freedom. In this context, Catholic colleges and universities must first of all be true and good colleges and universities in the American sense even before they can be Catholic. The proposed norms are incompatible with the American notion of academic freedom and university autonomy.[59]

The fourteen presidents of leading Catholic universities in a separate response claim in strong language that secularist critics would find that their most searing criticism of Catholic universities had been confirmed by the Vatican itself, because direct ecclesiastical control means that institutions are not universities at all but places of narrow sectarian indoctrination. Under the norms neither academic freedom nor institutional autonomy would exist. In addition, the proposed schema does not sufficiently account for the cultural and historical pluralism that exists in Catholic higher education through-out the world, and that, in keeping with recent Catholic documents, should be respected. Rome cannot and should not set down minute regulations to be followed in the same way in such diverse cultural and educational circumstances as exist throughout the world.[60]

The response of the conference of bishops in the United States has not been made public, but it apparently agreed in general with the reponses of the ACCU. Seven individual United States bishops, however, strongly supported the proposed norms.[61] Father Theodore Hesburgh was involved in the strong reactions against the document, but in another context he tended to downplay the proposed norms as just a "trial balloon."[62] Presumably aware that opponents of Catholic higher education in the United States might use the doc-ument against colleges and universities, he may not have wanted others to use the proposed schema to attack American Catholic higher education.[63]

On November 8, 1988, the Congregation for Catholic Education sent out a new draft of a document on Catholic higher education.[64] From the perspective of the leadership of American Catholic higher education this draft improved the earlier draft but still created great problems, especially in the area of academic freedom. Like its prede-cessor, this draft contains a long section on norms which when finally promulgated would become part of the law of the Catholic church. Recall, however, that some of these provisions are already contained in the new Code of Canon Law. The draft acknowledges that some Catholic institutions are "Catholic in inspiration," which means that they do not have to be juridically established by the Catholic church (art. 21). Such a recognition safeguards to some extent the autonomy of Catholic institutions of higher learning in the United States, but these institutions would still be subject to the norms proposed in this document.

On the question of academic freedom the draft opposes the generally accepted American understanding of the term. "Freedom in research and teaching is recognized and respected, so long as the rights of the individual and of the community are preserved within the context of the common good" (art. 23.1). Ecclesiastical authority has the right and the duty to intervene in order to protect the truth and integrity of the Christian message. Episcopal conferences will establish procedures for such interventions (art. 28.2 and 28.3).

In April 1989 the Congregation for Catholic Education invited delegates from around the world to discuss the draft at a meeting in Rome. This Third International Congress of Catholic Universities included ninety representatives of Catholic universities and institutions of higher learning throughout the world and thirty-seven representatives of different regional bishops' conferences. The major but not the only product of the meeting was a list of ten summary recommendations that were endorsed by the congress with near unanimity. Also, a committee of fifteen delegates (including three Americans) was chosen to assist in the writing of the final draft, which will be presented to the voting members of the congregation and ultimately to the pope, who is scheduled to promulgate the final document soon. The American representatives were enthusiastic and very hopeful about both the format and the substance of the meeting.[65]

Some of the ten recommendations give a firm basis for the very favorable response by the delegates of American Catholic higher education.[66] The first recommendation maintains that the final document "should be positive, inspirational, and future oriented." Whatever normative principles are included should be few in number, general in nature, and take into account regional laws and institutional statutes (recall that most of the problems in the earlier drafts came from the quantity and specificity of norms). Recommendation 3 calls for a clear distinction between the church's mission of evangelization and the teaching and research mission of the Catholic university.

However, the compromises in these recommendations are evident, and threats to academic freedom remain. The word academic freedom does not appear. Freedom of teaching and research is conditioned by "the rights of the individual and of the community" within the context of the common good (recommendation 2). Many commentators in the past have used the common good of the church as a reason to limit academic freedom. Recommendation 9 recognizes without any nuances that Catholic theology should be faithful to the magisterium of the church. Recommendation 7 acknowledges institutions in which church authority does not enter into the internal governance of the university, but bishops, never to be seen as external agents, are participants in the life of the Catholic university. Such an understanding could justify the taking away of a canonical mission in accord with Canon 812.

Past history and the contemporary context make me more suspicious than euphoric about the work of this congress. Also, the congress does not speak for the congregation or for the pope, and the opening presentation to the congress made by the congregation strongly supported the previous draft.[67] The Roman authorities have yet to accept the American understanding of academic freedom.

This section has developed the approach taken to Catholic institutions of higher learning in the United States by the church's hierarchical leadership in the period of the 1970s and 1980s. In 1980 the conference of bishops in this country accepted the need for academic freedom and institutional autonomy. However, such support, especially in the light of developments in the 1980s now appears to be somewhat "soft." The Roman authorities throughout the last decade have strongly reinforced their position that Catholic theologians are subordinate to and delegated by the hierarchical magisterium. Such an understanding of the role of the theologian is opposed to the American concepts of academic freedom and institutional autonomy. What will happen in the future?

The Practical Context: The Present and the Future

To assess theoretical developments over the last twenty years and to have the background necessary for judging what might happen in the future to academic freedom and Catholic higher education in the United States, one must be familiar with the practical context within which these developments have occurred.

In the last decade a decided shift to a more conservative approach within the hierarchical leadership of the Roman Catholic church has taken place. In general, the pope and the Roman curia have resisted newer developments and recent calls for more change within the church. In the United States the divisions and differences between the Vatican and the American church are frequently discussed. In theory and in practice many American Catholics disagree to some extent with much of Catholic sexual teaching. There is much stress here between women religious and the Vatican. Bishops have been investigated by Rome; imprimaturs have been withdrawn from books; conservative bishops have been appointed to major dioceses throughout the country. However, to think that this tension exists only between the American Catholic church and Rome would be a mistake, for the tension is worldwide. In Latin America the theory and practice of liberation theology are the major topics of debate. In Africa many local churches want to adopt a greater inculturation of native customs into the liturgy. In the first world the role of women in the church is a burning issue.

Two recent books point out, from different perspectives, the fact that Rome is resisting many of the developments being proposed today throughout the Catholic world. *The Ratzinger Report: An Exclusive Interview on the State of the Church* gives the view of the Congregation for the Doctrine of the Faith's prefect, whose function is to protect and defend Catholic faith and morality. Most of the book emphasizes the dangers to the faith present in the modern world.[68] A group of more liberal Catholic scholars have contributed to *The Church in Anguish: Has the Vatican Betrayed Vatican II?* The strong subtitle makes a clear point. The hierarchical church leadership and especially the pope are strongly opposed to many recent trends in Catholic thought and practice.[69] I have often pointed out that such disagreements must be put in the proper context since for the most part they do not involve the heart and core of Catholic faith. However, the existence of many tensions within the Roman Catholic church must be admitted as a simple fact.[70]

As might be expected, papal and curial resistance to many recent proposals and developments has above all taken the form of the investigation and/or condemnation of theologians. Actions taken against theologians have received wide publicity.

The Holy Office, as the Congregation for the Doctrine of the Faith was formerly called, began in 1957 a file on Hans Küng, a Swiss-born theologian teaching in Germany who received his doctorate in that year. The congregation later informed Küng that his 1967 book, *The Church*, was being investigated, and for the next decade Küng was involved with investigations by the German bishops and by the Congregation for the Doctrine of the Faith. Finally on December 18, 1979, the congregation issued a declaration saying that Küng "can no longer be considered a Catholic theologian or function as such in a teaching role."[71]

Less publicized but even more drastic action was taken against the French Dominican theologian Jacques Pohier; in 1979 his book *Quand je dis Dieu* was condemned by the Congregation for the Doctrine of the Faith through its extraordinary process, which basically did not give the theologian any opportunity to defend himself. Pohier was also ordered to refrain from preaching, from public celebration of the Eucharist, and from all teachings in matters of faith.[72]

In September of 1968, it was reported in the press that the congregation had initiated proceedings against the Dutch theologian Edward Schillebeeckx. In 1976 another investigation started with regard to his book *Jesus*. After an exchange of letters, Schillebeeckx was finally called to Rome in December of 1979 to defend his positions in front of experts appointed by the congregation. Throughout the 1980s Schillebeeckx's work has continued to come under Vatican investigation, but no condemnations have been issued against him as a Catholic theologian.[73]

Liberation theologians from Latin America such as Gustavo Gutiérrez and Leonardo Boff have also been investigated by the Congregation for the Doctrine of the Faith. Boff was also called to Rome, amid great anxiety by many people from Latin America. In April 1985 the Congregation for the Doctrine of the Faith together with the Congregation for Religious informed the father general of the Franciscan order that Boff was silenced for an indefinite period of time, was relieved of his responsibilities to a Brazilian theological journal, and had to submit his writings to censors in advance of publication. Bishops and many other Brazilians reacted strongly against the treatment accorded Leonardo Boff. His silencing was relaxed somewhat and lasted about a year.[74]

I had been informed in the summer of 1979 that I was under investigation by the Vatican for my teachings in the area of moral theology, especially sexual ethics. After an investigation through correspondence the congregation concluded in the summer of 1986 that I was neither suitable nor eligible to exercise the function of a professor of Catholic theology.[75]

A comparison of the new code of canon law with the older 1917 law is most instructive. In the older code the relationship of the hierarchical teaching office to theologians was one of negative vigilance. In the new 1983 law a great change has occurred: the hierarchical teaching office positively deputizes the theologian, who functions only in the explicit relationship of being commissioned and sent by the hierarchical teaching office. The great danger arises that the theologian's function and charism in the church are absorbed by the hierarchical role. Traditionally, Catholic thought has seen the two roles as independent but complementary; the theologian must give due weight to official church teachings, but his or her role is based on academic ability rather than on a connection with an office or function in the church, as is the teaching role of pope and bishops.[76]

Tensions between the hierarchical magisterium and Catholic theologians have continued and even worsened. Two well-known and internationally respected Catholic theologians, Walbert Bühlmann and Bernard Häring, have published books describing their quarrels with Vatican congregations, especially with the Congregation for the Doctrine of the Faith. Both authors have vigorously protested how the Vatican often deals with theologians and stifles legitimate theological creativity.[77] In early 1989, 163 German-speaking theologians issued "The Cologne Declaration," which protested against three points: the imposition of bishops without regard for the wishes of the local churches; bans on theologians that prevented them from teaching in universities; and the tendency to give too much weight to the encyclical *Humanae Vitae*, which condemned artificial contraception.[78] After the Vatican spokesperson dismissed "The Cologne Declaration" as having no significance for the universal church, theologians from Belgium, France, Spain, and Italy publicly endorsed the document's perspective and concerns.[79] Over 750 North American theologians protested any contemplated Vatican action against me in 1986, and both the Catholic Theological Society of America and the College Theology Society strongly defended me.[80]

On February 25, 1989, the Congregation for the Doctrine of the Faith published a new profession of faith and oath of fidelity to be taken by many different people in the church, including teachers in any university who work in disciplines that deal with faith and morals.[81] A more simple and general profession of faith had been required according to the Code of Canon Law, but in practice such professions were apparently not made in Catholic institutions of higher learning. Most commentators interpret the new profession and oath as the attempt to exercise greater control over theologians and as a possible threat to academic freedom.[82]

From my perspective, there is one bright spot in all these developments. In 1989 the National Conference of Catholic Bishops in the United States passed a document that set up procedures to settle disputes between theologians and bishops. The procedures recognize existing tensions and the inadequate ways in which they have been resolved in the past. This document also does not insist that the theologian merely carries out and continues the teaching office of the hierarchical magisterium.[83]

Tensions between the hierarchical magisterium and Catholic theologians and canon law's new approach to the role of theologians have created much discussion and response within the Catholic church. No doubt, such approaches and actions are a part of a general trend within the hierarchical leadership of the church, especially in Rome, to regulate and restrict more stringently change and development within the church.[84] The control of theologians is an important means to prevent new developments from occurring. In light of this context, Roman documents and norms would be very unlikely to acknowledge academic freedom for Catholic theologians and for Catholic institutions of higher learning.

What has happened practically about academic freedom in Catholic institutions of higher learning in the United States in the 1970s and 1980s? Despite the existing tensions between theologians and the hierarchical magisterium, no confrontations over academic freedom in Catholic colleges and universities in the United States took place until the mid-1980s.

In the summer of 1985, four Catholic institutions of higher learning (St. Martin's College in Lacey, Washington; the College of St. Scholastica in Duluth, Minnesota; Boston College; and Villanova University) canceled previously scheduled addresses or seminars by Professor Daniel Maguire of Marquette University. An investigating committee of the American Association of University Professors concluded that the message given to the academic community was that the schools' invitations were withdrawn because Maguire had signed statements and spoken publicly against the hierarchy's official teaching on abortion. He was a leading figure in a group of Catholics who had published a statement in the *New York Times* in the fall of 1984 that called attention to a diversity of Catholic opinion on the matter of abortion. This statement caused great controversy among Catholics in the United States and between the women religious who had signed the statement and the Vatican. In the Maguire case, the investigating committee disagreed with the four institutions' decision to cancel the scheduled talks or institutes, for the cancellations violated academic freedom.[85] The Maguire case did not involve the dismissal of a faculty member, but it highlighted the pressures felt by administrators of Catholic institutions on the sensitive question of abortion.

The most significant academic freedom case in the mid-1980s involved me and the Catholic University of America. Chapter 6 will discuss and explore this case in detail, but the basic facts need to be stated here in order to clarify the issues about academic freedom in Catholic institutions of higher learning.[86] I was a full or ordinary professor in the department of theology of Catholic University. The department of theology has an ecclesiastical faculty erected and approved by the Vatican and able to confer the ecclesiastical degrees of S.T.B. (bachelor of sacred theology), S.T.L. (licentiate in sacred theology), and S.T.D. (doctorate in sacred theology). The department of theology also has American accredited degree programs such as the M.A. (master of arts), M.Div. (master of divinity), D.Min. (doctor of ministry), and Ph.D. (doctor of philosophy). More than 75 percent of the students in my classes were in the American degree programs. In accord with the Apostolic Constitution *Sapientia Christiana* the ecclesiastical faculties at the university submitted to and received approval from the Vatican in 1981 for new statutes governing these faculties. One of the provisions in the new statutes was that professors needed a canonical mission from the chancellor of the university, but no canonical mission was actually given to any of the people already on the faculty. In August of 1986, the Congregation for the Doctrine of the Faith concluded that I was neither suitable nor eligible to exercise the function of a professor of Catholic theology, and it instructed the chancellor of Catholic University to take appropriate action.

Upon receiving the letter from the congregation, Archbishop James A. Hickey, chancellor of the university, announced that he was initiating the statutory process to take away my canonical mission to teach in an ecclesiastical faculty. In accord with the statutes and without waiving my rights that arose from my having served for years as a tenured professor without ever having had a canonical mission, I requested the due process procedure whereby a committee of faculty peers would conduct a hearing to determine if the chancellor had the most serious reasons required to take away my canonical mission. In October 1987, the faculty committee found that my canonical mission could be withdrawn only if I were to remain a tenured faculty member and continue to function as a professor in the areas of my competence, moral theology and ethics. The board of trustees took away my canonical mission, but would not allow me to teach theology. They offered me a teaching position in social ethics—only if I first agreed to accept publicly the Vatican letter that said that I was ineligible to teach Catholic theology at the university. However, Catholic moral theology is my area of competence. At their June 2, 1988, meeting the board of trustees passed a resolution stating that any assignment allowing Father Curran to exercise the function of a professor of Catholic theology in the face of the Holy See's declaration that he is ineligible to do so would be inconsistent with the university's special realtionship with the Holy See, incompatible with the university's freely chosen Catholic character, and contrary to the obligations imposed on the university as a matter of canon law. The Catholic University thus put itself on record as saying that authority external to the university can provide the reason for dismissing a tenured faculty member from teaching in her or his area of competence without academic due process. Not only did the university violate the principle and procedures of academic freedom through its action of constructive termination in my case, but it also issued a statement admitting that academic freedom does not and cannot exist in those areas at the Catholic University where the Catholic church claims to have the authority to intervene.

Jesuit Father William J. Byron, the president of the university, further developed the reasoning behind the statement of the board of trustees.[87] There is "an ecclesial limit on academic inquiry and communication in the field of Catholic theology. The ecclesial limit on Catholic theology is continuity with the tradition of the Catholic Church." Byron posed the issue as primarily one of religious freedom and not of academic freedom—the right of an institution to accept limits because of its religious commitments. Who is to make such judgments about a Catholic theologian in a Catholic institution? For Byron, "Ultimately it is for the church to make these determinations." Note the absence of any judgment by peers.

In the light of the present context, four very practical questions about the future of academic freedom in Catholic higher education can be posed: (1) What will be the position of the United States bishops in the future? (2) Will Canon 812 be applied in the United States? (3) Will the norms for Catholic higher education to be issued by the Congregation for Catholic Education violate the principles of institutional autonomy and academic freedom? (4) How will Catholic higher education respond to any new developments?

In the context of the declarations and actions of the Catholic University's board of trustees, many significant bishops have now adopted a position in contradiction to the Land O'Lakes Statement. The arguments proposed by the trustees and the president of Catholic University as well as the statements of some other bishops definitely and logically apply to all Catholic higher education. In the light of recent developments and the present climate, I doubt that many bishops today would give a resoundingly positive endorsement of the Land O'Lakes Statement or the principles expressed in it. I think a growing number of bishops are opposed to the theoretical and practical principles of academic freedom that are enshrined in that document.

The practical positions that might be taken by a bishop or bishops against academic freedom are more difficult to predict. The issue can be discussed primarily in terms of the invocation of Canon 812, which requires a mandate from competent ecclesiastical authority for all those teaching theological disciplines in any institution of higher education. Canon 812 has yet to be invoked as such in the

United States, although Canon 810, which calls for teachers in such institutions to be removed in accord with the statutes if they do not have the requisite qualities of doctrinal integrity and probity of life, has already been used in a case at the Catholic University of Puerto Rico at Ponce.[88]

A number of reasons help to explain why Canon 812 has not been used in the United States. The bishops have been warned that the invocation of the canon could well toll the death knell for Catholic higher education in the United States, because accreditation and public funding for Catholic higher education could be jeopardized. Prudent administrators, the bishops do not want to rock the boat. American canonists have raised the possibility that the new code's canons on Catholic universities and other institutions of higher studies are not applicable here because of specific characteristics of our Catholic colleges and universities such as civil charters, independent boards of trustees, and autonomy.[89] Some canonists also maintain that Canon 812 puts no obligation on the institution as such but only on the individual teacher to have a mandate.[90]

The Curran case at the Catholic University indicates that other cases might arise in the future at other Catholic institutions of higher learning. But perhaps not. Note that in the Curran case Canon 812 was not invoked by the archibishop of Washington, even though at one time in the process he threatened to invoke it. That the final action taken against me avoided its use indicates a continued reluctance on the part of American bishops to invoke Canon 812.

Without a doubt, the Catholic University would have taken no action against me had there not been an investigation and a decision from the Congregation for the Doctrine of the Faith that I was neither suitable nor eligible to teach Catholic theology. This is the classical case about academic freedom: whether a decision made by a church authority at the highest level can have an immediate juridical effect on the tenure of a university professor. However, such investigations and decisions by Roman church authoritites will probably remain somewhat rare; in the light of all the possible problems connected with outside interference by the church in the Catholic academy, most bishops would still probably remain reluctant to interfere.

I think the trustees at the Catholic University purposely avoided the use of Canon 812 and tried to protect the institution against the charge that it allowed outside forces to interfere in the university. The trustees themselves freely agreed that their institution has a special relationship to the Catholic church. As trustees of an American institution of higher learning, I do not think they can make such a commitment and still consider their institution to be a true American university, if by "special relationship" it is meant that the institution is bound by canon law and/or conscience to implement Vatican actions. However, they were careful to avoid the charge that an agency outside the university made the juridically effective judgment that I could not teach Catholic theology at the Catholic University of America. Since bishops for all practical purposes control the board of trustees at Catholic University, they could prevail upon the board to make such a determination.

An individual bishop invoking Canon 812 might be ineffectual in many cases. The independent board of trustees of the institution might not pay attention and go along with such an action. Such attempted action by a local bishop could thus create many practical difficulties that a prudent administrator would try to avoid. At the Catholic University it was much easier to have the board of trustees agree to take the necessary action. There continue to be many reasons against invoking Canon 812. But an individual bishop can decide at any time that he is duty bound to use it, and the Vatican could pressure a bishop to use it in a particular case.

The third area of concern for academic freedom in Catholic institutions of higher learning involves the norms to be issued soon by the Vatican. The leaders of Catholic higher education in the United States have opposed the norms as they were first proposed and will continue to do everything possible to prevent them from coming into effect. In present and future efforts, such leaders might not have the total support of the American bishops, which would make their work more difficult. In addition, these leaders must realize that the proposed norms are in harmony with the theory and practice of Roman authorities about the role of theologians in the church. Much more is at stake here than merely the American issue of academic freedom. Although even Theodore Hesburgh talks optimistically about changing the proposed schema, history argues the other way. The leadership of Catholic higher education tried in vain to have Canon 812 removed from the code of canon law. Since the canon is now in force, it will be much easier for church authorities to accept the proposed norms for Catholic higher education.

If unacceptable norms are adopted, Catholic higher education in the United States could ask for a dispensation from the norms because of the special circumstances existing in this country. It might be easier to obtain a dispensation than to block the legislation entirely, but in the present climate even obtaining a dispensation would not be easy. Another possibility involves working out a system so that any proposed church norms would work in a way compatible with academic freedom. For example, the mandate could be given automatically by the ecclesiastical superior to whomever is appointed by the institution to the theology faculty and could not be taken away by any action of the ecclesiastical superior. Such an approach would mean that for all practical purposes American Catholic higher education would continue to have full academic freedom, a position that might not be acceptable to the Vatican.

Conjecture about the future is always difficult. My best guess is that the future Vatican regulations on Catholic colleges and universities will be ambiguous on the matters of institutional autonomy and academic freedom. As a result, the leaders of Catholic higher education will say that they can live with such regulations. The real crunch will come if and when church authorities on the basis of such norms take actions that are violations of academic freedom.

A fourth area of concern for the future involves the reaction of Catholic higher education in general or of any one institution in particular to any norms or actions that would deprive the institution of academic freedom. Most Catholic institutions have independent boards of trustees who could legally say that they have no intention of following proposed norms or carrying out the directives of any ecclesiastical superior that are in opposition to academic freedom. The consequences of such action would be to put themselves in opposition to the local bishop or the Catholic church as a whole. Catholic colleges and universities in general would not want to put themselves into such a situation of opposition to the institutional church. Such opposition would hurt their relationship with some of their supporters and contributors. However, some institutions might be willing to take this step if the alternative was to lose their academic freedom and especially their continued existence.

The crux of the problem is that Catholic institutions of higher learning want to be both Catholic and universities. Today's mainstream maintains that such dual identity is possible and that being Catholic in no way detracts from what it means to be an American institution of higher learning. In this case the Catholic identity involves a moral reality without any juridical ties to the church as such. The college or university must be autonomous. However, the institutional church wants to have some control over the colleges and universities, especially in the area of theology.

The relationship of Catholic higher education to the drafting process for new Vatican norms illustrates the ambivalence of Catholic colleges and universities today. In accord with their own self-understanding as being autonomous and juridically independent of the Catholic church, these institutions should explain to Rome that while they have both an interest and a concern in what regulations come from Rome on this matter, such regulations would and could in no way affect these independent Catholic institutions. However, the leaders of Catholic higher education in the United States apparently do not want to make such a move since they would then seem to be in public opposition with the institutional church and might even be disowned by the official church structure. By cooperating in the drafting of norms for Catholic higher education, the leaders of Catholic higher education admit at least implicitly that they would and could be governed by such norms.

One can understand why Catholic college and university presidents do not want to give themselves any more problems than they already have at the present time. Catholic higher education earnestly hopes that a solution can be worked out with the church so that the academic freedom and autonomy of their institutions are safeguarded and protected. However, if the official church will not accept the necessary characteristics of an American institution of higher learning, then Catholic colleges will face a decision they obviously do not want to make. To continue as true American institutions of higher learning they will have to dissociate themselves from the institutional church. Their claim to be morally Catholic will be difficult to make if the Catholic church publicly and officially rejects them as being Catholic. The dilemma is obvious.

History shows a changing understanding of the role of academic freedom in Catholic colleges and universities. After the 1970s, it seemed that the leaders of the mainstream of Catholic higher education could feel confident in their judgment that academic freedom for Catholic higher education was totally compatible with the Catholic identity of their institutions. However, now the future is uncertain. Many clouds hang on the horizon. In this context it is necessary to propose as effectively as possible the rationale for academic freedom, the question to be addressed in the next chapter.

NOTES

1. *Tilton vs. Richardson,* 430 U.S. 672 (1971); *Roemer vs. Board of Public Works,* 426 U.S. 736 (1976). For an important commentary see Charles H. Wilson, Jr., *Tilton v. Richardson: The Search for Sectarianism in Education* (Washington, DC: Association of American Colleges, 1971).

2. College and University Department, National Catholic Educational Association, "Relations of American Catholic Colleges and Universities with the Church," *Catholic Mind* 74 (October 1976): 51–64.

3. Ibid., pp. 58, 59.

4. Joseph Dirvin, "The Catholic University in the Concrete," in George A. Kelly, ed., *Why Should the Catholic University Survive?* (New York: St. John's University Press, 1973), pp. 75–84.

5. Edward J. Berbusse, "The Catholic College Versus Academic Freedom," in Charles E. Curran and Richard A. McCormick, eds., *Readings in Moral Theology No. 6: Dissent in the Church* (New York: Paulist Press, 1988), p. 287. Germain G. Grisez, "American Catholic Higher Education: The Experience Evaluated," in Kelly, *Why Should the Catholic University Survive?* p. 55.

6. George A. Kelly, "Charles Curran and the ACCU," *Social Justice Review* 77, nn. 9–10 (September-October 1986): 158.

7. Germain G. Grisez, "Academic Freedom and Catholic Faith," *National Catholic Educational Association Bulletin* 64, n. 2 (November 1967): 20.

8. E.g., Grisez, in Kelly, *Why Should the Catholic University Survive?* p. 47.

9. Jeremiah Newman, "The Roman Document: The Catholic University in the Modern World Examined and Evaluated," in Kelly, *Why Should the Catholic University Survive?* pp. 67–73.

10. Christopher Derrick, *Church Authority and Intellectual Freedom* (San Francisco: Ignatius Press, 1981).

11. Grisez, *National Catholic Educational Association Bulletin* 64, n. 2 (November 1967): 15–20; Grisez, in Kelly, *Why Should the Catholic University Survive?* pp. 39–55.

12. Ronald Lawler, "Catholic Faith and Academic Freedom," in *Social Justice Review* 77 (1986): 170–176; S. Thomas Greenburg, "The Problem

of Identity in Catholic Higher Education: The Statement of the Question,'' in Kelly, *Why Should the Catholic University Survive?* pp. 24, 25; Vincent P. Miceli, ''Pope John Paul II and Catholic Universities,'' *Homiletic and Pastoral Review* 81 (1981): 8–18.

13. George A. Kelly, ''Introduction,'' in Kelly, *Why Should the Catholic University Survive?* p. xviii.

14. Lawler, *Social Justice Review* 77 (1986): 173, 174.

15. Grisez, in Kelly, *Why Should the Catholic University Survive?* pp. 47–50; Dennis Bonnette, ''The Effect of Secularism in Catholic Higher Education on American Society,'' *Catholic Educational Review* 66 (March 1968): 145–153. Other studies in opposition to academic freedom, in addition to those already mentioned, include: Damian Fedoryka ''The American Catholic University and the Vatican: Submission or Subversion?'' *Faith and Reason* 13 (1987): 105–116; Lynne C. Boughton, ''Catholic Colleges and the Vatican Proposal,'' *Homiletic and Pastoral Review* 88 (December 1987): 10–20; William E. May, ''Catholic Principles of Scholarship and Learning,'' *Homiletic and Pastoral Review* 88 (February 1988): 7–16. Paul J. Goda, ''Some Dissent About Dissent Within the Catholic Church in the Context of Catholic Universities,'' *Current Issues in Catholic Higher Education* 8, n.2 (Winter 1988): 15–21.

16. Andrew M. Greeley, William C. McCready, and Kathleen McCort, *Catholic Schools in a Declining Church* (Kansas City, MO: Sheed and Ward, 1976).

17. National Conference of Catholic Bishops, *To Teach as Jesus Did* (Washington, DC: United States Catholic Conference, 1973).

18. National Conference of Catholic Bishops, ''Catholic Higher Education and the Pastoral Mission of the Church,'' *Origins* 10 (1980): 378–384.

19. College and University Department of the National Catholic Educational Association, *Catholic Mind* 74 (October 1976): 51–64.

20. ''Catholic Higher Education and the Pastoral Mission of the Church,'' *Origins* 10 (1980): 380.

21. Ibid., p. 382. For an interpretation which sees this 1980 statement as limiting academic freedom and in basic agreement with the 1972 document of the bishops, see James John Annarelli, *Academic Freedom and Catholic Higher Education* (New York: Greenwood Press, 1987), pp. 68, 69.

22. Congregation for Catholic Education, ''Proposed Schema for a Pontifical Document on Catholic Universities,'' *Origins* 15 (1986): 706–711.

23. Congregation for Catholic Education, ''Summary of Responses to Draft Schema on Catholic Universities,'' *Origins* 17 (1988): 697.

24. Chapter 6 of this book contains a detailed account of the controversy between the Catholic University of America and me that resulted in the conclusion that I could not teach theology at the university.

25. Archbishop Daniel E. Pilarczyk, ''Academic Freedom: Church and University,'' *Origins* 18 (1988): 57–59.

26. Oscar H. Lipscomb, "Faith and Academic Freedom," *America* 159 (September 3–10, 1988): 124–125.

27. Bishop Donald W. Wuerl, "Academic Freedom and the University," *Origins* 18 (1988): 207–211.

28. Edward Boné, "The International Federation of Catholic Universities," *Lumen Vitae* 35 (1980): 176–183.

29. Theodore M. Hesburgh, "The Vatican and American Higher Education," *America* 155 (November 1, 1986): 247–250. The historical development traced in the following paragraphs can be found in Neil J. McCluskey, ed., "Introduction: This Is How It Happened," *The Catholic University: A Modern Appraisal* (Notre Dame, IN: University of Notre Dame Press, 1970), pp. 1–28; Robert J. Henle, "Catholic Universities and the Vatican," *America* 13 (April 9, 1977): 315–322; Ann Ida Gannon, "Some Aspects of Catholic Higher Education since Vatican II," *Current Issues in Catholic Higher Education* 8, no. 1 (Summer 1987): 10–24; Alice Gallin, "On the Road toward a Definition of a Catholic University," *The Jurist* 48 (1988): 536–558.

30. Land O'Lakes Statement, in McCluskey, *The Catholic University*, pp. 336, 337.

31. International Federation of Catholic Universities, "1968 Kinshasa Statement: The Catholic University in the Modern World," in McCluskey, *The Catholic University*, pp. 342–345.

32. McCluskey, "Introduction," in McCluskey, *The Catholic University*, p. 11

33. "1968 Kinshasa Statement," in McCluskey, *The Catholic University*, p. 345.

34. 1969 Congress of Delegates of Catholic Universities, "The Rome Statement: The Catholic University and the Aggiornamento," in McCluskey, *The Catholic University*, pp. 346–365.

35. Ibid., pp. 348, 349.

36. Ibid.

37. Ibid., p. 350.

38. McCluskey, "Introduction," in McCluskey, *The Catholic University*, p. 33.

39. International Federation of Catholic Universities, North American Region, "Freedom, Autonomy, and the University," *IDOC International* 39 (January 1972): 79–88.

40. John W. Donohue, "Catholic Universities Define Themselves: A Progress Report," *America* 128 (April 21, 1973): 355.

41. Congress of Delegates of the Catholic Universities of the World, Rome, November 20–29, 1972, "The Catholic University in the Modern World," in Kelly, *Why Should the Catholic University Survive?* pp. 108–129.

42. Jeremiah Newman, "The Roman Document: The Catholic University in the Modern World Examined and Evaluated," in Kelly, *Why Should the Catholic University Survive?* pp. 56–74.

43. Grisez, in Kelly, *Why Should the Catholic University Survive?* pp. 50–55.

44. Karen J. Winkler, "Catholic Educators Back Autonomy in Universities," *The Chronicle of Higher Education* (January 29, 1973): 5; Paul E. McKeever, "To Remain a Catholic University," *The Long Island Catholic* (January 25, 1973): 1.

45. For a similar judgment, see Donohue, *America* 128 (April 21, 1973): 355.

46. Letter of Gabriel Marie Cardinal Garrone, Prefect, "To the Presidents of Catholic Universities and the Directors of Catholic Institutions of Higher Learning," in Kelly, *Why Should the Catholic University Survive?* pp. 104, 105.

47. Hesburgh, *America* 155 (November 1, 1986): 248.

48. John W. Donohue, "Green Light for Universities," *America* 129 (July 21, 1973): 29.

49. Henle, *America* 136 (April 9, 1977): 319–320.

50. Declaration on Christian Education, par. 11, in Austin Flannery, ed., *Vatican Council II: the Conciliar and Post-Conciliar Documents* (Northport, NY: Costello Publishing Co., 1975), pp. 736, 737.

51. Pope Pius XII, *Deus Scientiarum Dominius, Acta Apostolicae Sedis* 23 (1931): 241–284.

52. Congregation for Catholic Education, *Normae Quaedem, Acta Apostolicae Sedis* 60 (1968): 10.

53. *Deus Scientiarum Dominus, Acta Apostolicae Sedis* 23 (1931): 251, art. 21.

54. James H. Provost, "Canonical Mission in Catholic Universities," *America* 142 (June 7, 1980): 475–477.

55. John Paul II, *Apostolic Constitution Sapientia Christiana On Ecclesiastical Faculties and Universities* (Washington, DC: United States Catholic Conference, 1979).

56. For a commentary on this canon and for its historical development, see James A. Coriden, "The Teaching Office in the Church," in James A. Coriden, Thomas J. Green, and Donald J. Heintschel, eds., *The Code of Canon Law: A Text and Commentary* (New York: Paulist Press, 1985), especially pp. 571–578.

57. Ibid. Also, Ladislas Orsy, "The Mandate to Teach Theological Disciplines: Glosses on Canon 812 of the New Code," *Theological Studies* 44 (1983): 476–488.

58. "Proposed Schema for a Pontifical Document on Catholic Universities," *Origins* 15 (1986): 706–711.

59. Association of Catholic Colleges and Universities, "Catholic College Presidents Respond to Proposed Vatican Schema," *Origins* 15 (1986): 697–704. For an opposing position see Kenneth D. Whitehead, "Religiously Affiliated Colleges and American Freedom," *America* 156 (February 7, 1987): 96–98.

60. Statement of Presidents of Leading Catholic Universities of North America on the Schema for a Proposed Document on the Catholic University,

sent to William Cardinal Baum, Prefect of the Congregation for Catholic Education, with a cover letter signed by Theodore M. Hesburgh on March 21, 1986.

61. Congregation for Catholic Education, "Summary of Responses to Draft Schema on Catholic Universities," *Origins* 17 (March 24, 1988): 597.

62. Hesburgh, *America* 155 (November 1, 1986): 247.

63. For less detailed summaries of the relationship over the years between the leaders of American Catholic higher education and the Vatican, see Gallin, *The Jurist* 48 (1988): 536–538; Gannon, *Current Issues in Catholic Higher Education* 8, n.1 (Summer 1987): 10–24.

64. Congregation for Catholic Education, "A Draft Document on Catholic Higher Education," *Origins* 18 (1988): 445–464.

65. Joseph A. O'Hare, "The Vatican and Catholic Universities," *America* 160 (May 27, 1989): 503–505; Edward A. Malloy, "From Rome with Hope," *America* 160 (June 10, 1989): 16.

66. Catholic Higher Education Congress, "Ten Recommendations," *Origins* 19 (1989): 16.

67. Archbishop José Saraiva Martins, "Address to Education Congress," *Origins* 19 (1989): 13–15.

68. Joseph Cardinal Ratzinger with Vittorio Messori, *The Ratzinger Report: An Exclusive Interview on the State of the Church* (San Francisco: Ignatius Press, 1985).

69. Hans Küng and Leonard Swidler, eds., *The Church in Anguish: Has the Vatican Betrayed Vatican II?* (San Francisco: Harper and Row, 1987).

70. Charles E. Curran, *Tensions in Moral Theology* (Notre Dame, IN: University of Notre Dame Press, 1988).

71. Leonard Swidler, ed., *Küng in Conflict* (New York: Doubleday, 1981); Peter Hebblethwaite, *The New Inquisition? The Case of Edward Schillebeeckx and Hans Küng* (San Francisco: Harper and Row, 1980).

72. Jean-Pierre Jossua, "Jaques Pohier: A Theologian Destroyed," in Küng and Swidler, *Church in Anguish*, pp. 205–211.

73. Ted Schoof, ed., *The Schillebeeckx Case* (New York: Paulist Press, 1984); Hebblethwaite, *The New Inquisition?*.

74. Harvey Cox, *The Silencing of Leonardo Boff: The Vatican and the Future of World Christianity* (Oak Park, IL: Meyer Stone Books, 1989); Leonardo Boff and Clodovis Boff, *Liberation Theology from Dialogue to Confrontation* (San Francisco: Harper and Row, 1986).

75. Charles E. Curran, *Faithful Dissent* (Kansas City: Sheed and Ward, 1986).

76. John A. Alessandro, "The Rights and Responsibilities of Theologians: A Canonical Perspective," in Leo J. O'Donovan, ed., *Cooperation Between Theologians and the Ecclesiastical Magisterium* (Washington: Canon Law Society of America, 1982), pp. 76–116; John P. Boyle, "Church Teaching Authority in the 1983 Code," in Curran and McCormick, *Readings in Moral Theology No. 6*, pp. 191–230. Note that Coriden does not understand the mandate as a formal commissioning or empowerment (Coriden, Green, and Heintschell, *Code of Canon Law*, p. 576).

77. Walbert Bühlman, *Dreaming About the Church: Acts of the Apostles of the Twentieth Century* (Kansas City, MO: Sheed and Ward, 1987); Bernhard Häring, interview with Gianni Licheri, *Fede, Storia, Morale* (Roma: Edizioni Borla, 1989).

78. "The Cologne Declaration," *Commonweal* 116 (February 24, 1989): 102–104.

79. "The Pope and the Theologians," *The Tablet* 243, n. 7769 (June 10, 1989): 659–660.

80. Curran, *Faithful Dissent*, pp. 282–284; See also chapter six.

81. Congregation for the Doctrine of the Faith, "Profession of Faith and Oath of Fidelity," *Origins* 118 (1989): 661–663.

82. Quentin L. Quade, "A University Perspective on the Oath of Fidelity," *America* 160 (April 15, 1989): 345–347.

83. *New York Times,* national edition, (June 18, 1989): 14.

84. Richard A. McCormick, "The Chill Factor: Recent Roman Interventions," *America* 150 (June 30, 1984): 475–481.

85. "Reports: Academic Freedom and the Abortion Issue: Four Incidents at Catholic Institutions," *Academe: Bulletin of the American Association of University Professors* 72, n. 4 (July-August 1986): 1a–13a.

86. See Curran, *Faithful Dissent*.

87. William J. Byron, "At Catholic U the Issue Is Religious, not Academic Freedom," *Washington Post* (June 5, 1988), Outlook Section.

88. "Academic Freedom and Tenure: The Catholic University of Puerto Rico," *Academe: Bulletin of the American Association of University Professors* 73, n. 3 (May-June 1987): 36.

89. Coriden, in Coriden, Green, and Heintschel, *Code of Canon Law,* pp. 571, 572.

90. Ibid., p. 576; Orsy, *Theological Studies* 44 (1983): 481, 482.

5. Rationale in Defense of Academic Freedom for Catholic Higher Education

Chapter 1 traced the development and understanding of academic freedom in American higher education and pointed out the strengths and weaknesses of this approach. The particularities of higher education in the United States have definitely influenced the understanding of academic freedom. Historically, the most serious threat to academic freedom came either from sponsoring bodies and financial contributors to private colleges and universities, or from the states in the schools they sponsored. The principles and procedures of academic freedom arose in the context of defending the freedom of the scholar from those individuals and groups who supported the institution. Many other threats to academic freedom exist, and it is necessary to recognize and deal with these other dangers arising, for example, from colleagues.

The principles and procedures of academic freedom that have been worked out and developed in this country by the American Association of University Professors (AAUP) are the generally accepted standards and processes of academic freedom that this chapter will defend. In the question of academic freedom for Catholic higher education, the primary problem concerns the freedom of the professor and the institution vis-à-vis church authority. Institutions that call themselves Catholic are often sponsored by religious communities, so that the threat to academic freedom in the academy comes from external church interference. The Land O'Lakes Statement in 1967 identified this problem and firmly stated that the Catholic institution of higher learning must have a true autonomy and academic freedom in the face of authority of whatever kind, lay or clerical, that is external to the academic community itself.[1] Church authorities can take no direct action of any kind that has immediate juridical effects in the academy.

This chapter defends the proposition that church authority of whatever kind should never directly interfere in the academy. The discussion will not deal with all aspects of academic freedom, but only with the troublesome question of the freedom of the Catholic academy from the direct interference of church authorities. In addition, the chapter will concentrate on the freedom of theology within the American Catholic academy; again, this forms only a small part of the total reality of academic freedom, but it is the part that is most seriously threatened by direct church intervention. The academic freedom of the theologian within the Catholic academy has been recognized by the leaders of Catholic higher education as the focal point of tension.[2] If the church should not directly interfere with the theologian, then no direct intervention should occur in other areas either.

No special limitation such as that in the 1940 AAUP statement is needed. The Catholic theologian in the Catholic college or university should have the same academic freedom as other scholars in their fields. This chapter will develop a defense for the academic freedom of Catholic theologians and Catholic institutions of higher learning that can be understood as the freedom from direct external intervention by church authorities in the work of the academy in general and especially in the hiring, promoting, tenuring, and dismissing of faculty.

Although much has been written on academic freedom in Catholic higher education, no in-depth defense of such freedom exists. James John Annarelli's *Academic Freedom and Catholic Higher Education* has been the most significant recent study in this area,[3] but he does not give a detailed justification of academic freedom for Catholic colleges and universities. In addition, I disagree with two important aspects of the brief justification he does provide. First, according to Annarelli, arguments based on the fact that academic freedom serves the good of the church should not occupy a central place in the discussion of the justification of academic freedom in the Catholic context. Second, he does not give special importance to the freedom of the Catholic theologian.[4] Annarelli's monograph also does not deal at length with the objections that have been raised against academic freedom by Catholic scholars in the past and even in the present.

In the responses by leaders of Catholic higher education to the new norms for Catholic colleges and universities that have been proposed by the Vatican Congregation for Catholic Education, the practical issue of survival for Catholic higher education has frequently been stressed. Many more Catholic colleges and universities are to be found in the United States than in any other country in the world. In the United States some smaller institutions have closed, but Catholic higher education has flourished. Even those opposed to academic freedom for Catholic institutions agree that many Catholic institutions could not survive without government aid and private grants from non-Catholic and secular sources. The leaders of Catholic higher education fear that financial aid and accreditation would be threatened if academic freedom and institutional autonomy were not to exist in Catholic higher education.[5] A minority maintains that accreditation and government funding would not be lost if Catholic institutions did not have full academic freedom and autonomy.[6]

The practical argument based on the growth and survival of Catholic colleges and universities as they exist today in the United States furnishes a strong reason for supporting academic freedom and autonomy, and one cannot blame the administrators of Catholic institutions for proposing such practical reasons. Such administrators know better than anyone else the financial problems facing Catholic higher education. They realize that without federal and state support the future of these institutions is in grave jeopardy. Administrators are rightly concerned that their institutions be both American colleges and universities and also Catholic. The continual survival of Catholic higher education is a good that should not be allowed to cease.

However, the survival of Catholic higher education as it now exists cannot be the ultimate reason for the defense of academic freedom in Catholic colleges and universities. In order to justify its existence academic freedom in itself should be for the good of Catholic higher education. From an ethical perspective, going out of business can be the proper choice if the alternative means going against one's principles in order to secure the institution's continuing existence. I am in no way criticizing the good faith of the leaders of Catholic higher education who have proposed the practical argument; they are convinced that their institutions exist for the good of the church and therefore their continuance is most signficant. However, this study steps back and proves that presupposition; namely, that academic freedom in Catholic higher education is ultimately for the good of Catholic higher education and the church. The main thrust of this section will be to attempt a proof and defense of the presuppositions of many leaders of Catholic higher education today.

Justification of Academic Freedom in General

What is the ultimate basis for the justification of academic freedom in American institutions of higher education in general? In my judgment, the justification is based on what is for the common good of society as a whole. One might call this a pragmatic justification for academic freedom rather than a doctrinaire or metaphysical justification. Academic freedom for institutions of higher learning is ultimately for the good of society itself. The fact that such freedom might be good for academic professors or good for the college or university cannot serve as the ultimate justification why academic freedom should be recognized by society at large as contributing to the good of society. Because academic freedom is good for the public at large, it should then be supported and recognized by society. Chapter one has shown how the AAUP documents and most commentators have accepted such a justification for academic freedom.

The pragmatic justification of academic freedom avoids some of the doctrinaire and overly metaphysical approaches that many Catholic commentators have objected to over the years. Academic freedom from my perspective cannot be based on an empiricism that recognizes only the scientific method. Such a narrow empiricism falsifies reality by refusing to admit the existence of anything that is not empirically verifiable. The empirical sciences have made a great contribution to progress and development in the nineteenth and twentieth centuries, but today humanity at large is conscious not only of the contribution but also of the limits of any one empirical science and of all of them together. The human being is more than empirical, and sometimes in the name of the human, one must say no to a particular science or to a particular technology. The ecological question has made us all conscious of the limits of our physical world and the need to say no to some proposed developments. The mere fact that technologically something can be done is no reason why it necessarily should be done. To be sure, American society in general in the last few decades has become more conscious of the limits of the empirical method and of the need for values and ethics in making the choices that will affect human existence in our world. In my judgment academic freedom cannot ultimately be grounded only in an empirical scientific method, and I doubt if anyone would seriously propose such a justification today.

Catholic opponents of academic freedom even to this day point to academic freedom's roots in the Enlightenment—its stress on reason and its denial of the spiritual and transcendental realms. However, the pragmatic defense of academic freedom based on its contribution to the good of society avoids such dogmatic arguments. No doubt a denial of the spiritual realm and of the possibility of belief in God could serve as a basis for academic freedom in some minds, but such a denial does not have to furnish the ultimate justification.

Some Catholics have objected to academic freedom because it absolutizes freedom, which must always be seen in relationship to truth and other values. Philosophically I agree with the judgment that freedom in the abstract cannot be absolutized. I also maintain that there is a danger on the American scene of giving too much importance to freedom and individual rights. It is interesting to recall that some Catholics in the 1930s joined their criticism of academic freedom to their criticism of the economic individualism that was so prevalent in American society. I do not want to use the metaphor of the free market of ideas to justify academic freedom and thus to associate it with individualism in economic matters. Robert Bellah and his coauthors have lately called attention to the danger of this individualism in our society and have appealed to the communitarian understanding proposed by biblical religion as an important antidote.[7] The recent pastoral letter of the United States Catholic bishops on the American economy also strongly disagrees with and highlights the dangers of a one-sided individualism that so often characterizes American approaches to the economic order.[8] The Catholic tradition of political economic ethics has tried to avoid the two extremes of individualism and collectivism and has repudiated both laissez-faire capitalism and totalitarianism. Thus the bishops call for a greater role for government in accord with the principle of subsidarity, and the pastoral letter admits not only political rights but also economic rights. The danger of absolutizing freedom is prevalent in the United States in general and in considerations of the economic order. But the pragmatic argument for academic freedom based on what contributes to the common good does not have to absolutize freedom.

The justification based on academic freedom's contribution to society skirts and avoids the problems of more doctrinaire approaches based on one particular epistemology or metaphysics and recognizes that in an intellectually pluralistic society one cannot expect to find agreement on one particular epistemological approach. Neoscholasticism in the past could not agree with the philosophical basis often proposed in defense of academic freedom. In the neoscholastic tradition the mind can know truths with certainty. Such a philosophical perspective cannot accept a relativistic epistemological support for academic freedom. Dogmatic metaphysical or theological arguments cannot find general acceptance among those who would use different approaches.

The justification of academic freedom based on its contribution to the common good of society not only avoids many problems connected with other possible justifications, but the approach also addresses the issues in the most satisfying and adequate manner. Academic freedom above all concerns the institutions of higher education in our American society and not merely the scholar as a private individual or the college or university as a private or public institution. All should admit that the individual scholar ought to enjoy freedom in research: to study, research, and write in accord with her or his own desires; to be free from any external coercion; and to have as the only legal limit that such work not be against civil law. Part of the fabric of society, institutions of higher education make a contribution to society as a whole through their teaching and research functions. Society today in many ways gives financial support to colleges and universities, and even private institutions receive some government funding; donors receive tax advantages. Since colleges and universities are social institutions affecting the body social, the justification for academic freedom rests on what is for the good of the society as a whole.

Of course, the nature of higher education must enter into the final judgment. Not every institution in society should enjoy academic freedom. The argument justifying academic freedom for higher education is thus a complex, inclusive, and pragmatic argument. In the light of what higher education is and should be, society is best served by recognizing and safeguarding the academic freedom of the academy. I have used the word pragmatic to describe this justification, but the description should not be understood to have a pejorative connotation. In addition, the pragmatic approach to academic freedom does not necessarily entail a utilitarian justification. The Catholic ethical tradition has often justified many of its positions and norms in social ethics by appealing to the common good or the end of political society. The argumentation proposed here and accepted by most theorists gives a proper emphasis to the historical, cultural, and social setting in which the college or university plays an important role.

Such a justification for academic freedom parallels the justification proposed for religious liberty and for the first amendment of the American Constitution by John Courtney Murray, the American Jesuit whose pioneering research prepared the way for the Catholic church's acceptance of religious freedom. Murray describes two possible ways of defending religious liberty, which is understood as the freedom from external coercion preventing one from acting in accord with one's conscience or forcing one to act against conscience in religious matters. One approach sees religious freedom as a moral or theological concept and then argues to the need for religious freedom in society; such a position could begin, for example, with the insight of the freedom of conscience or the freedom of the act of faith and then come to its own conclusion. Maintaining that such an approach is too abstract and deductive, Murray points out that it is divorced from the concrete reality of the sociohistorical context in all its particulars. Moreover, this way of justifying religious freedom can set off futile arguments about the rights of an erroneous conscience. Murray's understanding of religious freedom, on the other hand, begins with the dignity of the human person as he or she exists within the historical, cultural, and social reality of present circumstances. According to this view, religious freedom is formally a juridical or constitutional question that has its foundations in theology, ethics, political philosophy, and jurisprudence.

Murray's arguments for religious freedom also apply to academic freedom. Academic freedom like religious freedom is primarily a societal question and not merely an individual question. The danger exists of overtheologizing the concept of academic freedom by absolutizing freedom and failing to recognize that freedom always exists in a complicated web of concrete relationships that may at times limit freedom. In my judgment, academic freedom like religious freedom is a complex reality that is ultimately justified for the good of society in the concrete historical, cultural and political circumstances of the present societal situation.[9]

Murray had proposed a somewhat similar approach for the justification of the first amendment to the United States Constitution with its clauses of nonestablishment and free exercise of religion. Murray understands the two articles of the first amendment to be articles of peace and not of faith, the work of lawyers and not of theologians or even of political scientists, as only good law and not as true dogma in any sense of the term. No put-down, this is meant as high praise. All law is based on the common good. The primary criterion of good law is its necessity or utility for the promotion and preservation of the public peace under a given set of circumstances. Social peace assured by equal justice in dealing with possible conflicting groups is the highest integrating element of the common good. These two articles of the first amendment were not deduced a priori from first principles but arose from the historical and cultural circumstances of the United States. The existence of many different denominations in the United States in addition to the large number of unchurched citizens, the societal good resulting from the lack of persecution and discrimination, and the widening of religious toleration in England all contributed to the judgment that any other course except freedom of religion and separation of church and state would be disruptive, imprudent, impractical, and impossible.

The American experiment involves the establishment of civic unity in the midst of religious pluralism, and the first amendment is the practical means that assures that people of different and of no religious persuasion can join together in civic harmony and unity. Note again the pragmatic and concrete nature of the argument as opposed to a more doctrinaire, theological, or a priori approach. Murray contrasts his approach to the nonestablishment and free exercise clauses as articles of peace with the approach of those who treat the clauses as articles of faith. For some the first amendment enshrines certain ultimate beliefs and hence constitutes an article of faith. For many the first amendment is based on Protestant notions about faith, religion, religious truth, etc. The amendment thus almost becomes a religious dogma and norm of orthodoxy. For the secularist the first amendment is also an article of faith but of a different type of faith. Faith here is in the scientific empiricism that denies the existence of the spiritual, the transcendental, and even the metaphysical. Murray even finds a third distinct group, secularizing Protestants, who also see the first amendment as an article of watered-down faith. All these approaches overtheologize and overdogmatize the justification of the first amendment. The first amendment cannot be based upon the diverse faith commitments of different people but only on the contribution that it makes to society in the light of the concrete political, historical, and cultural realities of our American existence.[10]

So too with academic freedom. Academic freedom cannot be an article of faith or of dogma, and there is a danger of adducing overtheological or overmetaphysical arguments in favor of it. It is not to be deduced from a priori principles or understandings, but is better justified as a social institution precisely because it exists for the good of the society in which we find ourselves.

The reasons why academic freedom for higher education serves the good of society have already been developed in the literature on academic freedom. This chapter has emphasized the ultimate justification of academic freedom and the recognition that such a justification is in keeping with the Catholic approach to the analogous question of religious freedom. A proper understanding of the structure of the justification of academic freedom also responds to some of the objections of the past and the present that some Catholics have raised against academic freedom.

The Basic Defense of Academic Freedom in Catholic Institutions

The main thrust of this chapter is to justify academic freedom for Catholic higher education, a justification analogous to the justification of academic freedom in general. American society accepts academic freedom because such freedom is good for society: The Catholic church can accept academic freedom in Catholic higher education because academic freedom is good for the church in the concrete circumstances of the United States.

Catholic colleges and universities are supported and sponsored by entities of the Catholic church. As pointed out in chapter two, most institutions are sponsored by religious communities of women or men (e.g., the Sisters of St. Joseph or the Jesuits). Recall that on the whole, Catholic institutions of higher learning are today neither controlled nor owned by the church as such or by groups within the church such as religious communities. However, the Catholic church still views Catholic higher education as a part of the church's mission. Many Catholic religious communities make a sizeable commitment to Catholic higher education. These institutions also appeal to Catholics to support them in their endeavors. Thus the Catholic church continues to support Catholic higher education. Such institutions, despite their juridical independence, are looked upon as being for the good of the church. Logically, then, one has to make the argument that academic freedom in such institutions should be accepted because it too is for the good of the church. If academic freedom were harmful to the church, the church would not be able to support such freedom in church-sponsored institutions.

As previously noted, supporters of academic freedom for Catholic higher education have not really developed such a defense. To prove that academic freedom is good for the Catholic church is not easy, but it is necessary in order to justify academic freedom for Catholic higher education.

Based on the criterion of what is for the good of the church, my argument here will necessarily be inclusive, pragmatic, and concrete. The justification must consider all relevant factors that are involved in and will affect the good of the church. Such an approach cannot argue deductively from only one value or principle and by its very nature will be concrete. We are dealing with the understanding of academic freedom as it exists in the United States—as it has taken on a specific meaning in the light of the particular historical, cultural, and pedagogical circumstances of higher education in our country. The argument will not maintain that throughout the world all Catholic colleges and universities must have the same academic freedom as here, for the pragmatic and concrete aspects of justification limit the scope to just the United States. In other circumstances, other approaches could exist, and with good reasons. The thrust of my reasoning here is that on the American scene Catholic acceptance of academic freedom for Catholic higher education is ultimately for the good of the church itself. I specifically exclude seminaries as such; the freedom of all scholars—including theologians—in Roman Catholic seminaries is a very important and closely related topic, but we are here dealing with only academic freedom for all scholars at American Catholic colleges and universities.

Such an approach does away with some of the objectionable, more doctrinaire approaches to academic freedom. Academic freedom in the United States in general and academic freedom for Catholic higher education in particular do not rest on empiricism, the denial of the transcendent, an absolutizing of freedom, or an exaggerated individualism. However, the defenders of academic freedom for Catholic higher education must face squarely the task of showing why academic freedom is for the good of the Catholic church in the United States.

Further, the crux of the issue of academic freedom in Catholic education involves Catholic theology; contemporary history shows that the friction between the academy and external church authority is most acute in this area. Obviously academic freedom involves much more than theology, but if the academic freedom of the theologian within higher education is for the good of the church then the academic freedom of all other scholars in the academy will likewise be justified. The argument here will be limited to academic freedom for college and university Catholic theologians.

Such a defense of academic freedom will not be easy. Catholic self-understanding has always had a difficulty giving due importance to the reality of freedom in general. Catholic thought has traditionally opposed the absolutization of freedom. In addition, the concept of academic freedom on the American scene is very different from similar notions in other countries even in the Western world. For example, in 1989, one hundred sixty-three German-speaking theologians issued ''The Cologne Declaration,'' which was sharply critical of recent Vatican actions in appointing bishops and in appointing theologians to state universities and which also disagreed with the papal approach to and emphasis on the condemnation of artificial contraception. Although the German-speaking theologians strongly objected to Vatican interference in the appointement of professors to Catholic faculties of theology in state universities, they accepted as a matter of course that such theologians first be approved by the local bishop and given a canonical mission.[11] Their approach is in keeping with the existing custom and law in Germany as governed by concordats with the Vatican. Prior episcopal approval is totally contrary, however, to American standards of academic freedom. Thus the issue of academic freedom in the United States is a peculiarly American issue in which the people from the United States must convince the Vatican authorities that American theory and practice are in the best interests of the church in the United States. However, all recognize at the present time the tension that exists between the Vatican and the Catholic church in the United States.[12] At times some Americans forget that tensions also exist between the Vatican and many other particular churches throughout the world. In the light of these frictions it will be even more difficult to prove the point that must be made and accepted; namely, that academic freedom is ultimately for the good of the Catholic church in the United States. I will now try to make such an argument.[13]

The Role of Catholic Theology

First of all, some understanding of the role and function of Catholic theology is necessary. There has been much discussion and debate within Roman Catholicism in the past two decades about the proper role and understanding of the hierarchical magisterium and its relationship to the role and function of the Catholic church. The understanding proposed by many today is quite different from the approach often proposed in the pre-Vatican II era. Chapter three has already summarized some of the more significant and pertinent changes that took place in Catholic self-understanding at the time of the Second Vatican Council. The reasoning proposed here will try to synthesize much of what has already been written about the role of the hierarchical magisterium and of theologians in the church. In the light of the sources that will be used, e.g., the report of the joint committee of the Canon Law Society of America and of the Catholic Theological Society of America, it will be evident that the positions taken in this section are in no way radical or idiosyncratic but are well within the mainsteam of contemporary Catholic theology.[14] Some more conservative Catholic theologians might not agree, however, especially with some of the conclusions reached.

The teaching function of pope and bishops is a pastoral role conferred by office in the church. However, the hierarchical teaching office or magisterium is not absolute but is itself subject to the word of God and truth, as was taught in the Constitution on Divine Revelation of Vatican II.[15] The teaching authority through the inspiration of the Holy Spirit and using available human understandings discerns the word of God and the truth. Thomistic theology, an important part of the Catholic tradition, has always insisted that authority must conform itself to the truth and that authority is the servant of the truth. In morality the tradition maintained that something is commanded because it is good and not the other way around; the command in itself does not make something good. Thomistic understanding sees law not as an act of the will of the legislator but as an act of the practical reason of the legislator directing people to the good. For Thomas Aquinas an unjust law is no law and does not oblige in conscience. The lawmaker must conform her- or himself to what is the reasonable and good thing in itself.[16] The whole of Christian tradition in its prayer for rulers asked primarily for the gift of wisdom, not power. Thus within the Catholic tradition authority is always subject to the truth. Similarly, authoritative church teachers must always serve the word of God and truth; the hierarchical magisterium is not above the word of God.

In exercising its pastoral teaching role, the hierarchical magisterium needs theologians and all the people of God. In an earlier era theologians even had a vote in ecumenical councils, and all recognize the important work done by theologians at the Second Vatican Council. A complaint heard often today is that the hierarchical magisterium often relies on one school of theology and fails to recognize the plurality and diversity that exist in current Catholic theology. History shows that theologians have often prepared the way for hierarchical church teachings to follow. The reform of Vatican II would never have come about without the theological and pastoral developments which preceded it and encouraged it.

In addition, the hierarchical teaching office is not identical with the full teaching office of the church. The Pastoral Constitution on the Church in the Modern World states: ''With the help of the Holy Spirit, it is the task of the whole people of God, particularly of its pastors and theologians, to listen to and distinguish the many voices of our times and to interpret them in the light of the divine Word, in order that the revealed truth may be more deeply penetrated, better understood, and more suitably presented."[17] Through baptism all Christians share in the threefold office of Jesus as priest, teacher, and ruler. Just as the Catholic church now recognizes the priesthood of all believers together with a hierarchical priesthood, so too there exists a teaching role for all believers as well as the special hierarchical teaching function. The Constitution on the Church of the Second Vatican Council recognizes that all the holy people of God share in the prophetic office of Jesus.[18] The church has learned and continues to learn from its prophets. The Declaration on Religious Liberty in its opening paragraph implicitly admits that the teaching on religious liberty was true before a document was signed in Rome.[19]

In the light of these realities, some Catholic theologians have talked about a dual magisterium of hierarchical teachers and theologians or have stressed that a pluralism of magisteria or church teachers exists. I have usually avoided such terms, but I wholeheartedly agree with the ideas behind them.[20] Avery Dulles adopts and distinguishes a pluralistic theory of teaching authority in the church from hierocratic and democratic theories; several distinct organs of authority serve as checks and balances.[21]

One must also recognize various levels of hierarchical church teachings. Not all teachings carry the same importance or weight: some teachings are core and central to Christian and Catholic belief; other teachings are more remote and peripheral. The Second Vatican Council's Decree on Ecumenism recognizes a "hierarchy of truths."[22] Official Catholic teaching and canon law authoritatively approves the distinction between infallible teaching, which calls for an assent of faith on the part of the faithful, and authoritative noninfallible teaching, which demands religious respect of intellect and will. There has been discussion and debate about infallible teaching, but it is generally recognized that infallible teaching can be deepened, improved, and developed. Theologians especially have contributed to the development of church teaching, even of the infallible type. Infallible teaching is not the last word or the perfect word. Noninfallible teaching covers a great deal of diverse reality, and many more distinctions would be helpful. However, such teachings by their very nature might be wrong. The possibility of dissent from such teachings has been recognized by bishops and theologians alike.

The focus now shifts to the role and function of the theologian. The hierarchical teaching role is connected to an office in the church, whereas the theological function depends on the theological scholarship of the individual and the community of scholars. Catholic theology is a reflective, critical, systematic, and thematic human discipline thinking about Catholic faith and life. One can and should clearly distinguish the role of hierarchical teachers and theologians in the church even though the two roles sometimes overlap. The hierarchical teaching office needs the work of theologians and could not perform its teaching function adequately without the contribution of theologians. Catholic theologians as such must give the proper respect and response to hierarchical teaching. Thus it is easy to see why there has been and continues to be some stress within the Roman Catholic church between the hierarchical teaching office and theologians. In my judgment, such tension between the two roles will always exist, although all should work to avoid destructive conflicts.

To understand better both the role of the hierarchical magisterium and the role of the theologian, it is helpful to reflect on the Catholic self-understanding of its own faith. I have characterized the role of the church as one of creative fidelity to the word and work of Jesus. The church must always be faithful to Jesus' teaching and life, but such fidelity cannot merely repeat what Jesus said and did. A very distinctive aspect of the Catholic theological tradition is its *and*. Catholic thought has stressed scripture *and* tradition, faith *and* reason, grace *and* works, Jesus *and* the church, *and* Mary, *and* the saints. Elsewhere I have pointed out the dangers and problems that have arisen from the Catholic *and*, but on the whole I am deeply committed to this approach.[23] In a certain sense all of these couplets illustrate the Catholic insistence on mediation. The word and work of God is mediated to us in and through tradition, reason, our own humanity, and the church. The danger comes from absolutizing any of the second aspects and failing to see them as mediations. But God ordinarily comes to us in and through the human, as is illustrated by the Catholic emphasis on the human church with a sacramental system that celebrates the presence of God in the human meal of the Eucharist.

The proper understanding of the roles of scripture and tradition helps to explain the creative fidelity of the Catholic approach. The Catholic tradition has strongly opposed the axiom of the scriptures alone. The scriptures are historically and culturally conditioned. The word and work of Jesus must constantly be understood, lived, and appropriated in the light of the historical and cultural circumstances of time and place. Precisely for this reason, much development has occurred within the Catholic church over the years. The structure of the church itself as we know it today cannot be found as such in the New Testament. It was only in the fourth, fifth, and sixth centuries that the church came to its understanding about God as involving three divine persons and Jesus as being one person with two natures—human and divine. For the greater part of its existence the Catholic church did not accept and teach the existence of seven sacraments. Along the way, some developments and changes were repudiated by the church as unfaithful to the tradition. But that fact cannot deny the development that has taken place and must continue to take place. For example, the most renowned theologian in the Catholic tradition, Thomas Aquinas (died 1274), used the Aristotelian teaching that was just coming into the university world of Europe in order to understand better and explain the Christian faith; Aquinas was not satisfied with just repeating what past teachers and masters had said. Theology in the church constantly strives to know God's revelation in the light of the historical and cultural situation of the times. In regard to the work and word of Jesus, creative fidelity well characterizes the task of the whole church in general and of the theologian in particular.

The Catholic acceptance of faith and reason, and of grace and nature, also supports the emphasis on creative fidelity. An important question for any religion is its relationship to the human in general and to human reason in particular. The Catholic tradition has never seen grace and human nature in opposition to one another. According to a well-accepted and ancient theological and spiritual axiom grace does not destroy nature but builds on it. In this same vein, medieval Catholic thought insisted that faith and reason can never contradict one another. Such an affirmation recognizes the basic goodness and importance of human reason.

Precisely because of the acceptance of both faith and reason medieval Catholicism sponsored universities. The first scientists in that era were theologians. The church had nothing to fear from human reason. The church's continuing involvement in higher education bears witness to this traditional Catholic approach. The

Catholic acceptance of human reason is very well illustrated in moral theology. Catholic moral theology was heavily based on the natural law which maintains that human reason reflecting on human nature can arrive at true ethical wisdom and knowledge. The important role of reason in Catholic theology underscores the need for creative fidelity. It is true that historically problems arose between science and church teaching. The perennial problem of whose reason is right has never been solved, but still the Catholic tradition insists that faith and reason cannot contradict one another. In this light, faith is always using reason to try to arrive at deeper understandings and new knowledge.

The Catholic acceptance of scripture and tradition, grace and nature, and faith and reason grounds the need for creative fidelity from a theological perspective. From a philosophical perspective, historical consciousness (described in chapter three) has recently supplied a very crucial basis for creative fidelity and the need for theology in the church to understand, appropriate, and live the word and work of Jesus in the light of the historical and cultural situation in the present time.

Creative fidelity characterizes the approach of the church in general and of theology in particular. Theology will often be the scout who makes the first attempt to understand the gospel in the light of the contemporary scene. Bernard Lonergan, the most significant English-speaking theologian in this century, was fond of pointing out that the church usually arrives on the scene a little breathless and a little late. Some theologians might stress fidelity and be more critical of new developments, but theologians will always have a very important role to play in the development, change, and even correction of church teachings that are necessary for the good of the church.

Theology as a systematic, thematic, and critical reflection on Christian faith and life is very important for the good of the church. Theology rests on the faithful and creative scholarship of the individual and the community of scholars. History reminds us of the important role played by theologians in the life of the church. The church in apostolic times recognized the distinct role of the *didaskoloi* who teach in their own right and not merely as delegates of the *episkopoi* or *presbyteroi*. The Middle Ages recognized the magisterium of doctors or theologians in the church. The very term *mag-*

isterium, which now refers to the hierarchical magisterium, at that time was used primarily to refer to theologians. In the medieval universities and later on, the faculties of theology exercised an independent teaching authority. Recall that in some ecumenical councils in the past, theologians had a vote; at the Second Vatican Council theologians played a major role.

The understanding of the role of theologians developed here strongly disagrees with the understanding of the theologian as the one who teaches by reason of delegation or a mission given by the hierarchical teaching office. The hierarchical teaching office and the theological roles cannot be understood in terms of subordination and delegation. They are two distinct but interrelated functions. One recent study refers to the role of theologians as cooperative with and complementary to the hierarchical teaching role.[24] I have used the description of a somewhat independent and cooperative role to describe the theological function vis-à-vis the hierarchical teaching office, but recent official church documents insist that theologians teach in the name of the church and need a canonical mission or mandate.[25]

On the basis of the foregoing analysis, it follows that theologians need freedom in order to be true to their calling. However, the Catholic self-understanding gives a significant pastoral role to the hierarchical magisterium of pope and bishops. All Catholics must admit in theory that the hierarchical magisterium can at times legitimately intervene to protect and defend the faith by saying that the conclusions of a particular theologian are wrong or are not in keeping with Catholic self-understanding. Theologians have made many mistakes in the past and will continue to do so in the future. At times, as has happened in history, hierarchical intervention has been wrong; but no one can totally take away such a right and responsibility for teaching and oversight from the hierarchical teaching office in the Catholic church. From the perspective of Catholic self-understanding theology needs a legitimate freedom, but that freedom is still limited by revelation and by the role of the hierarchical teaching office. The academic freedom of the Catholic theologian as an academician is greater than the freedom of the Catholic theologian as a theologian in the church. To prove that academic freedom, including the academic freedom of the Catholic theologian in the academy, is good for the Catholic church, one must justify a greater level of freedom than is necessary for Catholic theology to carry out its function in the church.

Arguments against Academic Freedom for Catholic Theology

On the sole basis of the necessarily limited freedom of the Catholic theologian in the church, a strong case can be made against full academic freedom for Catholic theology. Chapter four developed the various reasons proposed against academic freedom in Catholic higher education in general. This section will summarize briefly three types of arguments—the theological, the historical, and the practical—that have been given to support the specific position that academic freedom should not exist for Catholic theologians in Catholic institutions of higher learning.

In Catholic self-understanding the pastoral teaching office of pope and bishops has the role of defending and protecting the faith. The hierarchical magisterium is greatly assisted in this teaching function by theologians, but authoritative judgments about faith and morals remain the province of the hierarchical magisterium. Pastoral judgments about faith and morals must be made by the official teaching office in the church.

In the light of Catholic self-understanding there is such a reality as revealed truth, and the church, especially through the hierarchical magisterium, has the responsibility for maintaining faithfulness both to that revealed truth and to its own pastoral task of sanctification. The church needs the contribution of theologians, but academics cannot take away the role that rightly belongs to the teaching officers of the hierarchical church. The university and the academy cannot tell people what is and what is not Catholic faith and cannot give direction to believers about their faith and their morals. If the theologian remains in the realm of speculation, there is no problem. But the theologian cannot assume the pastoral role of determining officially what is Catholic faith in giving direction to believers about their moral behavior. There will always be some tension and overlapping in the two functions, but the pastoral teaching office must exercise its role with regard to faith and morals.[26] In the Catholic church theologians do not have the last word or the official word in these areas.

Historically, the church has survived because the hierarchical magisterium has exercised its teaching function to protect the faith from error, which has arisen in the past and will continue to exist in the future. The hierarchical teaching function will always be needed to protect the church from error. History also indicates some abuse on the part of teaching authority in the church. The inquisition, the Galileo case, and even the processes used with regard to some contemporary Catholic theologians have been a source of embarrassment for some in the church. One does not and should not defend the abuse of authority in the past or in the present. However, as the ancient axiom says, the abuse does not do away with the use. We must make every effort to avoid abuses, but the role of the hierarchical teaching office is essential for promoting and preserving the faith of the Catholic church. The teaching office should function in many different ways; at times it must point out some positions as erroneous and outside the pale of Catholic faith.

From a practical perspective, the existence of full academic freedom for theology would create confusion and disturbance within the church and ultimately harm the church. Distorted and erroneous views on what is Catholic teaching will only confuse Catholics and non-Catholics alike. All the faithful have a right to know what is clearly the teaching of the church. Many Catholics have been upset by the statements of theologians that are often reported in the popular media; if theologians restricted themselves only to academic books and journals, the confusion might be less. But in reality, theological positions are often discussed in the popular media. The confusion about what Catholic teaching is, is harmful for all concerned. Theologians can at times lead people astray from the faith of the church. The Catholic church has the obligation to make sure that its faith and teaching are properly and clearly proposed and known. The confusion and doubt which would come from full academic freedom cannot be for the good of the church.

The Case for Academic Freedom in Catholic Theology

On the contrary, in my judgment these reasons for denying academic freedom are not convincing. I recognize some validity in the arguments that have been proposed, but what is of value can be preserved without denying full academic freedom for Catholic theology in Catholic higher education. Academic freedom is ultimately for the good of the church, even though theologians will make mistakes in matters of faith and morals. To build the defense of academic freedom for Catholic higher education and especially for Catholic theologians in the American Catholic academy, a cumulative argument will be developed in several steps.

Academic freedom for Catholic theology in Catholic colleges and universities in this context means that church authority cannot directly intervene in the affairs of the academy and specifically in the hiring, promoting, tenuring, and dismissing of faculty members. This chapter earlier discussed the role of the theologian in the church and pointed out that some freedom was essential for carrying out the theological task; academic freedom, however, goes beyond the freedom of the theologian within the church. In a true sense the Catholic academic theologian wears two hats—the theologian in the church and the theologian in the academy. The teaching office in the church has the right to point out what it believes to be erroneous teaching and to say that a particular theologian in some matters is wrong and does not speak for the church; but of course the church authority must make sure its own procedures are in accord with the demands of justice and truth. However, academic freedom means that the church and its authorities cannot directly intervene in the affairs of the academy.

My personal situation indicates very clearly what can happen in the hardest case scenario. The Congregation for the Doctrine of the Faith has declared that I am neither suitable nor eligible to be a professor of Catholic theology,[27] a situation that has never occurred before in the United States. I disagree with the decision made by the church authorities, but they have made it. That decision by church authority should not, however, have had juridical effect within the academy, for I can only be dismissed from a tenured academic appointment on the basis of a judgment on my competency made in the first instance by academic peers.[28] The Catholic theologian in the Catholic college or university enjoys a greater freedom than the Catholic theologian in the church. But on the American scene, defenders of academic freedom for Catholic institutions and for Catholic theology must prove that such freedom is actually good for the church. One must recognize the difficulty in proving this to the satisfaction of all in the church. Perhaps this difficulty explains the fact that most defenders of academic freedom for Catholic institutions have avoided what I think is the heart of the matter but also the most difficult aspect. I contend that acceptance of academic freedom for Catholic institutions in the United States is for the good of the church and has analogies with other lessons that the Catholic church has learned in the United States.

The first set of arguments here will indicate that the possible negative effects arising from academic freedom can be limited and handled effectively. Academic freedom means that the academy and the people in it are immune from direct intervention by outside authorities of any kind, in this case the hierarchy of the church. Church authorities cannot directly and immediately affect what happens in the academy, especially in the hiring, promoting, tenuring, and dismissing of faculty members. However, if they deem it necessary and prudent, they are always free to point out publicly that the position of a particular theologian is erroneous or not in keeping with the Catholic faith. The pastoral teaching office can still carry on its proper function in condemning what is judged to be erroneous or against faith. In this way the good of the church and its concern for the faith are safeguarded. It will be clear to everyone what official Catholic teaching is on a particular point, even though this particular teaching might still be wrong. The Catholic teaching office should be prudent and just in what it does, but the acceptance of academic freedom does not rule out the responsibility of the teaching office to point out errors in the work of a particular theologian who, as an individual member of the church, is related to the hierarchical teaching office. Academic freedom only means that such interventions do not and cannot affect in any way the theologian's status within the academy.

The scholar who enjoys academic freedom must always act responsibly and competently. The standards for accreditation of the Middle States Association of Colleges and Schools in discussing academic freedom thus speak about the teacher's responsibilities: "On the part of the faculty there is an obligation to distinguish personal conviction from proven conclusions and to present relevant data fairly to students because this same freedom serves their right to learn the facts."[29] The responsible Catholic theologian must always clearly and fairly portray and explain Catholic teaching. When disagreeing with such teaching, the theologian must clearly label her or his position as such. (Many theologians commenting on my case have claimed that *dissent* is not the best word to use to describe what I am doing.[30] While I recognize the negative connotations of the word, I always point out that such dissent should be seen as only one part of the whole theological enterprise, a part that exists within the context of assent. However, I continue to use the word *dissent* so that I can be very accurate and careful in distinguishing my position from official church teaching. Perhaps there is a better way to express this reality, but I have yet to find it.) The competent and responsible academic theologian must always clearly portray the teaching of the church and recognize his or her own positions for what they are, even though he or she holds them as true. Thus the responsibility of the academic theologian puts significant limits on how the theologian deals with official church teaching.

Another important limit on the possible errors and mistakes of a particular Catholic theologian comes from the criticism and inter-action of the theological community itself. Even before the existence of American universities vigorous debate had occurred among Cath-olic theologians. This debate became so rancorous at times that Catholic moral theology coined the phrase *odium theologicum* to describe a particularly bitter kind of hatred that at times existed among theologians. Lively debate will certainly put limits on the work and proposals of any individual theologian. Granted that the theologians at times will make mistakes, but the academy itself provides a context and milieu that promotes and somewhat safeguards the search for truth even in Catholic theology.[31]

What about the disturbance for some of the faithful that might arise because of academic freedom? The simple solution here is proper education. The theological enterprise is essential for the good of the church, but theologians are not official teachers in the church. In general, Americans strongly support academic freedom, but they do not blindly accept all that professors say. We all know that professors are often wrong, but they must have the freedom to explore truth. American Catholics do not lack sophistication; they are not going to accept everything that is said by an academician. Thus many of the possible negative effects of academic freedom on the good of the church can be alleviated.

The focus now shifts to the arguments in favor of academic freedom for Catholic colleges and universities and especially for the academic freedom of Catholic theology taught in these institutions. No one reason can prove beyond doubt that Catholic institutions of higher learning should accept academic freedom, but a number of reasons taken together can make the case for such academic freedom.

The question of the relationship between Catholic higher education and academic freedom forms only a part of the larger question of the relationship of the Catholic church to the American college or university. As described earlier, American institutions of higher learning, with their distinctive characteristics of autonomy and academic freedom, came into existence in the light of the particular historical and cultural circumstances of time and place. Can the Catholic church accept and use this cultural institution, or must it change the model to accommodate a "more Catholic understanding"?

The broadest aspect of the question concerns the relationship between the Catholic church and the culture in which it exists. The Catholic emphasis on the goodness of creation and the human, as underscored in the incarnation, posits a basic compatibility between the divine and the human. In the area of culture, Vatican Council II's Pastoral Constitution on the Church in the Modern World called attention to the rightful independence and autonomy of earthly affairs, for all creation has come forth from the hand of God. Created things and societies enjoy their own laws and values which must be deciphered, put to use, and regulated by human beings.[32] Since culture flows immediately from the spiritual and social nature of human beings, it needs a just freedom in which to develop. It also needs the legitimate possibility of exercising its independence according to its own principles. The council thus affirmed "the legitimate autonomy of culture."[33]

I have criticized the Pastoral Constitution on the Church in the Modern World for being too optimistic in general. Here, too, I would also point out that sin and evil can and do affect human culture and the institutions of culture. However, there still exists a proper autonomy for the institutions of human culture.

The history of the Catholic church in the United States shows how the church has learned the importance of the autonomy and independence of cultural realities. Take, for example, the very fundamental and basic reality of the state or the political order. The Catholic church since the Constantinian era of the fourth century had tended to see the state in the service of the church and to deny its autonomous and independent reality. The struggle over religious liberty at the Second Vatican Council was really a struggle over the role of the state. Only in 1965 did the Catholic church accept the state as an autonomous and independent reality that did not directly and immediately serve the church. An autonomous and independent state in the last analysis was the best solution, even for the good of the church itself.

A somewhat similar development occurred with regard to labor unions. Originally, Catholic teaching and practice held out for Catholic labor unions, a position that caused tension in the United States. Finally, secular labor unions were accepted in theory and in practice. The autonomy and independence of culture mean that Catholics and the church must accept and recognize basic human and cultural institutions as they exist in themselves; such institutions need not be changed in any way in order to make them Catholic—or even to serve the church. Both the theory proposed at the Second Vatican Council and the American Catholic experience support the general move toward the recognition and acceptance of the autonomy and independence of earthly and cultural realities. Again, I would add a word of caution. Some cultural institutions can reflect the power of sin. In general, however, one can see how the Catholic church in the United States would be open to accept the American institutions of the academy and see the necessity for Catholic colleges and universities to be first of all good colleges and universities; their being Catholic can add dimensions to what it means to be a good school, but being Catholic can never substitute for or do away with what is required to be a good school. Just as the state and labor unions best serve the church by being good institutions with their own autonomy and not by being directly subject to the church and clerical control, so too colleges and universities best serve the church by retaining their own autonomy. The church does not have to change the nature of the American academy in order to have the academy ultimately serve the church in an indirect way.

A possibly more significant analogy comes from Catholic journalism. There was a time when the national Catholic press, controlled by church authorities, was not truly open. The Catholic press was not to report all the news, but only what was edifying from the perspective of the church. However, the leadership of the Catholic press in the United States came to the conclusion that a truly open and honest press best serves the needs of the church. Many individuals in the Catholic press struggled at the time of the Second Vatican Council (1962–65) to make the Catholic press truly free and open. This reform applied especially to the Catholic News Service, which provides news for all Catholic publications in the United States. An analogous effort has gone on in Catholic higher education as the mainstream's leadership has struggled to make sure that Catholic colleges and universities are free and autonomous centers of study. In so many areas, the church has learned, in keeping with the best of the Catholic theological traditions, to accept the integrity and true autonomy of the institutions and realities of human culture. A very traditional Catholic theology recognized that grace does not destroy nature but builds on it. Catholic social workers must first be good, competent social workers. Catholic architects must be professionally accomplished architects. Such an argument as proposed here is not an absolute, since limitations and sin can affect any human and cultural reality, but there are good reasons for accepting the American institutions of higher learning as best serving the church precisely by first being good American colleges and universities.

The acceptance of American university standards and practices can provide a good contemporary illustration of the Catholic tradition's assertion that faith and reason cannot contradict one another. Yes, errors and mistakes will occur, but by accepting academic freedom the Catholic church in the United States will give visible witness to its traditional understanding about the relationship between faith and reason. Based on this same impulse the Catholic Church started universities in the medieval period. Now, in a different cultural setting, by accepting academic freedom the church can bear witness to its commitment to both faith and reason; Catholics have nothing to fear from the free search for truth. Catholic theology and philosophy rightly recognize the need for the individual and the community to pursue truth and to have confidence in the human ability to arrive at truth.

By recognizing the need for academic freedom, the Catholic church also bears witness to its fundamental belief in the freedom of the act of faith. No one can or should be forced or coerced into faith. Faith is a free, personal response to God and God's free gift of self. Especially in this day and age, people in our situation cannot be forced into faith. The acceptance of academic freedom is one way to reinforce the traditional belief in the freedom of the act of faith.

Contemporary Catholic thought recognizes that, in both theory and practice, Catholic life has not in the past stressed enough the importance and significance of freedom. Traditionally, Catholic theology and ethics have downplayed the role of freedom. Yes, freedom is not an absolute, and other considerations such as justice and truth are equally important. However, the church's record on supporting legitimate freedom has not been good. In history, the Catholic church has often had to apologize for its failure to support legitimate freedom. Past abuses by church authority still raise great anxieties among many American Roman Catholics. American Catholics remember the long struggle before the Catholic church finally accepted the understanding of religious freedom in the United States. Recall that Catholic support for democratic institutions and for human rights was late in coming. Catholics themselves have rightly been disturbed by the church's past failures to give enough importance to freedom. They are secure enough in their faith to accept academic freedom and to see such an acceptance as rightly making amends for errors of the past.

Catholic acceptance of academic freedom would also bear witness to non-Catholic Americans of the Catholic acceptance of the importance of freedom in general, and of the church's confidence in the power of the truth and in its own claims to truth. The Catholic church has often been criticized by others for the lack of freedom. To be sure, the Catholic church is not a democracy, and all truth is not up for grabs. But likewise the Catholic church is not a monarchy, and all truth is not fully possessed by the church. All religions recognize the need for some authority. Revelation is a gift from God and transcends merely human intelligence. However, the abuse of authoritarianism has often existed in the Catholic church in the past. By accepting academic freedom for Catholic higher education, the Catholic church could protect its own self-understanding while proving to the world that it is not afraid of truth and that it is committed to the principle that faith and reason cannot contradict one another.

The acceptance of academic freedom in Catholic institutions would in the long run make the church's hierarchical teaching office more credible. If everyone knows that academic freedom exists, that Catholic theologians enjoy freedom, and that theological interpretation in the academy is protected, then people within the church and outside it can have greater confidence in the teaching officers. For its part, the teaching office can profit from the theological dialogue that takes place within the walls of the academy, for vigorous theological debate allows all the issues to be raised and discussed. The hierarchical magisterium would obviously have to pay attention to these theological voices, but its own voice would come across as more acceptable. Academic freedom thus can actually help to support the hierarchical magisterium.

Academic freedom is accepted in the American ethos as a very important way for testing truth claims and arriving at the truth. The Catholic church in the United States will be more credible to its own members and to non-Catholics alike if it is willing to accept this same institution of academic freedom. Academic freedom for Catholic theology in Catholic higher education will at times have some negative consequences for the Catholic church, but these can be minimized and compensated for by the benefits that will accrue to the Catholic church from its acceptance of academic freedom on the American scene.

The Responsibilities and Competence of the Catholic Theologian

In the defense of academic freedom for Catholic colleges and universities, with its focus primarily on the discipline of Catholic theology, one further controverted issue needs to be discussed at length—the responsibilities of the professor of Catholic theology and the limits that flow therefrom. This question focuses on the competence of the scholar in the discipline of Catholic theology. The accepted principles of academic freedom recognize that a tenured professor can be dismissed for incompetency based on a judgment in the first instance made by academic peers.

The broader context of the present discussion is often phrased in terms of the limits on academic freedom. Is academic freedom an absolute? The AAUP's statements have always recognized the responsibilities of the faculty member that limit academic freedom. According to AAUP norms, a tenured faculty member can be dismissed for incompetency on the basis of academic due process which includes in the first instance a judgment by peers with the ultimate decision being made by the governing body of the institution on the basis of the record. As mentioned in chapter one, the AAUP has purposely left the concept of competency vague and without definition or description.

Both in theory and in practice, I have recognized that a Catholic theologian could be properly dismissed for incompetency in accord with the requisite due process. In practice, I have twice been personally involved in situations where my right to teach Catholic theology at the Catholic University of America has been at stake. In defending myself, I naturally took the position that best defended and explained my own rights. I have not dissented or disagreed with infallible church teachings, but only with a category of so-called noninfallible teaching. My defense has always centered on the right of Catholic theologians to dissent from such noninfallible teachings.[34] In these matters I clearly expressed the position as my own as distinguished from official church positions. But I also took the further step and insisted that my position in theory and in practice could be followed by one who claimed to be a good, loyal Roman Catholic. An important question arises: What if a Catholic theologian in the academy disagrees with a core or infallible teaching?

In my theoretical writings on academic freedom in Catholic theology, I have clearly recognized that a tenured professor of Catholic theology can be dismissed for incompetency in accord with academic due process. How have I understood the competency of the Catholic theologian? "Competency requires that one be true to the presuppositions, sources, and methods of the discipline."[35] I have also written: "Competency demands that a Catholic theologian theologize within the parameters of the Catholic faith. A Catholic theologian who does not believe in Jesus or does not accept a role for the pope in the church could rightly be judged to be incompetent."[36] Others have disagreed with me on this issue and pointed out that my position really means something less than the acceptance of full academic freedom. In the process of these discussions, I have come to refine and modify my position somewhat. However, the bottom line in my contention remains the same—Catholic theology is itself an academic discipline, and hence competency must be understood in the relationship to the specific discipline of Catholic theology. Catholic theology is not the same as religion or Christian theology.

In general, how is competency to be judged in any discipline? The accepted normative statements and processes accepted in the

American academy do not spell out how competency is to be determined. However, as pointed out in chapter one, many commentators understand competency primarily in terms of method. I can accept method as the norm by which to measure competency, even in the area of Catholic theology.

The Catholic theologian's competency is spelled out in terms of the use of the method of Catholic theology. One does not have to be a member of the Catholic church to teach Catholic theology. There can be no requirement of formal faith as a criterion of the competency for the Catholic theologian in the American academy; a Protestant or an atheist could be a Catholic theologian. Earlier, I had maintained that the substance of one's teaching could be the basis for a judgment of competency. I think now it is better to limit competency to the question of method. There will always be debate about the proper interpretation of substantive teachings. Even core and infallible teachings are open to development and better understanding. Fundamental beliefs about God, Jesus, and the sacraments have developed over the centuries. Questions about substantive issues (e.g., the divinity of Jesus, the role of the pope in the church) logically involve methodological concerns and are best dealt with on the level of methodology. In this light and in accord with the greater number of commentators, I think it is better to rest the competency of the Catholic theologian on the use of a proper method of the discipline. However, the method of Catholic theology must give due weight to revelation and to the teaching office or hierarchical magisterium in the church. The criterion of due weight to the sources of Catholic theology by necessity will be somewhat vague. All must recognize that this is a part of the method of the discipline of Catholic theology, which should be the ultimate criterion of competence in the judgment made by peers.

To object that such an understanding of academic freedom and the competency of the professor in his or her discipline is not in accord with the accepted American norms of academic freedom, one would logically have to deny the existence of Catholic theology as a discipline. Many reject religion and are opposed to religion. However, even the secularist could still recognize religion in general or Catholic theology in particular as a legitimate discipline even though personally she or he does not accept the existence of the transcendent. Certain presuppositions are necessary to accept the discipline of

Catholic theology as such; but other disciplines today have presuppositions which might be rejected by others. Think, for example, of black studies and women's studies. Both disciplines have definite presuppositions and very distinctive methods that might not necessarily be accepted by all. Today the American academy seems more open to disciplines with presuppositions not shared by all. Programs in Jewish studies, Islamic studies, and Catholic studies exist in American colleges and universities. In addition, the discipline of Catholic theology has been in existence for a very long time. If one accepts Catholic theology as a legitimate discipline, then in accord with the accepted norms and procedures of academic freedom, one must admit that a professor whose methodology is faulty is not competent as a Catholic theologian.

In this light, I will continue the dialogue with some who have disagreed with my position on this matter. Written and oral discussion with James Annarelli of St. John's University has caused me to clarify and modify somewhat my understanding of competency as seen in terms of method. (I still do not think that he would agree with me.) In his discussion of theology, Annarelli gives very little attention to Catholic theology as such, while concentrating on other forms of theology. He acknowledges no distinctive aspect of competency for the Catholic theologian as Catholic.[37] Annarelli insists that theology must respect the criterion of public accessibility or at least not construe public accessibility in a narrow way.[38] However, there are presuppositions to Catholic theology that are not publicly accessible to all. This dialogue illustrates that the ultimate question is the existence of the discipline of Catholic theology as such. If this is a legitimate discipline, and I claim that it is and that a Catholic institution should recognize it as a legitimate discipline, then a specific competency is connected with this discipline.

The same central point of discussion arose in the position taken by Lonnie D. Kliever, Professor of Religious Studies at Southern Methodist University, in response to an earlier paper of mine on this topic. According to Kliever, Curran's understanding of institutional autonomy and academic freedom are seriously deficient on two counts. First, freedom of inquiry is compromised by requiring fidelity to any authority; Curran proposes a freedom only within the constraints of a ruling ideology or governing body. Second, procedures of due process resting on peer review do not sufficiently safeguard academic freedom where ideological concerns or institutional aims constrain scholarly inquiry.[39] According to Kliever, my restricted view of academic freedom is consistent with the limitations clause for religious affiliated institutions in the 1940 Statement but not with full academic freedom.

In response, I would reiterate that my clarification of competency is to be identified in terms of method and that the method of Catholic theology involves giving due weight to relevation and hierarchical magisterial teaching. The freedom I propose is limited by the need for a competent method, but not directly by "the constraints of a ruling ideology or governing body." Our differences come down to the fact that Kliever in reality cannot accept Catholic theology as a legitimate university discipline. According to him, the modern American university devotes itself to critical intelligence and "methodological skepticism—the habit of mind that remains open to radical challenge and revolutionary changes." Such an understanding would not be able to accept Catholic theology as a discipline, and many other disciplines would also be in jeopardy. If the distinctive method of feminist studies were challenged, then feminist studies itself would truly no longer exist.

Two other comments occasioned by the dialogue with Kliever are appropriate. As mentioned in chapter one, the judgment by peers is not a foolproof system. People in the academy know many cases in which they believe peers have erred. However, the fact of the matter is that the American academy today relies heavily on peer judgment. Peer judgment in general and in judgments about competency is the best available and only feasible system at the present time.

The concept of *peers* deserves some further attention. In any academic judgment made by peers (e.g., hiring, promoting, tenuring), there are two types of peers. Peers within one's own institution are not just the peers in one's own discipline. School or university-wide committees make judgments about someone not in their own field. These people are peers and can rightly make such judgments. However, they must consult widely and in depth with the immediate peers in one's specific area of academic competence. *Peers* can and should be understood in both these senses.

The second comment raised by Kliever's position concerns the limitations clause for church-related institutions in the 1940 Statement. I see no need for Catholic institutions to adopt such a clause. Catholic theology can and shoud be treated in the same way as any other discipline. No need exists for any limitation of academic freedom beyond the fundamental professional responsibility of competency as enunciated in terms of method.

The Catholic tradition has often employed casuistry in attempting to deal with specific questions. Casuistry has been abused, but it still has a very important use.[40] Some casuistry about the preceding discussion might be helpful.

The theologian in the academy like any other scholar must be responsible and competent. Responsibility means that the theologian must present the official teaching of the Catholic church as such and label her or his own position as a personal position. Such a person is a competent scholar and no grounds exist for a charge of incompetency. Even if a scholar were to disagree with a core teaching of the church but clearly label the disagreement as a personal position and not the official teaching of the church, such a scholar is both responsible and competent.

Many proponents of limits on the freedom of the theologian both in the academy and in the church make a distinction between the speculative and the practical realms. The church needs the work of theologians, but such work is speculation and has no direct effect on the realities of the present order. As long as theologians stick to speculation, no problem arises with what they do.[41] In reality the friction between the Catholic church and scholars has usually come to the fore when scholars, including myself, have gone beyond this point. What if the theologian maintains that the church should change its own teaching and adopt a scholar's position as its own? What if the academician maintains that on a moral matter one can follow the dissenting position in practice and still be a loyal Roman Catholic?

Areas of practical tension arise when theologians advocate their position as a legitimate position in the church. Here the judgment about responsibility and competency must be settled on the basis of a judgment by peers about method. The questions involving core teachings or infallible teachings constitute the most difficult issues. However, one could claim that one's own method is still correct. Thus, for example, Hans Küng has denied the church's teaching on infallibility, but he still maintains that his position is in accord with the First Vatican Council.

The whole point of this casuistry is to show exactly where the problems might arise and how they should be solved. In reality the possible problematic situations occur less frequently than one might have imagined.

The casuistry must also go one step further into the area of prudential judgment. Recall that the process for dismissal of a tenured faculty member on the basis of incompetency must be instituted by the president of the institution. When should the president make such a decision? Even from the viewpoint of the church, prudence would seem to argue ordinarily against the instigation of such a process. Even in the cases of the advocacy of positions contrary to core teachings, prudence indicates that the best policy is to allow academic discussion to take care of itself. Catholics in the United States should be accustomed to such academic debate and are not so naive as to accept on faith whatever a theologian says. By calling attention to such cases one often gives them recognition. From personal experience I can testify to the fact that the Vatican action against me has given me a greater audience and greater attention than I would have had without such action. In March of 1986 just before my tension with the Vatican became public I spoke at a well-known private college in New England. There were some added problems on campus at the time, but about fifteen people showed up for the talk. Since then I have never had fewer than a hundred.

I believe that at the present time a number of Catholic college and university presidents have followed such prudent advice. By instigating a process for dismissal one often creates more problems and tensions and calls greater attention to the particular question and institution. The old axiom of letting sleeping dogs lie is most apt in these cases.

Thus in practice prudence would often argue against instigating a dismissal proceeding against a Catholic theologian. However, despite my practical reluctance in some cases to institute dismissal proceedings, I still maintain that Catholic theology is a legitimate academic discipline with its own distinctive understanding of competence.

The basic thesis of this book defending academic freedom for Catholic institutions of higher learning rests on two fundamental positions: Catholic colleges or universities can and should be colleges and universities in the full American sense of the terms; Catholic theology is a legitimate university discipline. This position can be and has been attacked from two different perspectives. On the one hand, some Catholics maintain that academic freedom cannot exist in Catholic colleges and universities because of the special nature of theology and the role of the teaching authority of the church in theology. On the other hand, some will not accept the legitimacy of Catholic theology as a discipline with its own specific and distinctive methodology. Catholic theology should enjoy total and complete academic freedom. Such academic freedom is limited by the responsibilities of the professor and by competency as enunciated in terms of the method. Thus Catholic theology should be treated no differently from any other university discipline.

This chapter has attempted to situate properly the argument for academic freedom for Catholic colleges and universities and then to prove the compatibility between Catholic institutions of higher learning and academic freedom. To show that academic freedom should exist and flourish in Catholic higher education one must prove that academic freedom is for the good of the church. The primary area of friction between academic freedom and the good of the church concerns Catholic theology. Thus the crux of the question is the academic freedom of Catholic theology. Note how such an understanding of the issue is analogous to the defense of academic freedom in American society based on the fact that academic freedom ultimately exists for the good of society at large. In past commentaries and discussions, these aspects of the issue have not been developed in depth. In developing such a justification this chapter recognizes that some possible negative effects on the church might come from academic freedom in Catholic higher education, but these can be minimized and outweighed by the positive advantages accruing to the church from its recognition of academic freedom for Catholic theology in Catholic higher education. If even in the most troublesome area of theology, academic freedom in Catholic higher education is good for the church, then the Catholic church can and should accept academic freedom for all of Catholic higher education.

NOTES

1. Land O'Lakes Statement, in Neil G. McCluskey, ed., *The Catholic University: A Modern Appraisal,* (Notre Dame, IN: University of Notre Dame Press, 1970), pp. 336ff.

2. E.g., Theodore M. Hesburgh, *The Hesburgh Papers: Higher Values in Higher Education* (Kansas City, MO: Andrews and McNeel, 1979), pp. 37, 38, 75.

3. James John Annarelli, *Academic Freedom and Catholic Higher Education* (New York: Greenwood Press, 1987).

4. Ibid., pp. 198–205.

5. Association of Catholic Colleges and Universities, "Catholic College Presidents Respond to Proposed Vatican Statement," *Origins* 15 (1986): 706–711.

6. Kenneth D. Whitehead, "Religiously Affiliated Colleges and American Freedom," *America* 156 (February 7, 1987): 96–98.

7. Robert N. Bellah, et al., *Habits of the Heart: Individualism and Commitment in American Life* (Berkeley, CA: University of California Press, 1985).

8. United States Catholic Bishops, *Economic Justice for All: Pastoral Letter on Catholic Social Teaching and the U.S. Economy* (Washington, DC: National Conference of Catholic Bishops, 1986).

9. John Courtney Murray, *The Problem of Religious Freedom* (Westminster, MD: Newman Press, 1965), pp. 7–22.

10. John Courtney Murray, *We Hold These Truths: Catholic Reflections on the American Proposition* (Kansas City, MO: Sheed and Ward, 1960), pp. 45–69.

11. "The Cologne Declaration," *Commonweal* 16 (February 24, 1989): 102–104.

12. For the papers given at a special meeting of the pope, Vatican officials, and U.S. archbishops, see *Origins* 18 (1989): 677–728.

13. The Canadian situation is quite similar to that of the United States, but the number of Catholic institutions of higher learning in Canada is much smaller than in the United States.

14. Leo O'Donovan, ed., *Cooperation Between Theologians and the Ecclesiastical Magisterium: A Report of the Joint Committee of the Canon Law Society of America and the Catholic Theological Society of America* (Washington, DC: Canon Law Society of America, 1982). See also Francis A. Sullivan, *Magisterium: Teaching Authority in the Catholic Church* (New York: Paulist Press, 1983); and Sullivan, "Magisterium and Theology," *Proceedings of the Catholic Theological Society of America* 43 (1988): 65–75.

15. Dogmatic Constitution on Divine Revelation, par. 10, in Austin Flannery, ed., *Vatican Council II: The Conciliar and Post-Conciliar Documents* (Northport, NY: Costello Publishing Co., 1975), p. 756.

16. Thomas Aquinas, *Summa Theologiae* (Rome: Marietti 1952), *Ia IIae*, q. 90–97.

17. Pastoral Constitution on the Church in the Modern World, par. 44, in Flannery, *Vatican Council II*, p. 946.

18. Dogmatic Constitution on the Church, par. 12, in Flannery, *Vatican Council II*, p. 363.

19. Declaration on Religious Liberty, par. 1, in Flannery, *Vatican Council II*, p. 799.

20. For a presentation of many different perspectives on the magisterium, see Charles E. Curran and Richard A. McCormick, *Readings in Moral Theology No. 3: The Magisterium and Morality* (New York: Paulist Press, 1982); *Readings in Moral Theology No. 6: Dissent in the Church* (New York: Paulist Press, 1988).

21. Avery Dulles, "Doctrinal Authority for a Pilgrim Church" in Curran and McCormick, *Readings in Moral Theology No. 3*, pp. 247–270.

22. Decree on Ecumenism, par. 11, in Flannery, *Vatican Council II*, p. 462.

23. Charles E. Curran, *Critical Concerns in Moral Theology* (Notre Dame, IN: University of Notre Dame Press, 1984), pp. 148ff.

24. "In Service to the Gospel: A Consensus Statement of the Joint Committee," in O'Donovan, *Cooperation Between Theologians and the Ecclesiastical Magisterium*, pp. 175–189.

25. Charles E. Curran, *Faithful Dissent* (Kansas City, MO: Sheed and Ward, 1986), pp. 52ff.

26. This particular argument has been made especially by Daniel Pilarczyk, "Academic Freedom: Church and University," *Origins* 18 (1988): 57–59.

27. For the history and documentation of the action taken against me by the Congregation for the Doctrine of the Faith, see my *Faithful Dissent*.

28. William J. Rewak, "Dissent in Catholic Universities," in *Current Issues in Catholic Higher Education* 8 (1987): 46–50; Rodger Van Allen, "The Implications of the Curran Case for Academic Freedom," in William W. May, ed., *Vatican Authority and American Catholic Dissent: The Curran Case and its Consequences* (New York: Crossroad, 1987), pp. 144–159.

29. Commission on Higher Education: Middle States Association of Colleges and Schools, *Characteristics of Excellence in Higher Education: Standards for Accreditation* (Philadelphia, PA: Middle States Association of Colleges and Schools, 1982), p. 5.

30. E.g., Kevin Kelly, "Obedience and Dissent II: Serving the Truth," *The Tablet* 240 (June 21, 1986): 647.

31. For a defense of public moral discourse as a necessary condition for the faithful search for moral truth, see Margaret A. Farley, "Moral Discourse in the Public Arena," in May, *Vatican Authority and American Catholic Dissent*, pp. 168–186.

32. Pastoral Constitution on the Church in the Modern World, par. 36, in Flannery, *Vatican Council II*, p. 935.

33. Pastoral Constitution on the Church in the Modern World, par. 59, in Flannery, *Vatican Council II*, p. 964.

34. These personal involvements will be discussed at greater length in chapter 6. For a full discussion and explanation of the defense of dissent from the papal encyclical *Humanae Vitae* as being academically acceptable, see Charles E. Curran and Robert E. Hunt, et al., *Dissent in and for the*

Church (New York: Sheed and Ward, 1970); and John F. Hunt, Terrence R. Connelly, et al., *The Responsibility of Dissent: The Church and Academic Freedom* (New York: Sheed and Ward, 1969).

35. Charles E. Curran, *Moral Theology: A Continuing Journey* (Notre Dame, IN: University of Notre Dame Press, 1982), p. 25.

36. Charles E. Curran, *Tensions in Moral Theology* (Notre Dame, IN: University of Notre Dame Press, 1988), p. 47.

37. Annarelli, *Academic Freedom and Catholic Higher Education*, pp. 174–179.

38. Ibid., pp. 178–79.

39. Lonnie D. Kliever, "Academic Freedom and Church-Affiliated Universities," *Texas Law Review* 66, no. 7 (June 1988): 1478.

40. Albert R. Jonsen and Stephen Toulmin, *The Abuse of Casuistry: A History of Moral Reasoning* (Berkeley, CA: University of California Press, 1988).

41. For a refutation of the role of the theologian as mere speculator, see Richard A. McCormick, "The Shape of Moral Evasion in Catholicism," *America* 159 (October 1, 1988): 187.

42. Hans Küng, "Appeal Statement," in Peter Hebblethwaite, *The New Inquisition? The Case of Edward Schillebeeckx and Hans Küng* (San Francisco: Harper and Row, 1980), p. 165. See also Leonard Swidler, ed., *Küng in Conflict* (New York: Doubleday, 1981).

6. My Personal Involvement in Struggles for Academic Freedom

Academic freedom in Catholic higher education involves a most significant theoretical and practical issue. Catholic scholars and leaders in Catholic higher education, together with all those concerned about higher education in the United States, have been and are interested in the topic. Many of those concerned about academic freedom in Catholic higher education have been personally involved in the practical aspects of the issue.

My interest in and concern for academic freedom has similarly been both professional and personal, and my experiences have frequently plunged me into academic freedom questions. My practical involvement has unquestionably led me to pursue an in-depth study of academic freedom. This book would probably never have been written were it not for the history of my own experience with issues of academic freedom.

All of us scholars are called to be self-critical and to raise pertinent and critical questions to ourselves and to our own ideas. I do not pretend to be neutral on the issue of academic freedom: I am committed to the theoretical and practical truth of the proposition that academic freedom is essential and necessary for Catholic higher education in the United States. Some kinds of contemporary philosophy and theology emphasize the importance of experience and reflection upon experience. In the past, the ideal of objectivity demanded that the noninvolved, neutral observer dispassionately weigh pros and cons before coming to a decision. In reality, however, none of us can ever be totally neutral and objective in that sense, for we are all the products of our own backgrounds, upbringings, environments, and experience. I can see advantages and disadvan-

192

tages in the two different starting points of an involved participant or a neutral observer. Current discussions about feminism illustrate the issues well. I consider myself a feminist. White, middle-class, male academics in the United States did not as a whole recognize and give sufficient attention to the needs of blacks, the poor, or women. The narrowness of the experience of white, middle-class males obviously affected their thinking and their research. But possible dangers as well as advantages attend the perspective of an involved participant. Some feminists might not give enough importance to realities other than the feminist experience. Yes, an involved participant must always be self-critical and conscious of her or his own presuppositions and narrowness, but she or he can be just as true a scholar as the detached observer. Many who have written on behalf of academic freedom for Catholic higher education have themselves been very much involved in the practical effort to secure such freedom. All of us must be conscious of our own narrowness and blinders, and open to self-critical questions, but practical involvement does not necessarily cast doubt on the academician's or scholar's consideration of the issues involved.

Academic freedom has been an important issue ever since I first came to the Catholic University of America (CUA) in 1965. I strongly disagree with the declarations and actions of the board of trustees of CUA in 1987 and 1988 that on the basis of the declaration from the Congregation for the Doctrine of the Faith I could no longer teach Catholic theology at the university; the board's action proves that academic freedom does not exist now at CUA. However, I will always remain grateful for all that I learned and experienced during my career teaching theology at the Catholic University. In this setting and from my colleagues in many different disciplines I first learned and experienced what it means for an institution to be an American university and what it means to protect and cherish the rights of academic freedom. In my most recent disagreement with the board of trustees and administration of the university, I was not trying to remake the institution in accord with my own understanding of academic freedom. I maintain rather that the trustees and administration have changed the institution by their recent determination that on the basis of a declaration from the Congregation for the Doctrine of the Faith I am not able to teach

Catholic theology anywhere at the university. The story should speak for itself.

Three major and well-publicized events thrust me into the struggle over academic freedom at CUA. These incidents once again show that the real crux for academic freedom in Catholic higher education concerns the role of Catholic theology. This chapter will tell the story of three personal experiences: my nonreappointment and the subsequent university-wide strike in 1967; the public and organized dissent from the encyclical *Humanae Vitae* in 1968 with the subsequent judgment of the faculty board of inquiry that the Catholic University scholars had acted responsibly; Catholic University's determination in 1988 that as a matter of religious conviction and canon law, CUA could not allow me to teach Catholic theology anywhere at the university because of the declaration of the Vatican's Congregation for the Doctrine of the Faith that I was neither suitable nor eligible to be a professor of Catholic theology.

My Nonreappointment and the Strike of 1967

To understand the events of 1967, some historical background is necessary. I was ordained as a priest for the diocese of Rochester, New York, in 1958. After my college education at St. Bernard's Seminary and College in Rochester, New York, I finished my seminary training in Rome at the Gregorian University, an institution with faculties (departments) almost exclusively in the sacred sciences and without the expansiveness of American universities. Subsequently I earned an S.T.D. (doctorate in sacred theology) from the Gregorian University and an S.T.D. with specialization in moral theology from the Academia Alfonsiana, another pontifical institution in Rome. In September 1961, I began teaching moral theology at St. Bernard's Seminary. Thus I had had no firsthand experience or understanding of an American university before coming to the Catholic University as an assistant professor in the fall of 1965.

Thanks to the faculty of the Academia Alfonsiana, especially Bernard Häring and Domenico Capone, and to Joseph Fuchs at the Gregorian University, I had been exposed to a new approach to moral theology. In reaction to the legalism and minimalism of the neo-scholastic manuals of moral theology, the new approach stressed the biblical, personal, dynamic, communitarian, and liturgical dimensions of the discipline. A short time later, this renewal swept through Roman Catholicism at the Second Vatican Council (1962–65). On the faculty of St. Bernard's Seminary in the interesting and exciting times of the early 1960s, I approached theology differently from most of the other faculty members. My professors in Rome and some of my colleagues at St. Bernard's urged me to do some scholarly research and writing. In the first several years, I published a few pieces that could aptly be described as high-level popularizatons which did not claim to be strict academic scholarship. However, I was invited to give a paper on Catholic moral theology at the historic Roman Catholic–Protestant Colloquium sponsored by Harvard University in March 1963.[1] My first inclination was to decline the invitation because of my youth and inexperience, but the organizers convinced me that I was the person they wanted. During my four years at St. Bernard's, I continued to publish articles and essays. I received offers to teach from the school of theology of CUA, the department of religious education at CUA, and the department of theology at the University of Notre Dame. As a priest belonging to the diocese of Rochester, New York, I needed my bishop's permission to accept any of these invitations; Bishop James E. Kearney, my superior, said I was needed at the diocesan seminary and could not be released to go elsewhere.

However, there was another side to the story. My progressive and newer approaches to moral theology attracted some controversy, and on three different occasions diocesan officials told me to be careful to avoid controversy. One source of opposition to my orthodoxy, Hugo Maria Kellner, a Catholic layman living near Rochester, objected to much of what was happening at the Second Vatican Council; he mailed out mimeographed tracts to Catholic cardinals, bishops, and other leaders that attacked many of the newer ideas proposed at the council. Kellner strongly disagreed in particular with the positions of Cardinal Joseph Ritter of St. Louis, Cardinal Lawrence Shehan of Baltimore, Bishop Emmett Carter of London, Ontario, and myself. In letters to the rector of St. Bernard's Seminary in February in 1965, he urged that appropriate action be taken against me because of my progressivism and lack of orthodoxy. Copies of his letters were sent to many others involved in seminary education in the United States.

In the fall of 1964, I wrote that I disagreed with the Catholic church's teaching condemning artificial contraception for married couples and urged a change in Catholic teaching. Later I maintained that such couples could use artificial contraception in a responsible way and still be loyal Roman Catholics. I also spoke publicly on this issue at a number of conferences in this country and in Canada. My position on artificial contraception was the last straw for Rochester's diocesan officials. In late July of 1965, the auxiliary bishop Lawrence B. Casey informed me that I could no longer teach at the seminary because of my positions, especially because of my dissent on artificial contraception. He urged me to accept the offer to teach in the school of theology at CUA. Bishop James E. Kearney—my superior, a member of the board of trustees of CUA and a recent recipient of an honorary degree—gave me permission to go to the Catholic University and wrote to the rector that I was now free to accept their offer. Arrangements were quickly made, and I arrived at CUA in September of 1965.

Catholic University had a fascinating history of its own. CUA was incorporated as a civil institution of higher learning in the District of Columbia but also had received a charter from the pope. In 1965 the university was a pontifical university and its civil by-laws recognized some church control. The board of trustees included all American archbishops and was heavily dominated by the clergy. The rector (president) was appointed by the Holy See, the Vatican's central governing office with its different congregations and tribunals that assist the pope.

Catholic University stood out among American Catholic institutions of higher learning because of its unique relationship to the church and because of its emphasis on graduate study. Before World War II, CUA was for all practical purposes the only Catholic university with graduate programs across the board. The university had achieved distinction in a number of areas and had managed to attract some very well-known faculty. Many of the doctoral students, but by no means all of them, were priests and religious who were preparing to teach in the colleges or seminaries of their communities or dioceses.

All was not well at CUA in the 1960s. In 1963 the administration forbade Catholic theologians associated with the more progressive ideas represented at the Second Vatican Council from speaking on campus. This censorship received nationwide publicity and added to the grievances of the CUA faculty.[2] A 1963 "Report of a Special Committee on Departures from Proper Academic Procedure" that had been commissioned by the faculty of the graduate school of arts and sciences condemned the administration for avoiding intellectual controversies in sensitive matters. The subject areas for administrative actions included biblical studies, liturgy, ecclesiology, relations with non-Catholics, evolutionary theory, population problems, and sexual behavior. A ''policy which seeks to avoid these subjects in research, teaching, or educational discussion because they are in some sense controversial is incompatible with the declared aims of this University or university institutions in general.''[3] Thus the faculty of the major school of CUA expressed its dissatisfaction with the administration of the rector, William J. McDonald.

I arrived on the scene in September of 1965 with a two-year contract as an assistant professor, but without a familiarity with the workings of an American university and without an awareness of the recent history of the Catholic University. My education began in earnest shortly after my arrival. On September 7, Hugo Maria Kellner wrote a letter to the administrators and all the clerical members of the university's faculty. He concluded that my becoming a faculty member at CUA was a black day for an institution that had been a citadel of Catholic orthodoxy, and he also included his earlier letters about me.[4]

On September 27, 1965, the vice-rector (vice-president), Monsignor Joseph B. McAllister, called me to his office for a conference occasioned by the Kellner letter.[5] The dean of the school of theology, Father Walter J. Schmitz, who had invited me to Catholic University, had already talked to me about the letter. I explained to the vice-rector that I had told Father Schmitz that I did not want to embarrass CUA. I was not teaching in the area of sexual ethics, so that my dissent would not come up in my classes.

On December 20, 1965, I was again called in by the vice-rector Msgr. McAllister to discuss my participation in a White House Conference on Population. Together with four other Catholic participants, I had submitted a statement pointing out that the Catholic spokespersons at the conference had failed to make the necessary distinction between Catholic moral teaching on family planning and public policy in a religiously pluralistic society. Catholics can accept public policy provisions for artificial contraception even though they have a different position on the morality of artificial contraception. This statement was then reported in the Catholic press. In signing the statement I had not even identified myself as teaching at CUA. McAllister did not threaten me in any way, but he reminded me (without any agreement on my part) that there was a need to consult the rector before signing any such statements. I think we both realized at the time that no one paid any attention to that particular directive.

In September 1966 I was again summoned to the vice-rector's office, this time because of a story in the *National Catholic Reporter* about a series of lectures I had given that summer in Oklahoma. I stood by what I said and what was printed in the article but admitted some distortion in the context. I wanted to talk to the rector personally about this but was not invited to do so. According to the notes Msgr. McAllister took at this meeting, I emphasized my eagerness not to embarrass the rector or the university, but I had to be honest and had to use my academic freedom to express myself in my scholarly area.

I had discussed these meetings with some of my faculty colleagues in the school of theology. At its October 1966 meeting, the faculty of the school of theology unanimously passed a resolution that expressed confidence in my teaching and orthodoxy and objected to unspecified charges made against me and the consequent harassment of me.[6]

In June 1966, I gave a paper at the annual meeting of the Catholic Theological Society of America that disagreed with the official Catholic teaching that masturbation is always wrong and involves grave matter (evil). Fides Publishers of Notre Dame agreed to publish a book of my essays which appeared in late 1966 under the title *Christian Morality Today*. On the basis of these publications and my teaching, I applied for promotion to that rank of associate professor beginning in September of 1968 when my first two-year contract ceased. In November, the faculty of the school of theology voted unanimously for my promotion, and the academic senate of the university did likewise on March 21, 1967.

Only later did I learn that other, more ominous, events were occurring at the same time.[7] On Monday morning, April 17, 1967, I was called to the rector's quarters. In the presence of other administrators and Father Schmitz (who to this day has remained a staunch supporter and close friend), the rector, Bishop William J. McDonald, informed me that the board of trustees had decided not to renew my contract but no reasons were given. I protested that I should have had a hearing and threatened to make the matter public. I agreed not to make the matter public for twenty-four hours, but felt free to consult with my colleagues in the meantime. My colleagues reacted with outrage and consternation. The theology faculty met on Tuesday at noon. A steering committee of students scheduled with faculty help a rally for Tuesday evening in which over four hundred people heard about the situation from my colleagues.

On Wednesday morning, over two thousand faculty and students held a rally in front of the rector's quarters. Many students were already boycotting classes, and the momentum was building. The theology faculty met at noon again on Wednesday, April 19, and the twenty-two members present voted unanimously for a resolution that pointed out that the decision of the trustees repudiated the professional judgment and integrity of both the school of theology and the academic senate; the action by the trustees jeopardized the academic freedom and security of every professor at CUA. The resolution continued: "Under these circumstances, we cannot and will not function unless and until Father Curran is reinstated. We invite our colleagues in other schools of the university to join with us in our protest." The faculty of theology had gone on strike and urged their faculty colleagues to do likewise. On Wednesday afternoon, I met with the press together with Father Schmitz and Father Eugene Burke, a long-time theology professor. We explained our positions and underscored that the people involved were not anarchists, but committed Catholics and conscientious academics who were strongly protesting the violation of academic freedom and due process.

By Thursday morning, the boycott or strike was almost total. Only the school of education conducted classes, but few if any students attended. On Thursday noon the entire faculty of the university met and voted 400 to 18 to support in its entirety the resolution passed by the school of theology. "We cannot and will not function as members of our respective faculties unless and until Father Curran is reinstated." The strike and boycott totally closed down CUA. The tone and style were determined, very respectful, and dignified. Students and faculty worked together to organize events, picket, stage rallies, and encourage the participation of all. In no way did the organizers and sponsors want to give the impression of a radical, militant, and anarchistic movement. Picketers were neat in their appearances and respectful in their words and deeds.

The strike came to a successful conclusion on Monday evening, April 24. Father Schmitz had met with the university's chancellor (Archbishop Patrick A. O'Boyle), the rector, and others during the morning of April 24. The chancellor and rector set up a meeting with the faculty of the school of theology for 4 PM. The administration was initially not willing to do more than say that my reappointment would be reconsidered. The faculty was adamant. Finally, the chancellor and rector agreed that the action of the board of trustees would be abrogated, and I would be given a new contract and promoted to associate professor beginning September, 1967. The chancellor and the rector then made this solution known to the crowd of three thousand students and faculty gathered in the dusk in front of Mullen Library. I finally spoke, thanked all for their support, and pointed out that the issue went beyond any one person. I called for the dedication and work of all to make the Catholic University a true institution of higher learning in the service of the Catholic church and the country. At the time of the strike, I did not know everything that had transpired within the board of trustees. Although no reasons for my nonreappointment were given, it was common knowledge that my progressive, more liberal teachings in general, and especially on artificial contraception, had been the real reason. Subsequent newspaper reports, the minutes of the April 1967 board of trustees' meeting which I saw only eighteen months later, and memoranda prepared by Msgr. McAllister which I first saw in 1987 filled in many important details.

Newspaper reports at the time of the strike indicated the influence of the pope's apostolic delegate to the United States, Archbishop Egidio Vagnozzi, in the matter. A few years later, Roy Meachum, a journalist who had covered the strike, wrote in the *Washingtonian* that in an interview Archbishop Vagnozzi said he was responsible for my firing because Rome wanted to make an example out of a liberal American priest.

The relevant board minutes and the memoranda of the vice-rector provide further important details. On October 20, 1966, at the executive committee of the board of trustees, Archbishop John J. Krol of Philadelphia had raised questions about my teachings. In accord with the current statutes, a committee of three bishops was appointed to investigate and make a final determination if I had offended against Catholic doctrine. The three members—Archibishop Krol, Archbishop Phillip M. Hannan of New Orleans, and Bishop McDonald—met on March 17, 1967, and agreed that I should be terminated as of September 1. Archibishop Krol reported the decision of the committee to the board of trustees at their meeting in Chicago on April 10, 1967. Archbishop Paul J. Hallinan of Atlanta was the only board member who voted against the resolution.

A successful strike at a major university was unprecedented in modern times, and it had long-lasting structural effects at the Catholic University. As part of the settlement of the strike, the board of trustees agreed to meet with the faculty of theology and again with elected representatives of the entire faculty; these meetings with the special committee of the board of trustees took place in May of 1967. In the final analysis, the meetings with faculty representatives had more lasting effects. The general faculty submitted four "demands": a new rector, a reconstitution of the board of trustees, a reconstitution of the academic senate, and direct faculty representation to the board of trustees.[8] At the same time, the committee from the Middle States Association of Colleges and Schools pointed out that CUA's structure of Vatican control of the institution was incompatible with contemporary American understandings of a university. During the 1967–68 academic year, the survey and objectives committee of the board of trustees chaired by Dr. Carroll A. Hochwalt of St. Louis met regularly to implement changes at Catholic University. Ulimately, the structure of the institution was radically changed.[9]

The first fruits of the structural changes involved a statement of objectives that went through university channels including the academic senate and was approved by the board of trustees in July of 1968. According to this statement, CUA is "a free and autonomous center of study" where "the only constraint upon truth is truth itself"; the objectives include the language of the Land O' Lakes statement of 1967 about the need for academic freedom and institutional autonomy as essential characteristics of all American universities including Catholic universities. The trustees of CUA accepted "the standards and procedures of American institutions of higher learning" and CUA "seeks to achieve distinction within the academic world."[10] The work on the revised statutes and bylaws for CUA continued in 1969 until they were finally approved by the board of trustees and by the Congregation for Catholic Education in Rome in January of 1970. Rome no longer had control over the university. Debates within the board of trustees revealed that a group of influential churchmen, including Cardinals John J. Krol of Philadelphia, Patrick A. O'Boyle of Washington, and James F. McIntyre of Los Angeles opposed the changes. The Congregation for Catholic Education in Rome insisted that language be put into the objectives about fidelity to the word of God as it comes to us through the magisterium of the church, but no one at the time saw that as affecting the basic change that CUA was no longer controlled by the church. The whole purpose of the change was to insure that CUA was an autonomous institution controlled by its own board of trustees and not by the church. The board of trustees was now comprised of half clergy members and half lay members, and the rector was no longer appointed by Rome. In the understanding of many at CUA at the time the university, now "depontificalized," had become an autonomous American university with three pontifical ecclesiastical faculties—theology, philosophy, and canon law.[11] However, the final adoption of the new statutes goes beyond an important development that occurred in the summer of 1968.

Dissent from *Humanae Vitae* and the Faculty Board of Inquiry

The issue of artificial contraception for married couples had been a burning topic among Catholics in the 1960s. Finally, on June 29, 1968, Pope Paul VI released his encyclical *Humanae Vitae*, which condemned the use of artificial contraception for Catholic spouses.[12] The afternoon the encyclical was released, some colleagues and I obtained copies and studied it.[13] We decided to issue a statement about the document that asserted the right of Catholics to dissent in theory and in practice from the particular condemnation of artificial contraception and still remain loyal Roman Catholics. That night, we telephoned colleagues throughout the city of Washington and the country asking for signatures for the statement that we had drawn up. The next morning I acted as spokesperson at a press conference at which the statement was released in the name of the eighty-seven original signers. It concluded: "Therefore, as Roman Catholic theologians, conscious of our duties and our limitations, we conclude that spouses may responsibly decide according to their conscience that artificial contraception in some circumstances is permissible and indeed necessary to preserve and foster the values and sacredness of marriage."[14] Ultimately over six hundred scholars signed this statement, twenty-one of them faculty members at CUA. This unprecedented statement of dissent was closely identified with theologians at CUA because we were among the original drafters and organizers.

This episode gave the Catholic University the challenge and opportunity to live up to its new statement of objectives. Cardinal Patrick A. O'Boyle, the archbishop of Washington, was, ex officio, the chancellor of CUA. In his diocese, O'Boyle took more punitive action against his priests who disagreed with the encyclical than any other bishop at the time. On the day the encyclical was issued, Cardinal O'Boyle released a statement calling for absolute obedience to the encyclical "without equivocation, ambiguity, or simulation."[15] In August, O'Boyle publicly accused the dissenters of "setting the church on fire."[16] The Reverend John P. Whalen, the acting rector of CUA, recognized that the statement and the involvement of the CUA faculty members had raised a significant issue for the institution. He arranged with me to gather a group of theologians and bishops to discuss both the pastoral aspects of the encyclical and the dissent from it. I arranged for seven dissenters to attend a meeting at the Statler Hilton Hotel in New York on August 18 and 19. Seven who disagreed with the dissent, including four bishops, also attended. The discussions were cordial but inconclusive. In the meantime Cardinal O'Boyle, through a special delivery letter, summoned the faculty of the school of theology, the department of religious education, and in particular the CUA faculty members who had signed the statement of dissent to a meeting at the university on August 20. O'Boyle was accompanied by the university's civil lawyer and a canon lawyer. A court reporter took down all that was said. The chancellor asked those present to comment in regard to the problems they thought the theologians' statement might raise for the university. The dissenting theologians cited approved Catholic authors who had recognized the possibility of dissent from noninfallible hierarchical church teaching. No charges were made against the signers of the statement at this meeting. A special meeting of the board of trustees of CUA was called for September 5, 1968. The divisions in the trustees that emerged in the development of new university statutes and bylaws surfaced again. At the beginning of the meeting Cardinal James F. McIntyre of Los Angeles introduced a resolution stating that the utterances of Father Curran and his associates constituted a violation of the professors' profession of faith, and hence justified their termination. This motion was not adopted. In the course of the meeting, Cardinal O'Boyle produced a letter from the Vatican Secretary of State that he interpreted as support for his position that action should be taken against the dissenters who refused to recant. Cardinal O'Boyle swore those present to secrecy about the letter, and no mention of it was made in the minutes of the meeting. The existence of the letter came to light in my suit against Catholic University in December 1988 and was ultimately produced for the court by lawyers for the chancellor. Actually, the letter said that no disciplinary action should be taken immediately against the dissenters, but that efforts to make them recant should be made.

The trustees were obviously conscious of the strike in 1967 and of their commitment to ensure that Catholic University was truly an American university with institutional autonomy and academic freedom. In the end, this conviction guided the action taken by the trustees with regard to the dissenting theologians, but not without some contradictions and concessions. The trustees knew that the reputation of Catholic University as an American institution of higher learning was at stake, and they were now in the spotlight of much publicity and concern.

At 9 PM on September 5, Dr. Carroll A. Hochwalt, the chair of the board of trustees, issued a press release that described the board's action. The statement noted the board's full adherence to the teaching authority of the pope, but also affirmed "the commitment of the Catholic University to accepted norms of academic freedom in the work of teaching and to the due process protection of such freedom." The dissenting faculty members do not speak for the university. Moreover, the style and method of organizing the dissent raised questions about what was done. The board then made three conclusions. First, final judgments concerning theological teachings belong to the bishops of the church. Second, the acting rector was directed "to institute through due academic process an immediate inquiry as to whether the teachers at this university who signed the recent statement of dissent have violated by their declarations or actions with respect to the encyclical *Humanae Vitae* their responsibilities to the University under its existing statutes and under their commitments as teachers in the University and specifically as teachers of theology and/or other sacred sciences." Third, only those who agreed to abstain during the inquiry from any activities inconsistent with the pronouncements of the ordinary teaching authority of the church would be allowed to continue to teach. Those unable to accept this condition would receive their salary but could not teach, a conclusion that the board erroneously claimed was in accord with the norms of the American Association of University Professors (AAUP) that allow for the suspension of a faculty member from teaching when the continued teaching is a source of immediate harm to others. The statement closed by repeating the intent of the board of trustees to protect its faculty from harm to its academic freedom and to protect the Catholic community from harm to the authentic teaching of the church.

The trustees' statement set the inquiry process in motion. A committee of the academic senate prepared a process in accord with academic due process that was accepted by the academic senate on October 16, 1968. The board of inquiry was to consist of five members, including one from outside the university who was competent in the sacred sciences and an alternate, all to be elected by the faculty. The final committee, chaired by Professor Donald E. Marlowe, dean of the school of engineering, was often referred to as the Marlowe Committee.[17]

What about the process mandated by the board of trustees and fleshed out by the academic senate? In general, the process underscored the strong commitment of CUA to academic freedom and institutional autonomy. Church authority could not directly intervene in the academy to dismiss Catholic theologians. The scholars as academicians had a right to be judged by their peers in accord with accepted norms of academic responsibility. In carrying out its task, the board of inquiry followed very closely existing academic norms, especially those developed by the AAUP. The very fact of the inquiry proved CUA's commitment to academic freedom. The dissent from the encyclical was unprecedented, but the trustees did not allow church authorities to intervene directly in the academy.

However, we, the subject professors, noted three distinct problems with the process itself. First, the choice of silence or suspension that the board of trustees gave us: if we would keep silent about the encyclical, we would not be suspended. Such a condition was not in accord with AAUP standards, despite the fact that the statement by the trustees referred especially to AAUP documents. The subject professors through counsel informed the acting rector that they could agree to the trustees' conditions only insofar as they were consistent with the AAUP principles. We agreed to silence concerning the proceedings of the inquiry itself, but to no more. On September 13, the university announced this agreement in a press release. However, the acting rector subsequently informed the board of trustees that we, the subject professors, had agreed to the original conditions of silence. Even at the conclusion of the inquiry, the trustees thanked us for observing the conditions of silence.

A second problem with the proceedings was the fact that no specific charges were made against us, and we had to prove our innocence. We proposed that a representative from the board of trustees be a party to the proceedings to make sure that we did not have the burden of proof. The academic senate procedures made no mention of charges, but rather proposed a two-sided structure to the inquiry—the parties to the inquiry were the dissenting professors and a person designated by the university's administration who would ensure full and complete development of the issues before the inquiry board. Despite our protests, specific charges were never brought against us, so we were left with the burden of proving our own innocence. Finally in December of 1968, Bishop James P. Shannon, a member of the board of trustees and former president of the College of St. Thomas in St. Paul, was named as the other party mentioned in the procedures. In February, with the agreement of the subject professors and Bishop Shannon, the inquiry board adopted findings of facts.

A third problem concerned the changing focus of the inquiry. On September 5, the board of trustees mandated an inquiry into "our declarations and actions with regard to the encyclical *Humanae Vitae*." The acting rector, John P. Whalen, on behalf of the trustees, had informed the subject professors that anyone who recanted would be spared from the inquiry. In response to our continued request for specific charges, the board of trustees through a letter of comment from the new acting rector Brother Nivard Scheel attempted on December 23, 1968, to clarify and particularize the September 5,

1968, press release. The letter claims that the board had not questioned the right of the scholars to have or to hold private dissent on noninfallible papal teaching; the inquiry would focus on the style and method of the dissent.

In the judgment of the subject professors, this constituted a new focus. The faculty board of inquiry itself agreed, for it considered the fact of the dissent itself in its final report. The board's changed focus obviously resulted from some ensuing developments. The dissenting theologians had made many people aware of the possibility of legitimate dissent from noninfallible hierarchical teaching. In November 1968, the American bishops issued a pastoral letter "Human Life in Our Day," which accepted the legitimacy of public dissent from noninfallible teaching under three conditions—that there exist grave and serious reasons, that the teaching office of the church would not be impugned, and that no scandal would be given.[18] The December 23 focus left out what had been part of the original focus, but the Marlowe Committee in its final report also dealt with the fact of the dissent itself.

Hearings before the board of inquiry began in December. In the inquiry, the subject professors were fortunate to have as their legal counsel John F. Hunt and Terrence R. Connelly of the New York law firm of Cravath, Swaine, and Moore. The subject professors can never adequately express their gratitude for such legal help and dedication. Our academic counsel was Professor Robert K. Webb, professor of history at Columbia University and managing editor of the *American Historical Review.* Professor Webb generously gave of his time and counsel, thereby illustrating his own commitment to the principles and procedures of the American academy. The inquiry board also had its own legal counsel. Eight days of hearings before the inquiry board generated over three thousand pages of exhibits, testimony, and background material. The board heard thirty-eight witnesses, including all the subject professors. At the request of the subject professors a number of witnesses from outside the university appeared and testified about aspects of the case. Walter J. Burghardt, S.J., of Woodstock College, John T. Noonan, Jr., of the University of California at Berkeley, Gerard S. Sloyan of Temple University, and John F. Hotchkin of the staff of the United States Bishops' Conference all testified on theological, historical, ethical, and ecumenical aspects of the issue. President John C. Bennett of Union Theological Seminary, President Robert Cross of Hunter College, President Victor Yanitelli of St. Peter's College, Jersey City, Father Clarence Friedman of the National Catholic Educational Association, and Father John Thirkel, dean of theology of St. Mary's Seminary and University in Baltimore, all testified about the norms and procedures of academic freedom and the responsibilities and duties of academics. Kenneth Woodward of *Newsweek* testified about how the media handles religious questions and what expectations it has. In addition, Professor Bernard Lonergan of Regis College, Toronto, and President Theodore M. Hesburgh of the University of Notre Dame submitted written testimony to the board. The committee asked Father Austin Vaughan of New York to testify, since he opposed the dissent. In addition, we subject professors submitted briefs to the inquiry board that pertained to both the theological and the academic freedom aspects of the case. Later we published the materials in a revised format in two volumes.

The issues involved in the case fit under the AAUP norms governing extramural utterances. The statement of dissent was not teaching or research as such, but an extramural statement that involved an immediate, public, and organized dissent to the papal encyclical. However, the dissent raised an issue concerning our competence to teach Catholic theology.

On April 1, 1969, the board of inquiry submitted its final report to the academic senate and to the subject professors. The report itself was seventy-one pages in length, and a seven-page summary gave the board's unanimous recommendations and conclusions.[19] The board of inquiry made five recommendations. First, the commentary made by the subject professors in their July 30, 1968, statement was adequately supported by theological scholarship, and their actions in composing, issuing, and disseminating the statement did not violate the professors' commitments and responsibilities. Second, no further proceedings should be instituted against the professors with regard to their dissent from *Humanae Vitae*. Third, the university should incorporate into its statutes, bylaws, and regulations the norms of academic freedom and academic due process of the AAUP that were recommended in the report. Fourth, the report criticized the threat of suspensions made by the board of trustees. Fifth, while acknowledging the ultimate canonical jurisdiction and doctrinal competence of the hierarchy, the trustees should remain sensitive to the devastating effect of any exercise of ecclesiastical power in the resolution of academic difficulties (Summary, pp. 1, 2).

In its report, the Marlowe Committee recognized that the existing statutes (first adopted in 1937) contained provisions that were no longer acceptable. With regard to those statutes, the board of inquiry saw only the profession of faith as applicable to the declarations and actions of the professors. "All other statutory admonitions are inapplicable, either being not germane, not enforced in practice, or not made known to the subject professors at the time of their appointment. Further, some provisions of the statutes are patently incompatible with modern American university practice" (Summary, p. 3). In this connection, for example, the board determined that the requirement in the 1937 statutes that professors in the pontifical schools needed a canonical mission from the chancellor no longer applies (p. 9). In all their judgments, the board gave primacy to the 1968 statement of objectives and interpreted all else in the light of these objectives.

The academic senate of the Catholic University unanimously approved the report and forwarded it to the acting rector for transmission to the board of trustees, which was scheduled to meet in Houston, Texas, on April 12 and 13, 1969. After deliberations the board voted to receive the report and appointed a five-person committee chaired by Cardinal John Krol of Philadelphia to study the report and make recommendations to the full board at their June meeting. After the conclusion of the Houston trustees' meeting, the academic senate directed that the report be made public. The press correctly reported that the subject professors had been vindicated by the faculty report. In June, the trustees met and discussed a six-page document submitted by the Krol committee. Later we learned that the committee's report was accepted by the trustees but never made public. Instead, the trustees once again issued a public statement to the press. The trustees accepted the board of inquiry's report "insofar as it pertained to the academic propriety of the conduct of these faculty members." However, the trustees claimed that their action did not represent their approval of the theological position expressed in the dissenting statement. It was also reported in the press that the trustees supported the chancellor in his decision to refer the matter of the orthodoxy of the dissenters' position to the appropriate committee in the National Conference of Catholic Bishops.[20]

Despite some qualifications, the bottom line was clear—the subject professors could and did continue to teach at the Catholic University. We who were involved recognized some of the shortcomings and deceptions in the whole process, but the fundamental principles of academic freedom and academic due process were established and preserved. The university itself, in its report to the Middle States Association in 1970 and 1980, pointed with pride to this incident as proof that academic freedom exists at CUA.[21] Committee A of the AAUP cited the board of inquiry report and used it to support its contention that it no longer endorses the need for church-related institutions to take advantage of the limitations clause with regard to academic freedom as found in the 1940 Statement.[22] Our continued teaching at Catholic University after our respectful, immediate, public, and organized dissent from the conclusions of a papal encyclical was living proof, or so we thought, that academic freedom and institutional autonomy existed at CUA.

The Declaration of the
Congregation for the Doctrine of the Faith in 1986

Some tensions involving academic freedom remained at Catholic University in the 1970s, but both inside and outside the campus the pervading sense was that the battle for academic freedom had been won. If academic freedom in theology existed at the national Catholic university, then academic freedom would exist in all Catholic higher education. For many, I became the symbol of academic freedom at CUA. Part of my commitment to stay at CUA despite other offers and feelers was based on loyalty to those who had stood with me in the struggles for academic freedom. In the 1960s, I had learned what a university is from some of these colleagues.

However, in August 1986, I was again in the middle of a controversy over academic freedom. On August 18, 1986, I was given a letter from Cardinal Joseph Ratzinger, the prefect of the Congregation for the Doctrine of the Faith, declaring that after a lengthy investigation, the congregation concluded that I was neither suitable nor eligible to teach Catholic theology.[23] The action of the congregation had been approved by the pope. This letter was handed to me by James A. Hickey, the archbishop of Washington and thus ex officio chancellor of the Catholic University. Later I learned that the chancellor also received a letter from Cardinal Ratzinger that instructed the archbishop to take appropriate action. The chancellor then informed me that he would institute the process for taking away my canonical mission to teach on an ecclesiastical faculty. According to the canonical statutes for ecclesiastical faculties, I could ask for a due process hearing to determine if the chancellor had the requisite "most serious reasons" to take away the canonical mission.

To understand these and subsequent events, some historical and contextual information is needed. I was informed in August 1979 by a letter from Cardinal Franjo Seper, then prefect of the Congregation for the Doctrine of the Faith, that I was under investigation because of errors and ambiguities in my writings. The letter was handed to me by Cardinal William W. Baum, then chancellor of CUA and archbishop of Washington. The investigation and process took place by mail. The congregation claimed that my theological dissent from noninfallible church teachings failed to give the requisite respect or obedience of intellect and will due to such teachings. Specifically, the congregation disagreed with my nuanced and moderate dissent on such questions as artificial contraception, masturbation, divorce and remarriage, abortion, premarital sex, and euthanasia. (The story of this investigation has already been published in detail.) In a letter dated September 17, 1985, and given to me in October by Archbishop Hickey, the Congregation for the Doctrine of the Faith declared that if I did not recant my positions I could no longer be considered a Catholic theologian. I met four times thereafter with Archbishop Hickey, the chancellor of CUA, and Cardinal Joseph L. Bernardin of Chicago, the chair of the board of trustees. We talked about ways to address the problem and about possible compromises. I proposed that I would voluntarily agree not to teach any courses in sexual ethics, which was the major area of the problems that the congregation found in my writings. I told the two churchmen very forthrightly that I had not taught this subject in at least ten years, and I had shifted the focus of my interest in writing to social ethics in the mid-1970s. I hoped this compromise might provide a way out for all concerned.

Early in September of 1984, I had proposed another compromise as a way to solve what I thought might become a thorny problem.

I proposed that I move from the department of theology, which has an ecclesiastical faculty, to the department of religion and religious education, which has no ecclesiastical faculty and grants only civil degrees. (These differences will be explained later in greater detail.) And in January of 1987, I offered another compromise whereby I would become a professor-at-large within the university. The compromises I offered then and later were an effort both to ward off potential problems and to keep the academic freedom of CUA intact. If the university itself or any outside church authority forced me to move off the theology faculty and assigned me to religion and religious education or forbade me to teach sexual ethics, academic freedom would have been breached; I could, however, volunteer to do these things without violating the principle of academic freedom. Together with many others, I had worked to gain the acceptance of academic freedom at CUA, and I wanted to protect that hard-won victory. However, no compromise was accepted. Further, the compromise about not teaching sexual ethics was proposed to the congregation in Rome and rejected.

Although the Congregation for the Doctrine of the Faith told me that their formal process had finished, I attended an informal meeting with the officials of the Congregation in Rome in March of 1986 and again proposed the compromise of not teaching courses in sexual ethics. After the meeting, the congregation issued a joint press release agreed to by them and myself that described the meeting. I returned to the United States and held a press conference to explain the entire situation. In August I received the final letter from the congregation with a notice from Archbishop Hickey that he was going to institute the process to take away my canonical mission to teach on an ecclesiastical faculty.

An explanation of the structure of CUA is now necessary. Before 1970, the Catholic University was an ecclesiastical university under the control of the church. With the change in the statutes in 1970, the university is no longer controlled by the church but by its own board of trustees. Nevertheless, the university still has three pontifical or ecclesiastical faculties which grant ecclesiastical degrees recognized by Rome. These faculties are governed by special canonical statutes that are also part of the civil bylaws of the institution. The three pontifical or ecclesiastical faculties are theology, philosophy, and canon law. In 1979, Rome issued an apostolic constitution *Sapientia*

Christiana that gave the principles and norms for ecclesiastical universities and faculties.[24] Each institution was to draw up its own statutes in accord with these norms and submit them to Rome for final approval. *Sapientia Christiana* recognized that in drawing up these statutes, the faculties in question could adapt to the local academic customs.[25]

In this context, CUA and the three ecclesiastical faculties began the process to come up with new statutes. The chancellor of the university then was Archbishop James A. Hickey. The role of the chancellor in the entire university, according to the bylaws, is to serve as a liaison with the Holy See and with the National Conference of Catholic Bishops. However, with regard to the ecclesiastical faculties, the chancellor has special powers and responsibilities.[26]

In 1979, the three ecclesiastical faculties did not form one operating unit at the university. The department of theology and the department of canon law were parts of the school of religious studies, which also included the departments of religion and religious education, biblical studies, and church history, none of them an ecclesiastical faculty. Philosophy was a separate school by itself. In addition, the departments of theology and canon law, as well as the school of philosophy, also offered nonecclesiastical or civil degree programs. In fact at that time, less than twenty percent of the students in the department of theology were in the ecclesiastical degree programs—the S.T.B. (baccalaureate in sacred theology), the S.T.L. (licentiate in sacred theology), and the S.T.D. (doctorate in sacred theology). The civil or American degree programs included the M.A., the M.Div., the Ph.D., and the doctor of ministry.

Sapientia Christiana called for all full-time Catholic faculty members to receive a canonical mission from the chancellor. The canonical mission was described as a mission to teach in the name of the church and was conferred by the chancellor on all the members of the faculty. The canonical mission could also be withdrawn. Also, before tenure could be obtained, a *nihil obstat* (literally, a declaration that nothing stands in the way) had to be given by the Holy See (sec. III, art. 27).

The faculty of the department of theology was in general quite negative and wary about these provisions of the apostolic constitution *Sapientia Christiana*. The two provisions seemed to oppose the principles and procedures of academic freedom. The provision of the need for a canonical mission was looked upon as most threatening, especially to those who were already tenured members of the faculty. The earlier apostolic constitution governing ecclesiastical faculties since 1931, *Deus Scientiarum Dominus*, had also required a canonical mission for all who teach in ecclesiastical faculties. When I first came to Catholic University in 1965, however, I was not given a canonical mission and no mention was ever made of it. In the 1968–69 academic year, the Marlowe Committee explicitly addressed the issue of the canonical mission. The committee concluded that the provision of a canonical mission was not applicable to the subject professors; and, even if it were, it would have to be interpreted in the light of American academic principles and procedures.[27] Thus from my perspective, I never had a canonical mission and I did not need to have one.

The theology faculty voted to ask the chancellor to obtain a dispensation from Rome from the requirements of canonical mission and *nihil obstat*. The general feeling was that both requirements were in opposition to the American notions of academic freedom and institutional autonomy. *Sapientia Christiana* allowed for individual institutions to adapt to local traditions and circumstances, but the chancellor insisted that the statutes could not be approved by Rome without these two provisions.[28]

Some of us continued to resist the requirements of canonical mission and *nihil obstat*. However, in the light of the position of the chancellor, the majority of the three ecclesiastical faculties concerned did not fight his position but worked to get the protections of academic freedom and academic due process written into the canonical statutes. In the final statutes, adherence to the principles of academic freedom was explicitly made, but this recognition existed side by side with the requirements of canonical mission and *nihil obstat*. These norms and practices concerning appointments to the "Faculties are intended to insure fidelity to the revealing Word of God...and to safeguard academic freedom"[29] (Canonical Statutes, part V section 11). The chancellor is charged to exercise his responsibility to protect the doctrine of the church in collaboration "with the Faculties as a matter of collective responsibility and in accord with recognized academic procedures."[30] In addition, academic due process was specifically written into the statutes for the withdrawal of the canonical mission. The faculty members involved had the right to choose a hearing by a faculty committee of peers (not just from the ecclesiastical faculties of the university) to determine if the chancellor had "the most serious reasons" to withdraw the canonical mission. The faculty committee report would ultimately be sent to the board of trustees for final action.[31]

Adaptations were also made in the requirement of obtaining the *nihil obstat* prior to receiving tenure. The university's board of trustees[32] and the administration did not want to have the decision of the *nihil obstat* made by the Roman congregation, a procedure that was thought to violate the autonomy of the institution and that might raise some problems concerning accreditation and government funding. The process that was finally accepted called for the *nihil obstat* to be given by the bishops on the board of trustees. However, the faculty later found out that the chancellor would first check with Rome about the individual in question.

The faculty of theology was very conscious at the time about the possible tensions raised by the canonical statutes. I had shared with my faculty colleagues in the department under the promise of confidentiality the details of my investigation by Rome. The theology faculty clearly wanted to maintain the position in the canonical statutes that the theology department was more than an ecclesiastical faculty, and the canonical statutes as finally approved by the academic senate, the trustees, and the congregation in Rome clearly made this point. The statutes explicitly mention that the ecclesiastical faculties have other programs to which the statutes do not apply;[33] the specific canonical statutes for the ecclesiastical faculty of theology strongly insist that the department of theology is more than an ecclesiastical faculty, as is explicitly described in their title, "Statutes of the Pontifical Degree Programs of the Department of Theology."[34] Also, it is specifically mentioned that the department of theology *has* a pontifical faculty, not that it *is* a pontifical faculty.[35] Newer statutes were drawn up in 1984 but have never been approved. According to a letter from the congregation to Chancellor Hickey, the 1981 statutes are still in force even though they were originally approved for only three years.

When the question first arose in 1979 and 1980, the department of theology strongly resisted the new canonical statutes. The requirements of canonical mission and *nihil obstat* were seen as introducing something new that could easily be interpreted as violative of academic freedom. However, in the final version of the approved statutes, many in the theology department thought that academic freedom and academic due process were safeguarded because they were explicitly mentioned. In addition, the limits of the ecclesiastical faculty and of the role of the chancellor with regard to the other programs in the department of theology were clearly mentioned. The theology professors worked under the distinct impression that the statutes would not be retroactive. Chancellor Hickey later testified in court that he had never told anyone that the statutes would not be retroactive. After the statutes were approved, I wrote a letter to the university authorities pointing out that the statutes did not apply to me, since my tenure contract with the university was governed by earlier documents. The university could not unilaterally add new obligations that affected the very substance of my contract.[36] The university officials acknowledged my letter but did not express agreement.

Before my case in the fall of 1986, two other incidents involving tensions over the issue of academic freedom occurred at CUA. The school of religious studies was looking for a new dean to take over in September of 1985. The search committee and the faculty of the school voted for John P. Boyle, the director of the school of religion at the University of Iowa. However, Professor Boyle met with Chancellor Hickey who was not comfortable with Boyle's possible appointment, and Boyle withdrew from consideration. Apparently, Chancellor Hickey would have used his influence to prevent the appointment because Boyle had written a small book a few years before that called for a change in the Catholic church's teaching on sterilization.[37]

A second case involved a *nihil obstat* for Professor James H. Provost in the department of canon law. Provost was unanimously approved for tenure by all the requisite university bodies, including the academic senate. However, at first the bishops on the board of trustees, after consultation with Rome, voted to deny the *nihil obstat* to Provost. Finally on appeal, after Provost had clarified his positions, the board of trustees changed its mind and gave him the *nihil obstat*.

In August 1986, Chancellor Hickey handed me Ratzinger's letter declaring that I was neither suitable nor eligible to be a professor of Catholic theology. Archbishop Hickey informed me that he was going to begin the process to take away my canonical mission to teach in an ecclesiastical faculty. He gave me until the first of September to tell him if I wanted to take advantage of the due process proceedings provided for in the canonical statutes. I also reminded him that, as far as I was concerned, I never had a canonical mission and did not need one. I told him of the letter that I had written to university officials a few years before. At that time I also asked him to explain the relationship between the withdrawal of the canonical mission and my rights as a tenured faculty member. Hickey said that only the board of trustees could decide about that, but that he would obtain an answer for me. (Later Hickey testified in his deposition for the trial that it was his understanding from the very beginning that Ratzinger's letter meant that I could not teach Catholic theology anywhere at CUA, but he was going to go through all the procedural steps found in the statutes.)[38] I told the chancellor that the canonical statues did not apply to me, and that I had no canonical mission. Also, I reminded him that I was on sabbatical leave until January of 1987.[39]

I was faced with a decision. According to the canonical statutes, I had the right to a due process hearing before faculty peers to determine if the chancellor had "the most serious reasons" for the withdrawal of the canonical mission. The process was *mutatis mu-tandis*, the same process outlined in the statutes for a dismissal proceeding. I took counsel with a number of people. Above all, I was in contact with John F. Hunt, a partner in the New York law firm of Cravath, Swaine, and Moore. Hunt had represented the subject professors before the Marlowe Committee in 1968–69. The subject professors and their lawyers published two books dealing with the theological and academic freedom aspects of the case before the faculty board of inquiry. Cravath, Swaine, and Moore gave their services pro bono to the subject professors. I had stayed in contact with John Hunt over the years, and he assured me that he would be willing to represent me in any further proceedings that might arise. Paul C. Saunders, another partner in the firm, agreed to work on the case. At this mention of the firm of Cravath, Swaine, and Moore, and of Messrs. Hunt and Saunders, I must pause to express my deep appreciation and gratitude. I have worked closely with them and their associates for more than three years. Their dedication, competence, and concern have enabled me to see this whole problem through to its final academic and legal processes. In the hearing before the academic senate and in the legal process itself, Paul Saunders assumed the leading role since he is a litigator. I can never repay Hunt, Saunders, their associates, and their firm for all they have done. This book is dedicated to them as a small token of my esteem and gratitude.

Gratitude and truth call for another digression. In the course of the seven-year investigation by the Vatican and the three-year academic and legal process to retain my right to teach Catholic theology at CUA, I have benefited from the support and advice of many people. Throughout this decade I sought and was given counsel and encouragement from many people. I am well aware of the danger of mentioning names, but justice requires that such a risk be taken. The leadership of the Friends of American Catholic Theology (Johann Klodzen, Sally McReynolds, and Mary Zielinski Hellwig) together with the membership of FACT have been most dedicated and helpful. Some faculty colleagues especially the group of five theology faculty and all those who testified publicly on my behalf deserve my words of thanks. James A. Coriden and Robert T. Kennedy served as canonical counsel and friends throughout. Robert K. Webb again volunteered to be my academic counsel during the hearing at CUA. The five graduate students who became intervenor-plaintiffs in my legal case willingly gave much time and effort to my cause. The theme of my address at the successful end of the strike at CUA in 1967—that the whole affair and the ensuing challenge went beyond one person—remains true of our present controversy. I can never adequately express my gratitude to the many friends and colleagues who have supported me in these controversies about academic freedom. But now back to the narrative.

At the end of August, I informed the chancellor that I wanted the due process hearing to determine if he had the most serious reasons to withdraw my canonical mission. However in so doing, I did not waive my legal rights arising from the fact that I did not have a canonical mission and my contention that the canonical statutes did not apply to me. I felt this was the best way to obtain a hearing on the merits of the case. Thus the process began in September 1986.

I was frustrated by delays in the process. I had accepted the suggestion of the dean of the school of religious studies that I come back from sabbatical and teach one course so that the process could begin.[40] However, the administration did not accept that proposal. Even though I was on sabbatical, I was still willing to have the process get under way as quickly as possible. Negotiations took place between the lawyers about the exact process to be followed, since the canonical statutes described it as, *mutatis mutandis*, the process for dismissal of a faculty member for cause. The academic senate of the university was also discussing the process and proposing names for the committee. Only in February did the chancellor give his charge to the ad hoc committee.

I had received no official response from the university to my question about the relationship between the withdrawal of the canonical mission and my rights as a tenured faculty member. After an article by President William J. Byron appeared in the student newspaper, *The Tower*, in November, 1986 (an article reprinted from another journal without the personal knowledge of the president), I asked him for his official response to my question.[41] Byron responded that in his judgment tenure was understood broadly as tenure to the university, and not just to a particular department or school.[42] I also became aware of an intriguing development. The official letters of appointment (basically the contract) had always referred to me as a tenured professor in the department of theology, but the September 1986 letter of appointment referred to me as a tenured professor in the school of religious studies. However, before the due process hearing got off the ground, another problem arose—the suspension.

I was scheduled to come back from sabbatical and to teach three courses in the department of theology in the spring semester of 1987. A mimeographed handout sent from the department to the students in September listed me as teaching these courses. Chancellor Hickey, in Rome at the time, apparently learned of this and ordered my name and courses to be stricken. On October 3, the academic vice-president, John K. C. Oh, instructed the dean of the school of religious studies and the chair of the department of theology to remove my name from the schedule of courses.[43] My dean and chair protested, but without success.[44]

On December 19, the chancellor wrote me of his intention to suspend me from teaching in the second semester pending the hearing. As required by the statutes, he also asked the dean and theology's chair their opinion about the suspension. Both of them strongly opposed the suspension.[45] I too urged the chancellor to reconsider the suspension.[46] On January 9, the chancellor informed me that, in accord with the statutes, he was suspending me from teaching in the spring 1987 semester. On January 9, I wrote the chancellor acknowledging his letter but pointing out that he had no statutory authority to suspend me from teaching students in American or nonecclesiastical degree programs. I told him I would meet my classes, but inform the students in ecclesiastical degree programs that they could not take my courses for credit.

On January 13, the chancellor informed me that I was suspended from teaching in all programs of study. He insisted that only one faculty or body of teachers existed in the department of theology. If I insisted on teaching my classes to students seeking nonecclesiastical degrees, I had to show cause by noon on the following day why under his authority as archbishop of Washington he should not exercise his power under Canon 812 to prevent me from teaching theology anywhere in the university. (Recall that, according to Canon 812, anyone teaching theological disciplines in a Catholic institution of higher learning needs a mandate from the local ecclesiastical superior.) On January 14, the university ordered my classes canceled. I then responded that I would not attempt to teach my classes for two reasons. First, I did not want to occasion the invocation of Canon 812 over the matter of suspension; as I pointed out earlier, Canon 812 has never been explicitly invoked in the United States and its use might cause serious problems for Catholic higher education. Second, I did not want to make my students hostages to the actions taken against me. Students would suffer if they took my classes and later could not receive credit for them. However, I still insisted that the chancellor acted beyond his statutory rights in suspending me from teaching in the civil degree programs in the department of theology. He had the statutory power in "more serious and pressing cases" to suspend the teacher from ecclesiastical degree programs, but he had no power to suspend me from teaching in nonecclesiastical degree programs.[47] On February 27, 1987, I filed suit against the university in the Superior Court of the District of Columbia alleging that suspending me from teaching students in the ecclesiastical and especially in the nonecclesiastical degree programs was a breach of my contract.

Meanwhile, the due process hearing on withdrawing the canonical mission to teach on an ecclesiastical faculty was finally getting under way. On January 13, 1987, the academic senate, pursuant to the statutes, formally constituted the ad hoc faculty committee.[48] On February 11, the chancellor through his counsel formally made his charge or accusation. The sole reason cited for the removal of the canonical mission was that the "decision of the Holy See is a final, definitive decision by the highest authorities of the Catholic Church" and this "decision of the Holy See constitutes a most serious reason for the withdrawal of Father Curran's canonical mission to teach in the name of the church."[49]

The ad hoc committee finally met on April 20 to hear both sides discuss their understanding of the jurisdiction of the committee.[50] As mentioned earlier, I was represented by the firm of Cravath, Swaine, and Moore. In the previous fall, the university had retained the legal firm of Williams and Connolly. In this hearing, Kevin T. Baine and several of his associates in that firm represented the chancellor. Both sides submitted memoranda to the committee before the oral hearing on April 20. The chancellor maintained that the definitive declaration of the Holy See that I was neither suitable nor eligible to teach Catholic theology is not simply "a most serious reason" for the withdrawal of the canonical mission, but it is incontrovertible proof that the mission must be withdrawn. This decision of the Holy See, he argued, was binding upon the committee as a matter of canon law. Throughout the entire controversy the chancellor argued that canon law was the reason for all his actions, and that canon law was binding on all concerned. However, even if the committee were not bound by canon law, the Holy See's decision would in his view certainly constitute a most serious reason to remove Curran's canonical mission to teach in the name of the church. Curran cannot be permitted to retain a canonical mission to teach in the name of the church when the highest authorities in the church have declared him ineligible and unsuitable to do so. Under these circumstances, the committee need not hear testimony intended to demonstrate that other theologians hold views similar to Curran's, that he is a competent scholar in the eyes of peers, or even that he has been responsible in his presentation of Catholic teaching. The chancellor also contended that the university did not regard these proceedings as a dismissal proceeding. If the university were to terminate Curran's employment or his tenure, it would institute a separate proceeding for that purpose. Later in the hearing itself, the chancellor's lawyer affirmed that the withdrawal of the canonical mission in no way affected my tenure. According to the chancellor, the ad hoc committee had no responsibility or authority to resolve any and all questions that might be raised pursuant to my status in the university. The committee's sole function was to determine whether the chancellor has a most serious reason to withdraw the canonical mission.[51]

My position was that the canonical statutes incorporate the principles of academic freedom and academic due process. The committee sits as an academic committee. I have a right to a hearing on the merits of the case. The committee is under no obligation to accept the Vatican declaration as a most serious reason. It may so decide, but it does not have to. Due process and recognized academic procedures call for a hearing with the protection of due process as spelled out in the statutes and with a professional judgment on my suitability and fitness to teach made by my peers, by the committee, and ultimately by the board of trustees. The university provided for academic freedom and due process when it approved and promulgated the canonical statutes. These statutes themselves were approved by Rome. The committee must also consider the effects of the withdrawal of the canonical mission. We stated that both the committee and Professor Curran are entitled to know whether the result of this proceeding will lead to a constructive termination of employment.[52]

In accord with the understanding of academic freedom and academic due process, I thought the committee ultimately should make a judgment about my competency and fitness to teach moral theology. The Vatican letter was one element they could consider, but this letter ultimately had to be considered in the light of all other relevant factors touching on my competency. If I were competent and fit to teach Catholic moral theology, the canonical mission should not be taken away. I was following the theoretical interpretation of a canonical mission given by the Marlowe committee in 1969, even though the committee ruled that I did not have or need such a mission.

The ad hoc committee responded on April 22 and outlined its own understanding of its jurisdiction. The committee would not consider the procedural or substantive correctness or error of the Congregation for the Doctrine of the Faith's declaration concerning my suitability to teach Catholic theology. The committee would consider whether that determination constitutes "a most serious reason" for withdrawal of the canonical mission. The committee would also consider the effects of the withdrawal of the canonical mission and possible alternatives for implementation in the event that the committee should recommend that the canonical mission be withdrawn.[53]

The substantive hearing itself was scheduled for May 4, 5, and 6. I was pleased with the committee's understanding of its jurisdiction. The members did not see themselves as bound in canon law to accept the Vatican declaration as dispositive. Also, they would consider the effects of the withdrawal of the canonical mission. I also interpreted their understanding to mean that they would weigh the Vatican document as one element in their appraisal of my competency to teach Catholic moral theology.

However, when the hearing itself began on May 4, I realized that I was wrong on the last point. My lawyers and I were quite surprised when, at the outset, the committee said they would not take oral testimony from the witnesses we had called to testify about my competence. The final decision by the committee made it very clear that they were not going to judge my competence; in fact, in the end, they assumed it.[54]

First, it will be helpful to describe the committee and its operations. The committee consisted of seven senior faculty persons from Catholic University, only one of whom was in the field of Catholic theology. The chair was professor Urban A. Lester of the law school. John P. Arness of the Washington firm of Hogan and Hartson acted as counsel for the committee.

At the hearing on May 4, 5, and 6, the chancellor called no witnesses, but relied on the earlier and written testimony of Father Francis Morrissey, a canon lawyer from St. Paul's University in Ottawa. The chancellor rested his case on the determination of the Congregation for the Doctrine of the Faith. My attorney, Paul Saunders, requested that the chancellor be compelled to testify, but he refused and the committee declined to require him to testify. The committee itself called Professor Frederick R. McManus, a canon lawyer, former administrative official of the university, and the chief drafter of the canonical statutes, as well as Professor Carl J. Peter, who had been dean of the school of religious studies at the time of the drafting and approval of the new canonical statutes. The committee called these two witnesses to obtain their views on the canonical statutes and their application in this case.

The committee took live testimony from five witnesses proposed by my counsel—myself, Professor David N. Power (the chair of the department of theology), Professor William Cenkner (the dean of the school of religious studies), Sr. Alice Gallin (the executive director of the Association of Catholic Colleges and Universities), Robert K. Webb (professor and chair of history at the University of Maryland, Baltimore County, who was again generously serving as my academic counsel), and Father William J. Byron (the president of Catholic University). We had asked the committee to request Father Byron to testify, and testify he did, but only on a limited basis. However, the committee took only written testimony from the five witnesses who were to testify to my competency and the responsibleness of my positions. These witnesses were Professor Monika Hellwig of George-town University, Professor Richard A. McCormick of the University of Notre Dame, Professor Richard P. McBrien of Notre Dame, and Professor André Guindon of St. Paul's University in Ottawa. In addition, the committee received a short letter from Professor Bernard Häring of the Academia Alfonsiana in Rome testifying to my com-petency and responsibility.

The committee also had received about 150 letters from different groups, faculties, scholarly societies, and individuals. The vast ma-jority of these letters was supportive of me and urged that no action be taken against me. The boards of directors of the two largest theological societies that include Roman Catholics, the Catholic The-ological Society of America (CTSA) and the College Theology Society (CTS) strongly urged that no action be taken against me. The statement from the board of directors of the CTSA, which was later overwhelmingly approved by the membership at its annual meeting, stated in part:

> As the Board of the Catholic Theological Society of America, we affirm these stances of our Society's membership, and testify in the strongest possible way to Charles Curran's professional competence as a Catholic theologian, to the responsibility and integrity with which he fulfills his role as a Catholic theologian, and to the moderate character of his positions even where those positions disagree with the present official teaching of the church. Removing him from his

teaching post is incomprehensible on professional grounds, unjust in the singling out of this one scholar from many of his peers with similar opinions, and indefensible in the light of traditional understanding of what a theologian rightfully does.[55]

In the course of the three-day hearing, it became clear that the committee was not questioning my competence and was in no way going to weigh the declaration of the Congregation for the Doctrine of the Faith alongside other testimony about my competence.

After the hearing, both sides submitted briefs to the committee. The committee finally issued its report on October 9, 1987.[56] (Meanwhile, I had accepted a one-year appointment for the 1987–88 academic year as visiting Kaneb Professor of Catholic studies at Cornell University in Ithaca, New York.) In accord with the statutes, the report was sent to me and to the chancellor. If the chancellor disagreed with the report, he was to indicate his reasons for disagreement in writing and send it back to the committee for review. The sixty-one page report summarized the proceedings of the committee including the testimony it received, set forth the factual background, discussed the issues before the committee, and then made its conclusions and recommendations. The committee was keenly aware that the canonical statutes contain a potential conflict between the jurisdiction of the church and the institutional autonomy of the university (p. 58). The committee recognized the tension and possible conflict created in the canonical statutes between canon law and the general rules of academic autonomy and due process grounded in American civil law and the traditions and principles of American academic institutions. The canonical statutes profess a dual commitment "intended to assure fidelity to the revealing word of God as it is transmitted by tradition and interpreted and safeguarded by the magisterium of the church" as well as to "safeguard academic freedom." The committee concluded from this dual commitment that "the understanding of academic freedom in the case of a sacred discipline must be suitably nuanced" (pp. 51, 52).

The committee made no finding about my competence, but recognized "that Professor Curran is an outstanding scholar, teacher, speaker and writer in his field" (p. 2). "It is undisputed that Professor Curran's academic colleagues hold him in high esteem. Professor Curran has made extensive and continuing contributions to the functioning of the university and to the development of the field of moral theology. . . . Indeed, one witness described Professor Curran as 'one of the two most respected Catholic moral theologians in the United States today'" (pp. 35–36).

The committee understood the canonical mission to be an authorization to teach in the name of the church. The canonical mission in their judgment is a credential for a faculty member otherwise academically qualified for appointment to an ecclesiastical faculty (pp. 53–54) and a qualification conferred upon a faculty member by the official church (pp. 58, 59). The committee concluded that the canonical statutes and the repeated assertions of counsel to the chancellor show that the university did not seek to terminate Curran's employment or abrogate his tenure through the current action. As a result, in the process of withdrawing the canonical mission, the testimony of peers concerning academic competence did not have a direct relevance (p. 54).

The committee could not consider the declaration of the Congregation for the Doctrine of the Faith dispositive in this case, because such a disposition "at least potentially infringes on the institutional autonomy of the university, generally accepted principles of academic freedom, and Professor Curran's rights as a tenured member of the faculty" (p. 43). In the light of such an understanding, the committee made its recommendations (pp. 60, 61):

1. The canonical mission of Professor Curran may be withdrawn, provided his other rights are simultaneously affirmed, to wit: a. That he remain a tenured faculty member at the Catholic University of America, with all the rights and privileges to which that status entitles him; b. That he continue to function as a professor in the field of his competence, namely, as a professor in the area of moral theology and/or ethics.
2. If it is deemed impractical for Professor Curran to continue to teach in the department of theology, the committee recommends that arrangements for a suitable alternative academic position be made before Professor Curran's canonical mission is withdrawn.
3. If the foregoing recommendations cannot be implemented, the committee would oppose the withdrawal of Professor Curran's canonical mission and recommend against such action. In such circumstances, withdrawal of the mission would be unjust to Pro-

fessor Curran and would be harmful to the university and its mission.

My reaction in October of 1987 when I first read the report, and my continuing reaction, is that I was 75 percent satisfied with the report. As far as I personally was concerned, I would lose the canonical mission, but the report lauded my competence and assured me a tenured teaching position in the university in my area of competence. However, I thought the report was and is quite damaging to the department of theology. The bottom line was that academic freedom and institutional autonomy exist throughout the university in all parts except in the department of theology or in the other ecclesiastical faculties. The report leaned toward the chancellor's position that there could be only one faculty in the department of theology, although the possibility was not definitively excluded that one could teach students in nonecclesiastical degree programs in the department of theology even without a canonical mission (p. 56).

Faced with the dual commitments that had been written into the canonical statutes, the committee found that academic freedom in an ecclesiastical faculty had to give way to a decision by church authority. A faculty member could be removed from the ecclesiastical faculty without a judgment about one's competency and fitness to teach made by peers. For over two decades, I had fought for academic freedom for Catholic theology in general, and for the theology department at the Catholic University of America in particular. According to the committee's ruling the hard won victories of the past were now only history. The committee came up with a compromise that guaranteed me a tenured position teaching in my area of competence, but acknowledged that academic freedom as understood on the American academic scene does not exist in the ecclesiastical faculty of theology at the Catholic University. It had been my contention all along that withdrawal of the canonical mission had to be interpreted in relation to one's competency and fitness to teach. The Marlowe Committee in 1969 had taken the same position. I do not know what went into the committee's deliberations. The dual commitments of the canonical statutes were a compromise that tried to smooth over the inevitable tension between church authority and academic freedom. Undoubtedly, the committee felt constrained by the definitive declaration of the Congregation for the Doctrine of the Faith, but as a result they effectively excised the ecclesiastical faculty of theology from the rest of the university. At that stage, I had no further input into the committee.

The chancellor received the report on October 13, 1987. According to the statutes, if the chancellor agreed with the report, he would send it to the board of trustees. If the chancellor objected to the report, he should indicate to the committee the reasons for his disagreement and the committee should respond. Finally, on December 14, the chancellor wrote the committee agreeing with their decision that the canonical mission could be withdrawn, but objecting to the conditions that the canonical mission could be withdrawn only if I continued to function as a tenured professor in my area of competence—moral theology and/or ethics. He contended that the committee in imposing this condition went beyond its mandate, which was only to determine if the canonical mission could be withdrawn. Also, the rationale of the committee involved a fundamental inconsistency, he said. The committee acknowledged that canonical principles must be given precedence in determining the withdrawal of the canonical mission, but for reasons not connected with canon law concluded that "Curran should be permitted to teach theology somewhere in the university." The chancellor objected because the canonical principles were "subordinated to noncanonical considerations even in determining withdrawal of the canonical mission."[57]

My attorneys had cautioned me all along that the chancellor might use the hearing over the canonical mission to keep me from ever teaching theology again anywhere at the Catholic University. Paul Saunders strongly voiced this fear to the faculty committee.[58] Chancellor Hickey had told Dean Cenkner and Chair Power at the time of the suspension in January 1987 that I could not teach theology anywhere in the university.[59] Later I learned that the chancellor's deposition stated that he believed from the time he received Ratzinger's letter that I was unable to teach Catholic theology anywhere at Catholic University.[60] Although I had some disagreements with the faculty committee report, the chancellor had many more.

The ad hoc committee responded to the chancellor on December 21, 1987, and stuck by its conclusions: "If removal of the canonical mission, independently of any dismissal proceedings, were to terminate Professor Curran's functions as a teacher in the field of his competence, the removal would impinge upon his contractual rights and upon the proper autonomy of this university as understood in the context of the American academic tradition.''[61]

The committee report was sent to the board of trustees, which is required by the statutes to make the final decison in the light of the record. The trustees met on January 26, and in accord with the statutes an hour and a half was given to me to present my case. Paul Saunders, John Hunt, and I addressed the board. There was practically no discussion between the board and us after the presentations. That afternoon, the board met in executive session to discuss the matter. In accord with the procedures, if the board of trustees disagreed with the committee report, it had to send its objections to the committee. On January 27, Cardinal Joseph Bernardin, chair of the board of trustees, sent the response to the committee. The board determined that the canonical misson should be withdrawn. The board objected to the committee's condition that Curran continue to function as a tenured professor in his area of competence. In making that recommendation, the committee gave insufficient consideration to the declaration of the Holy See that Curran is neither suitable nor eligible to teach Catholic theology. In addition, the board concluded that the committee went beyond its scope in addressing these other issues. After withdrawal of the canonical mission, the president will be instructed to explore possible alternative teaching arrangements with Curran.[62] The board was apparently saying that I could not teach Catholic theology anywhere in the Catholic University. On February 3, I wrote to friends and supporters indicating that I thought the unviversity would not institute a dismissal proceeding against me, but would offer me a position outside my area of competence that I then could not accept.[63]

On February 16, 1988, the committee responded to the board of trustees. The committee reconsidered its report in the light of the objections stated by the trustees and reaffirmed its recommendations. The committee in its report was trying to do justice to the dual commitment of the canonical statutes to fidelity to the magisterium of the church and to academic freedom. Thus the committee made its two conclusions interdependent. The committee firmly restated its conclusions that the congregation's declaration ''is not controlling with regard to Professor Curran's ability to teach in any department outside an ecclesiastical faculty. In such departments the university must be guided by the American norms of academic freedom and tenure, including principles of academic competence and peer judgment, which the university has accepted and embodied in the faculty handbook.'' The committee suggested that the university enter into negotiations with me about alternative teaching assignments prior to withdrawing the canonical mission at the next board meeting, which was scheduled for April 12.[64]

In the meantime much consultation occurred on both sides. In December, we later discovered, a meeting took place in Rome attended by Archbishop Hickey, President Byron, their attorney Kevin Baine, Cardinal Ratzinger of the Congregation for the Doctrine of the Faith, and Cardinal Baum of the Congregation for Catholic Education.[65] Some time later, ecclesiastical pressure was applied on Matthew Clark, who as bishop of Rochester was my church superior, to bring me back to the diocese of Rochester or at least to take away my permission to teach at the Catholic University. Bishop Clark refused. On Holy Saturday, April 2, 1988, Archbishop Hickey was involved in a conference telephone call with Cardinal Baum, Archbishop Pio Laghi, the papal pro-nuncio, and several cardinals and archbishops on the board.[66] On April 5, a week before the trustees' meeting, Kevin Baine called and started negotiations with John Hunt about possible arrangements. Baine insisted that I would have to say publicly that I was bound by the Vatican declaration and would not teach Catholic theology at CUA. I would also have to accept Canons 750 and 752 which describe the response due to hierarchical teaching. Throughout these negotiations, my attorneys insisted on certain *conditiones sine qua non*. I could not accept the Vatican letter as binding on me; I could sign no loyalty oaths; and I would be teaching Catholic theology even though it might not be called that. Specifically by April 12 I was informed that the board of trustees would not offer me a position in religion and religious education, but in the department of sociology. I was willing to accept the title of professor of Christian social ethics in the department of sociology provided my courses were open to all nonecclesiastical degree program students interested in them and cross listed in all the announcements and catalogues of the department of religion and religious education. I also expressed my willingness not to teach courses in sexual ethics.

Another significant event occurred on April 5. In February 1987, I had filed suit against the university in the Superior Court of the District of Columbia for suspending me in the spring semester 1987 from teaching students in nonecclesiastical degree programs. Both sides agreed not to press the case while the faculty committee hearing process was under way. Once that concluded, the litigation process resumed, and the university moved for summary judgment and dismissal of my case because its decision was based on canon law and is thus immune from judicial review by a civil court. On April 5, 1988, Judge Bruce D. Beaudin of the Superior Court of the District of Columbia ruled that the university's positon was without merit and I had a right to have my contract case heard by the civil court.[67]

On April 12, counsel for the university dictated to my counsel the press release from the board of trustees. They withdrew the canonical mission, which barred me from teaching in the department of theology, but that action does not remove my tenure. The chancellor, the chair of the board, and the president were appointed as a three-person committee to enter into discussion with me about an alternative teaching assignment within an area of my professional competence.[68]

I issued a statement to the press that same day expressing my gratification that I was still a tenured professor at the Catholic University able to teach (or so I believed) in my area of competence. I urged that we move quickly to put this matter behind us and get on with our work.[69] I publicly said that I was 75 to 80 percent satisfied with the action. The problem remained the same one that had existed in the original report of the faculty committee. Academic freedom and institutional autonomy do not exist in the department of theology, but they exist in other parts of the university.

However, it soon became evident that there would be no agreement. The university did not accept my *conditiones sine qua non*. Perhaps a misunderstanding between the lawyers had occurred. Perhaps not. But the university insisted that I sign a statement saying that the congregation's declaration was binding on me and that I could not teach Catholic theology at CUA.

On April 13, 1988, Kevin Baine sent my counsel a proposed agreement. I had to sign a statement saying that the Vatican declaration bound me and that I would not teach Catholic theology at CUA. Also, I had to agree to give up my lawsuit on the suspension.

Any breach by me of any provision of the agreement would be adequate cause for my dismissal from the university.[70]

My counsel responded on April 19 expressing disappointment with the proposed settlement. "As we told you, there are certain *sine qua nons* to make this a true peace treaty. Your draft ignored all of them. Moreover, certain parts of it were offensive and demeaning to Curran, and violative of the principles of academic freedom." We then proposed an agreement along the lines discussed earlier.[71] On April 29, counsel for the chancellor responded with another offer that again demanded that I accept the congregation's decision as binding upon me and that I could not teach Catholic theology at the university.[72] To accept such a condition would contradict the very principles for which I stood. My aim was not to gain a job for myself, but to prove that academic freedom existed at the Catholic University. A declaration from the Congregation for the Doctrine of the Faith that I was neither suitable nor eligible to teach Catholic theology could not have direct, immediate, juridical effect in the academy. I could only be dismissed from my position as a tenured professor teaching Catholic theology on the basis of a judgment by peers about my competence. My counsel told Kevin Baine that if we did not hear by May 10, we would consider their April 29, 1988 offer to be final.[73] We had no response and on May 17, 1988, I publicly announced that the Catholic University had unilaterally broken its contract with me by refusing to offer me a tenured position in my area of competence.[74] In later weeks, there was some further correspondence from President Byron about a teaching position, but I had to agree to accept the Vatican declaration as binding on me and to agree that I would not teach Catholic theology at Catholic University.

In the course of the discussions, one other point of contention arose. In its recommendations, the committee concluded that I should continue to function as a tenured professor in the field of my competence "namely, as a professor in the area of moral theology and/or ethics." The chancellor in his December 14, 1987, letter to the committee explicitly understood the committee to mean that I should be allowed to teach theology elsewhere in the university. The university officials later interpreted the committee report to mean I could teach ethics so long as "ethics" did not include "theology." I strongly disagreed. My training, competence, writing, and reputation are not in the area of philosophical ethics as such, but of theological ethics or moral theology. Elsewhere in the report, the committee referred to moral theology as my area of competence.

For a short time I thought that the university might make its case against me on these grounds. The board of trustees would accept the recommendation of the ad hoc faculty committee and offer me a position teaching social ethics but not Catholic theology. Such a strategy had much to offer from the viewpoint of CUA because they could then claim to be following the recommendation of the ad hoc committee. However, by insisting that I sign or publicly agree to a loyalty oath not to teach Catholic theology at CUA they went beyond and against the recommendation of the ad hoc committee. I do not know why CUA finally decided not to take the route of claiming to follow the faculty committee. Perhaps they recognized that it was a subterfuge or would not stand up in court. Perhaps the board of trustees wanted to make a very strong and public statement about the limits on academic freedom at Catholic University. I only know for sure that in the final analysis CUA rejected this approach for the more radical position of saying very clearly that full academic freedom in the American sense of the term does not exist at Catholic University.

On June 2, 1988, the board of trustees met and passed a new resolution. "The board accepts the declaration of the Holy See as binding upon the university as a matter of canon law and religious conviction." "[A]ny assignment allowing Father Curran to exercise the function of a professor of Catholic theology despite the Holy See's declaration that he is ineligible to do so would be inconsistent with the university's special relationship with the Holy See, incompatible with the university's freely chosen Catholic character, and contrary to the obligations imposed on the university as a matter of canon law."[75] As President Byron phrased it in the *Washington Post*, there is "an ecclesial limit" on theological exploration and communication at CUA. Byron and others pointed out that the autonomy of the university is not threatened by such a condition because the trustees and the institution have freely chosen this limit.[76] However, in the light of the accepted American understanding of academic freedom, a university cannot voluntarily agree to accept an outside authority as definitive in determining who can teach on its faculty.

Chapter 1 pointed out that autonomy and academic freedom do not mean exactly the same thing. Autonomy can be and has been invoked in a way that unnecessarily limits academic freedom. Ever since the Land O'Lakes Statement of 1967 Catholic educators have often coupled academic freedom with institutional autonomy. In the light of the broader discussion on academic freedom and of the actions in my case Catholic educators should be more careful in spelling out the exact meaning of autonomy so that autonomy cannot be used to limit academic freedom. The Catholic institution rightly needs autonomy with respect to the institutional church and interference by the church. However, the college or university especially as represented by its board of trustees or administration cannot autonomously make decisions that restrict the freedom of the faculty.

There is another important aspect to my controversy with CUA—the legal aspect. The legal case has attracted much attention in the press and in articles in legal reviews.[77] I do not have the competence to discuss the case in depth, since I am not trained as a lawyer. Here I will briefly describe the lawsuit I brought against Catholic University and the decision reached by Judge Frederick H. Weisberg of the Superior Court of the District of Columbia.

I first filed suit against CUA in February 1987 to challenge the action of the university in suspending me from teaching students in nonecclesiastical degree programs in the department of theology and from teaching theology elsewhere in the university. I was represented by the firm of Cravath, Swaine, and Moore of New York with Paul C. Saunders having the primary responsibility for the case. CUA was represented by Williams and Connolly of Washington with Kevin T. Baine as the primary lawyer. Both parties agreed at that time to concentrate their efforts on a speedy resolution of the hearing at CUA before the ad hoc committee, and no action was taken immediately on the lawsuit itself. The hearing before the ad hoc committee of the academic senate at CUA took place in April and May 1987, but the final decision was not made known until October 1987. I have described earlier what occurred before the final decision of the board of trustees of CUA in June of 1988 that I could not teach Catholic theology anywhere at Catholic University.

Paul Saunders agreed not to press our litigation until the board of trustees' meeting in January 1988 and then extended that until March 1, 1988. On March 1, Kevin Baine filed a motion to dismiss the case or for summary judgment.[78] CUA argued that the decision by the chancellor to suspend me was a matter of canon law and that the civil court had no authority to review this decision or the chancellor's interpretation of canon law. On March 18, 1988, my lawyers opposed the motion.[79] Our position was that the dispute was not an intra-church issue governed by canon law but rather involved a contract between me and a civilly incorporated higher educational institution in the District of Columbia.

On April 5, 1988, Judge Bruce D. Beaudin of the Superior Court of the District of Columbia ruled in my favor.[80] The Court found that my claim was indeed based on a contract governed by the civil law of the District of Columbia and not by church law. As Judge Beaudin put it: "Curran has properly turned to this Court for a determination in this case."

A week later, the board of trustees withdrew my canonical mission, and two months later determined that on the basis of the declaration of the Congregation for the Doctrine of the Faith I could not teach Catholic theology anywhere at Catholic University. On June 10, 1988, we amended our complaint to allege that CUA had constructively terminated my appointment in violation of my tenure contract as a professor of theology.[81]

Interrogatories were posed and depositions were taken, including lengthy depositions from me, from Cardinals Hickey and Bernardin, and from President Byron. Meanwhile, five graduate students in the nonecclesiastical degree programs of the department of theology filed suit against CUA for interfering with their rights and their academic freedom because of the actions taken against me and other actions taken by CUA. These students were added as intervenor-plaintiffs to my case.[82] I was grateful for the support of these students and for their willingness to go through all the strains of a lawsuit.

On November 2, 1988, the attorneys for the university filed another motion for summary judgment, again arguing that the decision made by CUA in my case was based on religious conviction and canon law, and that on the basis of the first amendment's separation of church and state the civil court had no jurisdiction over the case.[83] On November 17, 1988, my attorneys filed a long trial brief and a memorandum in opposition.[84] We claimed that the case involved a broken contract and that CUA's actions were not immune from judicial scrutiny because of its claimed rights to the free exercise of religion.

We knew all along that one of the most difficult parts of our case was the request for specific performance; namely, we were asking the court to order the Catholic University to reinstate me as a professor of theology. Specific performance is ordinarily very difficult to obtain in a case of breach of contract, especially one relating to an employment contract. Ordinarily, the courts just award monetary damages, but I made it clear throughout that my primary concern was not for money or a financial settlement. I had brought the lawsuit because of the principle involved. I had fought for academic freedom at the Catholic University for over twenty years. I thought academic freedom existed at Catholic University, and I wanted the court to make such an acknowledgment not so much for my benefit, but, in spite of itself, for the university's.

The nonjury trial was held before Judge Frederick Weisberg from December 14 through December 23, 1988. At the beginning of the trial the attorneys for CUA again asked for summary judgment, and the court again denied it. In his opening statement Judge Weisberg set the limited parameters for the case: it was a dispute about the nature of the tenure contract entered into by the parties.

Others with the requisite competence will no doubt describe the ten days of the trial and explain the evidence and the legal arguments made by both sides. Many have already commented about the distinctive and remarkable features of the case. The trial presented witnesses and issues not ordinarily seen in such a court. Two cardinals of the Catholic church testified. In my judgment, Judge Weisberg was concerned, cautious, and interested. The judge had to grapple with questions of theology, canon law, church history, and academic norms and procedures as well as the legal issues involving contracts. Nothing the judge said gave us a clear indication of how he would rule, but I had been cautioned throughout that even getting the case to trial should be considered a victory and that we had an uphill battle.

Judge Weisberg handed down his decision on February 28, 1989.[85] The bottom line was very clear—I had lost the case. He ruled that my contract did not include a right to academic freedom. In my judgment the Catholic University lost much more in the process.

In his decision Judge Weisberg avoided all arguments based on the first amendment. The sole issue was the nature of the contract, the documents describing and expanding upon the contract, and the expectations of reasonable people at the time. The judge decided that there was no requirement for me to have a canonical mission before 1981. However, when the new canonical statutes went into effect in 1981 they could be applied retroactively to me over my objection, and therefore from that date forward I was required to have a canonical mission. (I had argued that I had never been given a canonical mission; that the requirements of the 1981 statutes affecting the essence of my contract could not be unilaterally added to my contract by the university ten years after I was tenured; and that the requirement of a canonical mission in the 1981 canonical statutes was not retroactive for those faculty members already at the university.) Since I had to have a canonical mission to teach on an ecclesiastical faculty, the court concluded that CUA did not break my contract when it took away the canonical mission to teach in an ecclesiastical faculty.

Did the university have an obligation to permit me to teach students in nonecclesiastical degree programs in the department of theology? No, because I had not proved that there were or should be two different teaching bodies in the department of theology. What about its obligation to allow me to teach theology in other parts of the university? There was no such legal obligation because my tenure was to the department of theology and not to the university as a whole or to any other place in the university. More importantly, the court said that any reasonable faculty member entering into a contract with CUA should have known that in the case of a definitive declaration from the Holy See that the professor is not suitable to teach Catholic theology, the university would enforce such a declaration. In addition the judge ruled that, even if he had decided in my favor, he never would have granted specific performance.

The judge's decision made it very clear that the real crux of the issue was the Catholic University's attempt to have it both ways by asserting both its commitment to academic freedom and its unwavering fealty to the Holy See. On some issues, and this case certainly is one of them, he said, "the University may choose for itself on which side of that conflict it wants to come down, and nothing in its contract with Professor Curran or any other faculty member promises that it will always come down on the side of academic freedom.''[86]

I was disappointed by the judge's decision. Has there ever been a judicial decision where one of the parties was not disappointed? My fundamental difference with Judge Weisberg's decision centers on his judgment that full academic freedom did not exist at CUA after the events of the late 1960s. But this is not the place to enter into an in-depth analysis and criticism of the judge's decision.

The question I faced on hearing the decision was whether or not to appeal. Paul Saunders read me the decision over the telephone. I had already considered the question of appeal with my lawyers and with other friends and advisors. Over the two and a half years of the academic and legal phases of my case I had made no decisions without lengthy consultation with my lawyers. However, within three minutes I decided not to appeal, and Paul Saunders and John Hunt were in complete agreement.

Why did I decide not to appeal? First as a legal matter, success on appeal was far from certain and the careful judicial opinion made it far less likely. The decision was not based on great constitutional questions of law such as the first amendment, and technically the trial had been flawless. Even if we could win an appeal, the chances of obtaining specific performance were very low. More importantly, the board of trustees said in 1988 and Judge Weisberg confirmed its right to say that full academic freedom in the American sense of the term does not now exist at Catholic University. My appeal would not change that reality. The courts could not force the board of trustees to change the positions they took in 1988. I had told friends and advisors that even if I won specific performance, I probably would not want to stay for a long time at Catholic University because the action of the trustees in 1988 had significantly changed the nature of the institution as far as I was concerned. Also, I was tired, and it was time to move on. As long as the case was in court it would be difficult for me to accept a full-time tenured position in an American institution of higher learning. I have been fortunate in securing visiting professorships at Cornell University for the 1987–88 academic year and at the University of Southern California for the following two academic years. However, it was time for me to settle down on a more permanent basis.

The AAUP investigated both my case at Catholic University and the state of academic freedom at the institution. The investigating committee found that Catholic University had violated the principles and procedures of academic freedom, tenure, and institutional autonomy in my case.[87] Final action by the AAUP as a whole will be taken at the June 1990 annual meeting.

As usual there are questions and uncertainties about the future. What will happen to Catholic University?[88] Will the academic senate at CUA be able to bring about any change in the present position on academic freedom? What do the declarations and actions of the board of trustees at CUA portend for other Catholic institutions of higher learning in the United States? How will new legislation from Rome affect the academic freedom of American Catholic higher education? What is the future of Catholic higher education in the United States?

Two points are crystal clear. I cannot teach Catholic theology anywhere at the Catholic University of America. Full academic freedom does not exist there.

NOTES

1. Charles E. Curran, "The Problem of Conscience and the Twentieth Century Christian," in Samuel Miller, ed., *Ecumenical Dialogue at Harvard: The Roman Catholic-Protestant Colloquium* (Cambridge, MA: Harvard University Press, 1964), pp. 262–273.

2. For this incident and other interventions by ecclesiastical authorities in Catholic higher education, see John Tracy Ellis, "A Tradition of Autonomy?" in Neil J. McCluskey, ed., *The Catholic University: A Modern Appraisal* (Notre Dame, IN: University of Notre Dame Press, 1970), pp. 206–270.

3. "Report of a Special Committee on Departure From Proper Academic Procedure Commissioned by the Faculty of the Graduate School of Arts and Sciences, The Catholic University of America (1963)," p.12.

4. The letter in mimeographed form was addressed to "(Right, Very) Reverend and Dear Father."

5. In connection with the faculty hearing in 1987 to remove my canonical mission to teach in an ecclesiastical faculty, Catholic University provided me with the files of Msgr. Joseph B. McAllister, the vice-rector of the university when I was first appointed to that faculty. Msgr. McAllister made memos of all his conversations with me and also put together a long memo including all the aspects leading up to the strike in 1967 and its conclusions.

6. Minutes of the Faculty Meeting of the School of Theology of the Catholic University of America, October 16, 1966, Rev. George Kanoti, C.R., Secretary.

7. The history of these events at Catholic University in the spring of 1967 is recorded in Albert C. Pierce, *Beyond One Man* (Washington, DC: Anawim Press, 1967). See also, Charles E. Curran, *Ongoing Revision in Moral Theology* (Notre Dame, IN: Fides Publishers, 1975), pp. 272–278.

8. John F. Hunt, Terrence R. Connelly, et al., *The Responsibility of Dissent: The Church and Academic Freedom,* (New York: Sheed and Ward, 1969), p. 31.

9. Affidavit of Nivard Scheel sworn to Nov. 14, 1988, in *Charles E. Curran vs. The Catholic University of America,* pp. 17ff. (See below, n.39). Brother Nivard Scheel was associated with the administration of CUA for a number of years and was acting rector in 1968–69.

10. The Objectives of the Catholic University of America, Adopted by the Board of Trustees, July 26, 1968, in "Manual of Information for the Faculty: The Catholic University of America, 1968," p. ii.

11. Scheel Affidavit, pp. 16ff.

12. Pope Paul VI, *On the Regulation of Birth: Humanae Vitae* (Washington, DC: United States Catholic Conference, 1968).

13. The events summarized here are discussed in greater detail in Hunt, Connelly, et al., *Responsibility of Dissent;* and Charles E. Curran, Robert E. Hunt, et al., *Dissent in and for the Church: Theologians and Humanae Vitae* (New York: Sheed and Ward, 1969). See also my *Ongoing Revision in Moral Theology,* pp. 278–283.

14. Statement by Catholic Theologians, Washington, DC, July 30, 1968, in Hunt, Connelly, et al., *Responsibility of Dissent,* pp. 203–205.

15. National Catholic News Service (Domestic), August 1, 1968.

16. Letter dated August 2, 1968, from Patrick Cardinal O'Boyle to the Archdiocese of Washington.

17. The other members of the board of inquiry were Professors E. Catherine Dunn, Frederick R. McManus, Antanas Suziedelis, and Rev. Dr. Eugene I. Van Antwerp from the National Catholic Educational Association. Professor Kenneth L. Schmitz was the alternate board member.

18. National Conference of Catholic Bishops, *Human Life in Our Day* (Washington, DC: United States Catholic Conference, 1968), pp. 18, 19.

19. Report and Recommendations of the Faculty Board of Inquiry. The principal components of the report are recommendations, conclusions regarding the subject professors, conclusions regarding norms for licit dissent, and conclusions regarding other matters.

20. Hunt, Connelly, et al., *Responsibility of Dissent,* pp. 163–172.

21. Report of University Self-Study, 1978–1979, submitted to Middle States Association of Colleges and Schools, pp. 34ff.

22. Report of Committee A, *AAUP Bulletin* 56 (1970): 166, 167.

23. For the lengthy documentation and history of this investigation, see my *Faithful Dissent* (Kansas City, MO: Sheed and Ward, 1986).

24. Pope John Paul II, *Apostolic Constitution Sapientia Christiana, On Ecclesiastical Faculties and Universities* (Washington, DC: United States Catholic Conference, 1979).

25. *Sapientia Christiana,* p. 14.

26. Canonical Statutes for the Ecclesiastical Faculties of the Catholic University of America, 1981, III, 7, pp. 4, 5.

27. Report and Recommendations of the Faculty Board of Inquiry (1969), p. 9.

28. For the history and the development of new canonical statutes at the Catholic University of America in response to *Sapientia Christiana,* see the testimony of Professors Frederick R. McManus and Carl J. Peter, who were called to testify by the ad hoc committee hearing my case, in Oral Argument Before the Ad Hoc Committee, pp. 190–363; 852–930.

29. Canonical Statutes, V, n. 11, p. 10.

30. Ibid., III, 7g, p. 5.

31. Ibid., V, 8, p. 9.

32. Ibid., V, 6, p. 9.

33. Ibid., I, 1, p. i.

34. Ibid., p. 22.

35. Ibid.

36. Letter from Charles E. Curran to Vice-Provost and Dean of Graduate Studies Frederick R. McManus, August 12, 1982.

37. John P. Boyle, *The Sterilization Controversy: A New Crisis for the Catholic Hospital?* (New York: Paulist Press, 1977).

38. *Curran vs. Catholic University of America,* Deposition Transcript of Chancellor James A. Hickey, pp. 154, 157, 159, 160, 161, 177, 178.

39. For a more in-depth discussion of what transpired at this time, consult the transcript of the hearing at Catholic University before the ad hoc committee and the testimony given in the case of *Curran v. The Catholic University of America* heard before Judge Frederick Weisberg in the Superior Court of the District of Columbia in December, 1988. All the relevant documents submitted by me and CUA are part of the public record.

40. Letter from Dean William Cenkner to Charles E. Curran, Sept. 2, 1986.

41. Letter from Charles E. Curran to President William J. Byron, S.J., November 11, 1986.

42. Letter from President William J. Byron, S.J., to Charles E. Curran, November 14, 1986.

43. Confidential memo from Academic Vice-President John K.C. Oh to Dean William Cenkner, O.P., October 3, 1986.

44. Letter from Dean William Cenkner to Academic Vice-President John K.C. Oh, October 7, 1986; Memo from Chair David N. Power to Academic Vice-President John K.C. Oh, October 9, 1986.

45. Letter from Chair David N. Power to Chancellor James A. Hickey, December 22, 1986; Letter from Dean William Cenkner to Chancellor James A. Hickey, December 29, 1986.

46. Letter from Charles E. Curran to Chancellor James A. Hickey, January 7, 1987.

47. Letter from Charles E. Curran to Chancellor James A. Hickey, January 14, 1987.

48. The members of the ad hoc committee were Urban A. Lester, chair; Antanas Suziedelis, vice-chair; Maxwell Bloomfield, Lucy M. Cohen, Avery Dulles, S.J., Thomas Mastroianni, Elizabeth Timberlake.

49. Letter from Edward Bennett Williams to Professor Urban A. Lester, February 11, 1987.

50. A transcript of all the proceedings before the ad hoc committee was made and is a public document.

51. Edward Bennett Williams et al., Memorandum from the Chancellor, April 3, 1987; Edward Bennett Williams et al., Reply Memorandum from the Chancellor, April 10, 1987.

52. John F. Hunt, Paul C. Saunders, et al., Memorandum from Professor Charles E. Curran on the Jurisdiction of the Ad Hoc Committee, April 3, 1987; John F. Hunt, Paul C. Saunders, et al., Reply Memorandum from Professor Charles E. Curran on the Jurisdiction of the Ad Hoc Committee, April 10, 1987.

53. Letter from John P. Arness to Kevin T. Baine and to John F. Hunt and Paul Saunders, April 22, 1987. The ad hoc committee retained as its counsel John P. Arness of the Washington firm of Hogan and Hartson.

54. Transcript of the Hearing before the Ad Hoc Committee in Re Professor Charles E. Curran, May 4, 1987, pp. 159–188.

55. Statement of the Board of Directors of the Catholic Theological Society of America Submitted to the Board of Inquiry Committee of the Academic Senate at the Catholic University of America: Testimony Regarding the Case of Rev. Dr. Charles Curran. See also Testimony from the Officers and Board of Directors of the College Theology Society Regarding the Case of Professor Charles Curran which closes with the statement: "To affirm that Professor Curran cannot be considered a Roman Catholic Theologian is in effect to deny the legitimacy of the theological enterprise for Roman Catholics."

56. Report to the Chancellor from the Ad Hoc Committee of the Academic Senate of the Catholic University of America in the Matter of Professor Charles E. Curran, October 9, 1987.

57. Letter from Chancellor James A. Hickey to Professor Urban A. Lester, Chair, Ad Hoc Committee of the Academic Senate, December 14, 1987.

58. Transcript of the Oral Argument before the Ad Hoc Committee, pp. 976–987.

59. Ibid, pp. 436–439; 822.

60. See note 38.

61. Letter from Urban A. Lester, Chair of the Ad Hoc Committee to Chancellor Hickey, December 21, 1987.

62. Statement of the Board of Trustees of the Catholic University of America to the Ad Hoc Committee of the Academic Senate, sent under a

cover letter from Cardinal Joseph Bernardin, Chair of the Board of Trustees, January 27, 1988.

63. Memo from C.E. Curran, to Friends and Advisors Re Recent Developments, February 3, 1988.

64. Letter from Urban A. Lester to Cardinal Joseph Bernardin, Chair of the Board of Trustees, February 16, 1988.

65. Deposition of President William J. Byron in *Curran v. The Catholic University of America,* June 23, 1988, pp. 141–152.

66. Deposition of Chancellor James Aloysius Hickey in *Curran v. The Catholic University of America,* July 14, 1988, pp. 316–330.

67. Order of Judge Bruce D. Beaudin, in the *Curran v. The Catholic University of America,* Superior Court of the District of Columbia, April 5, 1988.

68. The Catholic University of America Press Release, April 12, 1988.

69. Statement of Professor Charles E. Curran Re CUA Board Action of April 12.

70. Letter from Kevin T. Baine to John F. Hunt and Paul C. Saunders, April 13, 1988.

71. Letter from John F. Hunt and Paul C. Saunders to Kevin T. Baine, April 19, 1988.

72. Letter from Kevin T. Baine to John F. Hunt and Paul C. Saunders, April 29, 1988.

73. This telephone conversation was confirmed in a letter from John F. Hunt and Paul C. Saunders to Kevin T. Baine, May 10, 1988.

74. Statement of Professor Charles E. Curran, May 17, 1988.

75. Resolution of the Board of Trustees of CUA, June 2, 1988.

76. William J. Byron, S.J., "At Catholic U. the Issue Is Religious, Not Academic Freedom," *Washington Post,* Outlook Section, June 5, 1988. For a more in-depth development, see William J. Byron, S.J., "Disciplined Inquiry: A Catholic Reflection on Academic Freedom," *Delta Epsilon Sigma Journal* 34 (March 1989): 4–13.

77. Judith L. Andrews, Phuong-Lien Dang, and Timothy M. McLean, "Recent Development: Church Licensed Professors: The Curran Controversy," *Journal of College and University Law* 13 (1987): 375–393. Michael Scott Feeley, "The Dissent of Theology: A Legal Analysis of the Curran Case," *Hastings Constitutional Law Quarterly* 15, no. 7 (1987); Michael Scott Feeley, "A Historical Account of the Curran Controversy," *The Catholic Lawyer* 32, no. 1 (1988): 1–26; Douglas Laycock and Susan E. Waelbroeck, "Academic Freedom and the Free Exercise of Religion," *Texas Law Review* (June 1988): 1455–1475.

78. Defendant's Motion to Dismiss or for Summary Judgment, *Curran v. Catholic University,* March 1, 1988.

79. Memorandum...In Opposition to Defendant's Motion, *Curran v. Catholic University of America,* March 18, 1988.

80. Judge Bruce D. Beaudin, Order, CA No. 1562–87, *Curran v. Catholic University,* March 27, 1988.

244 *Personal Involvement*

81. First Amended Complaint, *Curran v. Catholic University*, June 10, 1988.

82. The five graduate students involved in the suit were Julia Fleming, Kevin Forrester, Rose Gorman, Frederick Hayes, and Johann Klodzen.

83. Defendant's Motion to Dismiss or for Summary Judgment, *Curran v. Catholic University*, November 2, 1988.

84. Plaintiff's Trial Brief and Memorandum in Opposition to Defendant's Motion for Summary Judgment, *Curran v. Catholic University*, November 17, 1988.

85. Judge Frederick H. Weisberg, Opinion and Order, CA 1562-87, *Curran v. Catholic University*, February 28, 1989. The full opinion is also published in *Origins* 18 (1989): 664-672. On April 4, 1989, Judge Weisberg granted summary judgment to the university in the case of the five graduate students who had become intervenor-plaintiffs in my case.

86. *Origins* 18 (1989): 671.

87. "Academic Freedom and Tenure: The Catholic University of America," *Academe: Bulletin of the AAUP* 75 (Sept.-Oct. 1989), 27-38.

88. Frederick R. McManus, "Academic Freedom and the Catholic University of America," *America* 160 (May 27, 1989): 506-509; James H. Provost, Raymond H. Potvin, and Mary Collins, "In Rejoinder: What Next at Catholic U?" *Commonweal* 116 (May 5, 1989): 270-275.

Index

AAUP (Association of American University Professors). *See also* Catholic Higher Education: AAUP and
—Academic freedom and, 1, 12–13, 19, 106, 154, 205, 208; during the McCarthy era, 14, 16–17, 46
—Bulletin of (*Academe*), 13, 83
—censure by, 2, 13, 14; specific cases, 37, 46, 67, 68, 69, 70, 71–72
—Committee A, 12, 13, 69, 82–84, 109n. 42, 210
—investigations at Catholic institutions, 37–38, 67–74, 82, 141, 236
—origins of, 1, 8–9, 56
—Statements of, 1, 12, 17, 54, 157; 1915, 9–12, 14, 19, 21, 35–36; 1940, 1, 2, 12, 13, 21, 106; 1940, acceptance by Catholic groups/institutions of, 37, 68, 69, 84, 102, 210; 1940, limitations clause of, 36, 39–41, 81, 82–84, 109n. 42, 185–86, 210; 1958, 1, 2, 3, 4, 12, 13, 69, 79; 1967, 27; 1982 Updated Guidelines, 2
Abortion, 141, 211
Academia Alfonsiana, 194, 224
Academic Freedom, *See also* Catholic Higher Education; Research; Tenure
—aliens and, 19
—areas of/scope, 2, 11
—courts and, 8, 18, 19, 22, 23; Supreme Court, 104, 112–13, 133. *See also* Catholic University of America: Curran and: 1987–89, lawsuit.

—development in U.S. of, 6–13, 19, 35, 154; characteristics of, 3–6, 20; critique of 4, 5, 9, 13–23; history of, 6–10, 11–12, 14, 16–17, 21, 46, 56; radical scholars and, 14, 16–17, 19, 20–21, 46–49
—due process and, 1–2, 12–13, 14, 16–17, 21, 36, 37, 154; Curran and, 75, 199, 204, 208, 210; 1986–88 Curran case and, 142, 211, 216, 217, 218, 220, 222, 225; safeguards provided by, 5, 11, 23, 184, 204; specific cases involving, 67, 69
—duties correlative to, 2, 11, 39, 44, 175–76, 181–85, 188
—extramural utterances and, 2–3, 11, 17–18, 23, 208
—German concept of, 8, 164–65
—hiring and, 5, 15, 16, 82, 185; Catholic institutions and, 131, 155, 175
—institutional autonomy and. *See* Institutional Autonomy
—limits of: common good, 130; disciplinary, 50–52, 60–61, 77–78, 116, 122, 128; faculty responsibilities, 182, 183; moral law and, 35, 38; in religious institutions, 6, 41–42; in religious institutions, limitations clause and, 2, 36, 82–84, 109n. 42, 155; in religious institutions, Roman Catholic, 38–40, 42, 54, 116–17, 122–23, 143; in situations not

245

ered by AAUP documents, 4, 5, 14, 15
—peer review and, 3, 5, 11, 15, 23, 181; critique of, 16–17; Curran and, 184, 185, 205, 215; Curran and, 1986–88, 122, 143, 174, 217, 222, 230, 232; Darwinian debate, 7
—religious institutions and, 6, 41, 42, 53. *See also* Catholic Higher Education (academic freedom in); Limitations Clause (1940 AAUP Statement)
—statements governing. *See* AAUP: Statements of
—students', 8, 19, 44, 82; professors' academic freedom and, 10, 43, 61, 175
—theoretical justification for, 4, 7, 10, 21–22, 105–6; for Catholic theologians (in U.S.), 155, 164–65, 171, 174, 175, 176–77, 180–81, 183–84, 188; good of the church as, 155, 163, 173–81; in U.S. Catholic higher education, 76, 77, 78, 80, 85
—threats to: ecclesiastical, 35, 41, 56, 154; faculty, 5, 14, 17, 20, 22; funded research, 5, 20, 154; governing boards, 5, 7, 8, 9–10, 14, 15, 16, 18, 20, 23, 154; government, 50, 158
—violations of, 2, 5, 7–8, 9, 12; Catholic institutions and, 37, 67–74, 78, 119, 141; McCarthy era, 16–17, 46–47, 49. *See also* Catholic University of America: academic freedom in
Accreditation, 144, 156, 175, 215
Accrediting Associations, 2, 12, 13, 27, 81
AFL-CIO, 71
Alter, Karl J. (archbishop of Cincinnati), 72, 73
America, 31, 40, 47, 49, 72, 129
American Academic Freedom Project, 41
American Catholic Historical Association: AAUP 1940 Statement and, 37

American Catholic Philosophical Association: AAUP 1940 Statement and, 37; *Proceedings,* 44, 45
American Council on Education: 1925 Conference, 12, 36
American Economic Association: 1913 Joint Committee, 9
Americanist Heresy, 28, 92
American Political Science Association: 1913 Joint Committee, 9
American Sociological Society: 1913 Joint Committee, 9
Annarelli, James J., 155–56, 184
Arness, John P., 223
Association of American Colleges, 20, 45, 48, 50. *See also* AAUP: Statements of
Association of American Universities, 48
Association of Catholic Colleges and Universities, 27, 128, 131–32, 133, 224
Autonomy: of culture, 89, 90–92, 177–79; of universities, *see* Institutional Autonomy

Baine, Kevin T., 221, 226, 230, 231, 232, 234–35
Baum, William W. (cardinal), 211, 230
Beaudin, Bruce D., 231, 235
Bellah, Robert, 158
Bennett, John C., 207
Bernardin, Joseph (cardinal), 211, 229, 235, 236
Boff, Leonardo, 138–39
Bonnette, Denis, 72
Boston College, 78, 97, 141
Boyle, John, 216
Browne, Henry, 40
Bühlmann, Walter, 139
Bull, George, 32–33
Burghardt, Walter J., 207
Burke, Eugene, 199
Byrns, Ruth, 40
Byron, William J., 219, 224, 230, 232, 235; "ecclesial limit" on academic freedom at CUA and, 122, 143, 233

Byron, William J., 219, 224, 230, 232, 235; "ecclesial limit" on academic freedom at C.U.A. and, 122, 143, 233

Cahill, Joseph, 128
Caldwell, Richard, 69–70
Canonical mission, 130, 131, 165, 171, 209; Curran and, 142, 213, 214, 215, 237; Curran's, process to remove, 211, 212, 216–217, 218, 220–23, 226, 227, 228–30, 231, 235; mandate and, 137
Canon Law, 131, 140, 167, 225
—CUA's appeal to, 142, 145, 194, 221, 231; in motions for summary judgment, 231, 235
—1917 Code, 130, 139
—1983 Code, 135, 139, 144; Canons 750 and 752, 230; Canon 810, 133, 144; Canon 812, 131–32, 133, 136, 143–45, 220
Canon Law Society of America, 165
Capitalism, 21, 59, 158
Capone, Domenico, 194
Carnegie Commission on Higher Education, 95
Carroll, John (bishop of Baltimore), 26
Carter, Emmett (bishop of London, Ontario), 195
Casey, Lawrence B. (aux. bishop of Rochester), 196
Catholic Commission on Intellectual and Cultural Affairs, 95, 96
Catholic Educational Association, 27
Catholic Higher Education:
—AAUP and, 67–71, 74, 81–84; before 1960, 31, 35–38, 39–40, 54, 66
—academic freedom in, 23, 66, 114, 119, 122–23, 124, 129; Curran's justification for, 155, 157, 162–64, 173–81, 188; general acceptance of, 66, 114, 118, 123, 124, 210; justification for, for Catholic theologians, 155, 164–65, 171, 173–74, 175, 176–77, 180–81, 188; before mid-1960s, 34–

65; new interpretation of limitations clause and, 82–84; 1960s' cases concerning, 67–75; non-Catholic theorists views of, 35, 40, 41–42, 45, 53–54, 55, 81–84, 134; opposition to (after 1960), 80, 104, 114–18, 156, 158, 172–76, 188; opposition to (after 1960), church documents and, 120, 124, 125, 131; outside the U.S., 163–64, 165, 189n. 13; present and future prospects for, 136–48, 239; reasons for general acceptance of, 85–106, 112–13; Roman Catholic hierarchy and (1970s and 1980s), 118–36, 220; specific institutions acceptance of, 67, 71, 72–75; theoretical reflections and acceptance of, 75–80
—administration of, 68, 71, 133; ecclesiastical control, 99, 123, 124, 126, 132, 133, 134, 135, 147, 163; 1960s changes, 70–71, 99, 102–3; religious communities and, 30, 118, 119, 125, 132
—authority (church) and, 38, 144, 147, 154, 155, 164, 174, 175; Congregation for Catholic Education on, 126, 128, 131, 132, 134, 135; "Rome Statement" on, 125–26; significance of speculative/practical distinction for, 60–61
—church teachings in, 55, 114, 145; inculcation of, 55; theologian's treatment of, 80, 139, 175–76
—curriculum, 30
—development of, 26–29, 30–31, 81, 95–105, 106, 132, 133
—distinctiveness of, 79, 80, 98–99, 112, 147, 178
—faculty, 61, 119, 174, 175; faith commitment, 52; lay, 31, 97, 99–101, 104; personal lives of, 38, 133, 143. *See also* Catholic Higher Education: professionalism and
—federal aid and, 104, 112–13, 115, 123, 133, 144, 156–57, 215

—goals of, 29, 30, 51, 55, 59, 61, 96;
Grisez on, 117; after 1960, 77, 97–
99, 135–36
—graduate education and, 27, 32, 80,
96, 101, 196
—hierarchical teaching office and, 99,
116, 118, 136, 147; confrontations
(*see also* Catholic University of
America: Curran and), 72, 73, 80,
119–20; documents concerning, 120,
124, 126, 130–31, 136, 140; special
relationship in certain conservative
institutions, 114
—pastoral mission of the church and,
29, 55, 77, 92, 101, 119, 120, 126,
130–36
—professionalism and, 30–31, 39, 97,
98, 99–103, 104
—religious communities and, 103, 104,
125, 132, 154, 163; before 1960s,
27, 30, 32, 97, 99–100, 102, 118,
119, 125
—trustees in, 133, 144, 145, 146; shift
to, 103, 119, 125
—U.S. bishops and, 118–23, 133, 136,
143–44, 145; Canon 812, 144–45;
NCEA committee concerning relationship, 113; 1989 NCCB document, 140
—U.S. higher education and: Catholic
approaches to, 27–34, 97, 178;
Catholic attitudes concerning academic freedom in, before 1960s, 31,
34–35, 43, 44; Catholic attitudes
concerning academic freedom in
1960s, 70–71, 79, 80, 102–6, 112,
147; contemporary Catholic opposition to academic freedom, 115, 117;
Knapp/Breenbaum comparative
study, 96
—Vatican and, 118, 121, 123–36, 138–
42, 143, 145, 146, 147. *See also*
Catholic University of America
—view of academy, 59
"Catholic Higher Education and the
Pastoral Mission of the Church,"
120–21, 136

Catholic News Service, 178
Catholic Theological Society of America, 140, 165, 198, 224–25, 242n. 55
"Catholic University in the Modern
World," 127–29
Catholic University of America (CUA),
27, 39, 48, 95, 101
—academic freedom in, before 1967,
196–97, 198; 1967 Curran case and,
72, 73, 78, 199, 210, 212; 1968–69
Curran case and, 72, 74–75, 203–5,
210, 212; 1986–88 Curran case and,
119–20, 122, 194, 232, 233, 236,
237–38, 239; 1986–88 Curran case,
ad hoc committee report and, 227,
229; revision of canonical statutes
and, 215–16
—Academic Senate of, 216, 239; 1967
Curran case and, 73, 199, 201;
1968–69 Curran case and, 75, 205,
206, 208, 209; 1986–88 Curran case
and, 219, 220, 221, 234; Provost
case and, 216; revision of canonical
statutes and, 215
—Bans liberal theologians (1963), 73,
196
—board of trustees of, 196, 211; *nihil
obstat* given by bishops of, 215, 216;
1967 Curran case and, 73, 198, 200–
2, 204; 1968–69 Curran case and,
75, 203–4, 205, 206, 208, 209, 210;
1986–88 Curran case and, 143, 144–
45, 217, 222, 228, 229, 231, 235;
1986–88 Curran case and, CUA's academic freedom, 122, 142, 193, 233,
238; 1986–88 Curran case and, institutional autonomy and, 234
—canonical statutes, 209; Curran's due
process hearing and, 211, 217, 218,
219, 222, 225, 227, 229; revision of,
141–42, 241n. 28; Weisberg decision
and, 237
—Curran and: before 1967, 193–98,
214; 1967 (nonreappointment/
strike), 72, 73, 78, 194, 198–202,
204, 239n. 5; 1968–69 (Dissent

from *Humanae Vitae*), 72, 74–75, 202, 210; 1968–69, Marlowe Committee, 75, 83, 194, 205–10, 214, 222, 227, 240 nn. 17, 19; 1979–85 (investigation by Congregation for the Doctrine of the Faith, CDF), 210–11, 215, 218; 1986 (CDF declaration concerning), 142, 210, 230, 231, 235; 1986 (CDF Declaration concerning), CUA's claims about, 194, 222, 229; 1986 (CDF Declaration concerning), Hickey's transmission of, 210–11, 217; 1986 (CDF Declaration concerning), increase in Curran's audience and, 187; 1986 (CDF Declaration concerning), unique in U.S., 174; 1986–88 (removal of canonical mission), 122, 142, 144, 211, 212, 217, 218, 235; 1986–88 (removal of canonical mission), ad hoc committee and, 142, 220–30, 231, 232, 234, 241n. 39, 242n. 48; 1987 (suspension), 219–20, 228, 231, 234; 1987–89 (lawsuit), 204, 218, 220, 230, 232, 234–38; 1987–89 (lawsuit), student intervenors in, 218, 235, 244nn. 82, 85
—departments: Biblical Studies, 211; Canon Law, 129, 202, 212, 213, 216; Church History, 213; Religion and Religious Education, 195, 203, 212, 213, 230; Sociology, 230; Theology (formerly School of Theology), 129, 141, 212, 218, 224, 227–28, 231, 237; Theology, Curran's suspension from, 219, 219–20, 228, 231, 234; Theology, revision of ecclesiastical statutes and, 213, 214, 215, 216
—ecclesiastical faculties of, 141–42, 211, 226, 227–28, 216, 237; ecclesiastical degree programs in, 213, 220; few such in U.S., 129; 1937 statutes concerning, 209; 1969 CUA restructuring and, 202, 212; 1979 revision of statutes concerning, 141–42, 212–16

—schools: Arts and Sciences, 197; Education, 199; Philosophy, 129, 202, 212, 213; Religious Studies, 213, 216, 218, 219, 223, 224; Theology, 195, 197, 198, 199, 201, 202, 203
—structure, 196, 201–2, 212–16
—*Tower*, 219
—Vatican and, 144, 196, 201–2, 204, 213, 214, 221, 233, 235, 237. *See also* Congregation for the Doctrine of the Faith; CUA: canonical statutes of; CUA: ecclesiastical faculties of
Catholic University of Puerto Rico, 144
Catholic World, 72
Cenkner, William, 218, 219, 224, 228
Christendom College (Front Royal), 114
Church in Anguish: Has the Vatican Betrayed Vatican II?, 137
Church/State Separation, 28, 90, 91, 235
Clark, Matthew (bishop of Rochester), 230
Classicism, 85–86, 115
College of St. Scholastica (Duluth), 141
College of St. Thomas (St. Paul), 72, 206
College of Theology Society, 101, 140, 224–25, 242n.55
"Cologne Declaration," 139, 164–65
Common Good, 2, 39, 133, 136, 157–62
Commonweal, 49, 76, 78
Communism, 89, 93; academic freedom of Communists, 17, 19, 20–21, 40–41, 46–49, 53, 54. *See also* Academic Freedom: development, radical scholars and
Congar, Yves, 87
Congregation for Catholic Education, 113, 114, 123, 129, 202, 230; new norms for Catholic higher education proposed by, 121, 132–36, 143, 145, 156; "Rome Statement" and, 125,

Congregation for Catholic Education
(*continued*)
126; *Sapientia Christiana* and, 129–
31
Congregation for Religious, 138
Congregation for Seminaries and Educational Institutions, 123
Congregation for Seminaries and Universities, 123, 124
Congregation for the Doctrine of the Faith: Curran, declaration concerning, 120, 142, 174, 194, 210, 222, 225, 226, 230, 235; Curran, investigation of, 139, 210–11; investigation of other theologians, 138–39; oath of fidelity, 140
Connelly, Terence R., 207
Conscience, 59, 76, 90, 145, 160, 166
Constitution on Divine Revelation, 166
Constitution on the Church, 167
Contraception (artificial), 45, 73, 195–96, 197, 200, 211; *Humanae Vitae* and, 74, 84, 139, 164, 202–3
Coriden, James A., 218
Cornell University, 225, 238
Cravath, Swaine, and Moore, 217–18, 221, 223, 228, 231, 232, 234; representation of CUA dissenters from *Humane Vitae*, 205, 207
Cross, Robert, 208
Crosson, Frederick, 77–78
Curran, Charles E.: *Christian Morality Today*, 198; education of, 194–95; position on academic freedom, 157–62, 162–65, 171, 173–78, 192, 193, 227; St. Bernard's Seminary and, 194, 195–96. *See also* Catholic University of America: Curran and

Danforth Foundation Report, 81–82
Darwinian Debate, 7, 197
Davis, Jerome, 49
Declaration on Christian Education, 130
Declaration on Religious Liberty, 90, 167

Decree on Ecumenism, 170
Deferrari, Roy J., 48
Deus Scientiarum Dominus, 130, 214
Dewart, Leslie, 76
Dewey, John, 9, 48, 50, 53
Dismissal, 71, 131, 174, 175, 187
—Curran case and, 142, 174, 219, 221, 228, 232
—due process in, 1, 3, 4, 5, 11, 181. *See also* Academic Freedom: peer review
—reasons for, 3, 4 5, 11, 17; professional incompetence, 3, 5, 11, 17, 181, 182, 187
Dissent, 55, 76, 115, 119, 167, 186
—from noninfallible church teachings: Curran's 73, 176, 195–96, 211; *Humanae Vitae* and, 74, 83, 84, 194, 202–10
Divorce and Remarriage, 211
Donahue, Charles, S.J., 49–54
Donohue, John W., 129
Donovan, John D., 38, 97
"Draft Document on Catholic Higher Education," 133–136, 145–46, 147, 156
Due Process. *See* Academic Freedom: due process and
Dulles, Avery, 167, 242n. 48
Duquesne University, 72

Ecclesiastical Faculties, 129–31, 141–42, 214
Elderkin, George W., 32
Ellis, John Tracy, 95–96, 99
Empiricism, 41, 58, 117, 162; as justification for academic freedom, 4, 105–6, 157, 164. *See also* Darwinism; Scientific Method
Enlightenment, 115, 117, 158
Error, 42, 46, 87, 171, 173, 174; evolution and, 7; need to risk for good of church, 76, 179; rights of erroneous conscience, 160; students' right not to be taught, 61; Syllabus of Errors, 58

Euthanasia, 211
Extramural Utterances, 2–3, 11, 17–18, 23, 208

Faculty, 2, 3, 4–5, 8, 18–19, 20; civil rights of, 2, 11, 17, 18, 19, 22–23, 47, 51; university governing boards and, 4–5, 8, 9, 15–16
Fellowship of Catholic Scholars, 114, 115
Fleisher, Moses, 37, 63n. 30, 119
Fletcher, Joseph, 32
Fordham University, 32, 40, 49, 97, 98, 101
Freedom, 6, 50, 51, 92, 116, 130, 164, 177; absolutizing of, 158–59, 164; in Catholic thought, 58, 59, 88, 89–90, 93–94, 164, 180–81; truth as limit upon, 38, 39, 43, 44, 48, 61, 116–17. *See also* Academic Freedom; Religious Liberty
Friedman, Clarence, 208
Friends of American Catholic Theology (FACT), 218
Fuchs, Joseph, 194
Funding (University), 7–8, 20; federal, 115, 123, 133, 144, 156–57, 159; federal, Supreme Court cases, 104, 112–13

Galileo case, 173
Gallin, Alice, 224
Garrone, Gabriel (cardinal), 114
Georgetown University, 26, 33–34, 43, 78, 129, 224
Gleason, Philip, 29
Glennon, John (archbishop of St. Louis), 119
Gonzaga University, 68–69
Greeley, Andrew, 27–28, 62n. 7, 95, 101
Greenbaum, Joseph J., 96
Gregorian University, 194
Grennan, Jacqueline, 80
Grisez, Germain, 114–15, 116, 117, 128

Guindon, André, 224
Guthrie, Hunter, S.J., 33–34, 41, 43
Gutiérrez, Gustavo, 138

Hallinan, Paul J. (archbishop of Atlanta), 201
Halton, Thomas, O.P., 32
Hannan, Phillip (archbishop of New Orleans), 201
Häring, Bernard, 87, 139, 194, 224
Harnett, Robert C., S.J., 47–48
Harvard University (Roman Catholic/ Protestant Colloquium), 195
Hellwig, Mary Zielinski, 218
Hellwig, Monika, 224
Henle, Robert, 128, 129
Hesburgh, Theodore, 79–80, 84, 98, 103, 114, 208; Congregation for Catholic Education proposed norms and, 129, 134, 145; president IFCU, 124
Hickey, James A. (archbishop), 142, 211, 212, 218, 235, 236
—Curran case and: ad hoc committee, 218, 221, 223, 225, 227, 228, 232; board of trustees' committee, 231; meeting in Rome, 230; meetings with Curran, 211; suspension, 219, 220, 235; threat to invoke Canon 812, 144, 220
—revision of CUA ecclesiastical statutes and, 213, 214, 215–16
Hierarchical Teaching Office, 72, 74, 80, 114, 116, 204, 208, 225
—CUA canonical statutes and, 202, 225
—infallible teachings of, 55, 167, 182, 183, 186
—noninfallible teachings of, 55, 74, 114, 167, 183, 211
—relations with Catholic higher education. *See* Catholic Higher Education (academic freedom in, Roman Catholic hierarchy and; authority [church] and; hierarchical teaching office and; U.S. bishops and)

—role invoked to justify limits to academic freedom, 38, 116, 172–73, 188
—role of theologians and, 80, 168, 171, 174; theological competence and, 182, 183, 185, 186–87, 188
—Vatican II and, 87–88, 166–67
Higher Education Facilities Act, 112
Himstead, Ralph, 17, 46
Historical Consciousness, 85–86, 88, 170
Hochwalt, Carroll A., 201, 204
Hogan, Aloysius, J., 43
Holy Office. *See* Congregation for the Doctrine of the Faith
Hook, Sidney, 19, 40, 45, 48, 53, 54, 55
Hotchkin, John F., 207
"Human Life in Our Day" (NCCB), 207
Humanae Vitae, 84, 139; CUA dissent from, 74, 83, 194, 202, 203, 204, 205, 207, 208, 209, 210. *See also* Contraception (artificial)
Human rights, 61, 94, 117, 158, 175; John XXIII and, 58, 89; Murray and, 57, 94
Hunt, John, 207, 217–18, 229, 230, 238
Hunter College, 49, 208
Hutchins, Robert M., 96

Index of Forbidden Books, 77
Institutional Autonomy, 177–78
—CUA's, 201–2, 204, 205, 210; 1986–88 Curran case and, 225, 226, 229, 231, 233–34, 239; revision of the canonical statutes and, 214, 215
—German universities and, 8
—in Catholic institutions, 80, 81, 92, 103, 104, 111, 146, 147, 156; autonomy of culture and, 91, 178–79; Congregation for Catholic Education and, 123, 129, 132–33, 139, 144, 146; "Catholic University in the Modern World" and, 127; Kinshasa

Congress and, 124; Kliever's critique of Curran's view of, 185; Land O'Lakes Statement and, 78, 154, 201; NCCB documents and, 120, 121, 136; 1971 IFCU report and, 125
—medieval universities and, 6
Intellect, 60, 61
International Federation of Catholic Universities (IFCU), 78, 113, 123, 124, 125, 126, 131
—Kinshasa Congress 124–25, 126

Jesuit School of Theology (Berkeley), 129
John Paul I (pope), 130
John Paul II (pope), 130, 132, 135, 136, 137, 210
Johns Hopkins University, 9, 27
John XXIII (pope), 58, 89, 131

Kahn, Journet, 45–46
Kearney, James E. (bishop), 195, 196
Kearns, Francis E., 78
Kellner, Hugo Maria, 195, 197
Kelly, George A., 114, 117
Kennedy, John F., 93
Kennedy, Robert T., 218
Kerwin, Jerome G., 49
Kinshasa Congress. *See* International Federation of Catholic Universities.
Kirk, Russell, 54
Kliever, Lonnie, D., 185–86
Klodzen, Johann, 218, 244 n. 82
Knapp, Robert H., 96
Kreyche, Gerald F., 76–77
Krol, John J. (archbishop), 200–201, 202, 209
Küng, Hans, 138, 186–87

Labor Unions, 178
Laghi, Pio (archbishop), 230
Land O'Lakes:
—Conference, 79, 124

—Statement, 78, 79, 80, 84, 127, 143, 201, 234; Danforth Commission Report and, 82; opening of, 98
Lauer, Rosemary, 79
Leo XIII (pope), 28, 29, 56, 59, 92
Lester, Urban A., 223, 241n. 39
Liberalism, 34, 41, 50, 53, 59, 61–62, 89
Limitations Clause (1940 AAUP Statement), 36, 38–40, 81, 82–84, 109n. 42, 210; Curran's views of academic freedom and, 109n. 42, 185–86
Lipscomb, Oscar H. (archbishop of Mobile), 122
Lonergan, Bernard, 85, 170, 208
Lubac, Henri de, 87
Luther, Martin, 89

McAllister, Joseph B., 197–98, 200, 239n. 5
McBrien, Richard P., 224
McCarthy Era, 14, 17, 19, 46
McCormick, Richard A., 224
McDonald, William J. (bishop), 73, 197, 198, 199, 200, 201
Machiup, Fritz, 21
McIntyre, James F. (cardinal), 202, 204
MacIver, Robert M., 41–42, 45, 53–54
MacLaughlin, Leo, 98
MacMahon, Francis, E., 49
McManus, Frederick R., 230, 240n. 17, 241n. 28
McReynolds, Sally, 218
Maguire, Daniel, 141
Mallon, Wilfred M., 30–31, 38–39
Mandate (*See* Canonical Mission), 132, 133, 143, 146, 171, 220
Maritain, Jacques, 32
Marlowe, Donald E., 205; Marlowe Committee. *See* Catholic University of America: Curran and, 1968–69 (Dissent from *Humanae Vitae*)
Marquette University, 101
Marx, Karl, 59; Marxism, 49, 89; Marxists, 14, 21. *See also* Communism

Masturbation, 73, 198, 211
Mater et Magistra, 58, 89
Meachum, Roy, 200
Meade, Francis L., 44
Mercy College, 67–68
Metzger, Walter, 7, 21
Michaud, Paul M., 78
Middle States Association of Colleges and Schools, 72, 175, 201, 210
Morrissey, Francis, 223
Mullahy, Bernard, 44–45, 57, 61
Murray, John Courtney, 57, 87, 94, 160–62

National Association of Student Personnel Administrators, 19
National Association of Women Deans and Counselors, 19
National Catholic Educational Association, 35, 43, 76, 114, 208, 240n. 17; College and University Department, 113, 120, 121
National Catholic Reporter, 198
National Conference of Catholic Bishops. *See* Roman Catholic Church: U.S., hierarchy of
Natural Law, 38, 57, 58, 94
Neoscholasticism. *See* Philosophy
Newman Clubs, 32
Newman, Jeremiah, 128
New York Times, 141
Nihil obstat, 131, 213, 214, 216
Noonan, John, 207
Normae Quaedam, 130
North Central Association of Colleges and Secondary Schools, 28
Notre Dame (Maryland), 27
Nyquist, Ewald, B., 31

O'Boyle, Patrick A. (archbishop of Washington), 73, 200, 202, 203, 204, 210
O'Dea, Thomas, 196
Oh, John K. C., 219

Pacem in Terris, 58, 59

Parochial Schools, 27, 92–93, 104, 113, 118, 134; public schools and, 29, 61

Pastoral Constitution on the Church in the Modern World, 89, 90, 166–67, 177

Paul VI (pope), 74, 124, 130, 202

Peter, Carl J., 223, 241n. 28

Philosophy, 89, 112, 160, 179, 192; Cartesian, 5, 57; Catholic opposition to academic freedom and, 33, 44, 56–62, 105, 114; Donahue's views of academic freedom and, 50–53; Kantian, 57; Murray on the American proposition and Catholic philosophy, 57, 94; need for departments of in Catholic institutions, 199; neoscholastic, 29, 56–58, 61, 85, 86, 88, 163

Pilarczyk, Daniel (archbishop of Cincinnati), 122

Piux IX (pope), 58

Pius XI (pope), 130

Pius XII (pope), 86, 123

Pluralism, 161, 197; academic freedom and, 41, 49, 51–52, 54, 55, 159

Pohier, Jacques, 138

Power, David, 219, 224, 228

Power, Edward J., 27, 29

Premarital Sex, 211

Princeton University, 32

"Proposed Schema for a Pontifical Document on Catholic Universities," 132–34. *See also* "Draft Document of Catholic Higher Education"

Provost, James H., 216

Rabban, David, 20

Rahner, Karl, 87

Ramsey, Paul, 32

Ratio Studiorum, 30, 34

Ratzinger, Joseph (cardinal), 137, 210, 211, 216, 217, 228, 230; The *Ratzinger Report: An Exclusive Interview on the State of the Church,* 137

Reformation, 59

Religious Communities: administration of colleges, 27, 31, 31, 100, 103, 118, 119, 125; Catholic higher education and, 113, 132, 154, 163; community apostolate, 97, 102; faculty, 30, 31, 100; founding of colleges, 27, 118

Religious Liberty, 57, 93, 160–62, 181; CUA's appeal to, 143, 235; Vatican II and, 55, 90–91, 94, 167, 180

Renaissance, 57

"Report of a Special Committee on Departures from Proper Academic Procedure" (C.U.A., 1963), 196

Research, 195, 207
—academic freedom in U.S. higher education and, 2, 5, 7, 8, 11, 15, 20
—in Catholic higher education, 80, 101, 129, 135, 160; Land O'Lakes Statement and, 78, 127; before 1960, 30, 32, 39, 96, 100; "To Teach as Jesus Did" and, 120

Revelation, 33, 34, 45, 54–55
—*Constitution on Divine Revelation,* 166
—limits to academic freedom and, 35, 38, 52, 57, 60, 116, 122
—theology and, 86, 116, 120, 126, 169; theological competence, 180, 183, 185

Ritter, Joseph (cardinal), 195

Roesch, Raymond, 72–73

Roman Catholic Church, 137, 169, 180, 183. *See also* Vatican Council II
—U.S., Catholic-American problem, 28, 92–94, 147; character, 28, 35, 92–94, 95, 97, 187; good of and academic freedom, 76, 155, 162–65, 171–73, 180, 188; immigrants and, 28, 35, 93, 95, 97; Vatican and, 28, 93, 137–38, 139, 141, 165, 180
—U.S., hierarchy of, 28, 94, 136; Catholic higher education and, 118–23, 133, 140, 143, 145; Congregation for Catholic Education proposed norms and, 133, 134; joint NCEA

committee and, 113, 132; National Conference of Catholic Bishops, 118, 120, 121, 133, 134, 140, 158–61, 210, 213
"Rome Statement: The Catholic University and the Aggiornamento," 125–26

St. Bernard's Seminary (Rochester), 194, 195–96
St. John's University, 71–72, 78, 79, 114, 128, 184
St. Louis University, 37–38, 67, 103, 119
St. Martin's College (Lacey), 141
St. Mary's College (Winona), 69–70
San Diego College for Women, 72
Sapientia Christiana, 130–31, 141, 212–13, 241n. 28
Saunders, Paul, 217–18, 223, 228, 229, 234, 238
Scanlan, T. M., 22
Scheel, Brother Nivard, 206, 209, 240n. 9
Schillebeeckx, Edward, 138
Schmitz, Walter J., 197, 198, 199, 200, 240n. 17
Schrecker, Ellen, 14, 16–17
Schuster, George N., 48
Scientific Method, 48, 52, 58, 86, 117; academic freedom and, 4, 58, 105–6, 157–58, 164
Secularism, 29, 32, 50, 52, 55–56, 114, 117
Seminaries, 27, 102, 164, 195
Seper, Franz (cardinal), 211
Shannon, James P. (bishop), 206
Shehan, Lawrence (cardinal), 195
Shelton, Austin Jesse, Jr., 67–68, 70
Sisters of Mercy, 67
Sisters of St. Joseph, 163
Slaughter, Sheila, 14
Sloyan, Gerard, 207
Smith, Andrew, S.J., 44
Society of Catholic College Teachers of Sacred Doctrine. *See* College Theology Society

Society of Jesus (Jesuits), 30, 31, 47, 67, 166
Stace, Walter T., 32
State, 90, 91–92, 159, 177–78
"Statutes of the Pontifical Degree Programs of the Department of Theology." *See* Catholic University of America; canonical statutes
Students, Academic Freedom of. *See* Academic Freedom: students'
Subjectivism, 44, 48, 58
Supreme Court, 104, 112–13, 133
Suspension of faculty, 3, 205–6, 219–20, 228, 231, 234
Syllabus of Errors, 58

Tench, Richard T., 68–69, 70
Tenure, 68, 71, 181, 182, 185, 187
—AAUP and, 2, 5, 9, 11
—Catholic higher education and: Curran's at CUA, 142, 144, 226, 229, 235, 236, 237, 238; Curran's at CUA, question of relationship between tenure and canonical mission, 214, 217, 219, 221–22, 226, 228, 231; church and authorities and, 154, 174, 175; *nihil obstat* and, 213, 215, 216; before 1960, 31, 38
—critique of, 15–16
Theologian (Catholic), 202. *See also* Catholic Higher Education; Congregation for Catholic Education; Congregation for the Doctrine of the Faith
—academic freedom of: justification for, 155–56, 162–65, 171–72, 174, 177, 178, 181, 183, 188; Objections to, 172–73, 175, 178, 186, 188
—competence of, 181–88; Curran case and, 174, 222, 224, 226, 227
—role of, 165–72, 172, 174, 175–76, 181; as academic/as church member, 171, 174, 175, 186; as academic/as church member, church authorities and, 80, 126, 127; hierarchical magisterium and, 116, 140, 147, 165–68,

—Curran and. *See* Catholic University of America: Curran and; Curran, Charles E.
—federal funding and, 133
—importance of experience in some types of, 192–93
—liberation theology, 137–38
—moral theology, 94, 116, 170, 176; Curran and, 142, 194–95, 223, 226, 228, 232
—need for departments of in Catholic higher education, 99
—norms governing. *See* Canonical Mission; Canon Law; Congregation for Catholic Education; Mandate
—philosophy and, 56, 61
—professionalization and, 101–2
—Renaissance and, 57
—role of, 50, 116, 165–72, 175–76
—"To Teach as Jesus Did" and, 120
—before Vatican II, 85–86, 101, 179
Third International Congress of Catholic Universities, 135–36
Thirkel, Robert, 208
Thomas Aquinas, St., 56, 85, 86, 88, 166, 169
Thomism, 45, 51, 56–58, 88, 166
Tilton v. Richardson, 112–13, 133
Tos, Aldo, 39, 58
Totalitarianism, 59, 61–62, 89, 158
"To Teach as Jesus Did," 120
Trustees. *See* Universities: U.S., governing boards
Truth, 41, 61, 76, 87, 88, 166, 179, 180, 181; Donahue's theory and, 50, 51, 52; good of speculative order and, 59–60; hierarchy of, 167; *Mater et Magistra*, 58; opposition to academic freedom, before 1960, 32, 33, 35, 38, 39, 42, 43, 44, 48, 58; opposition to academic freedom, recent, 114, 116–17; Thomism and, 56–57
Tumulty, Philip A., 37

United Federation of College Teachers, 71

United States National Student Association, 19
Universities:
—German, 8, 10, 11, 130, 164–65
—medieval, 6, 46, 76, 169, 170–71, 179
—U.S. (and Colleges): Catholics in, 29, 31, 43, 48–49, 101; churches and, 6, 29, 35, 41, 56; denominational colleges, 29, 36, 42, 56, 79, 81–84; development of, 2, 6–8, 27, 29, 56, 81, 105–6; function, 10, 41–42, 51, 92; governing boards of (*see also* Academic Freedom: threats to), 4, 5; neutrality of, 7, 21; public trust of, 10, 21, 59. *See also* Catholic Higher Education
University of Chicago, 49
University of Dayton, 72–73
University of Notre Dame, 29, 45, 49, 77, 195, 224; Hesburgh and, 79, 84, 98, 124, 129, 208; lay trustees of, 103; 1966 Symposium, 77
University of Southern California, 238

Vagnozzi, Egidio (archbishop), 200
Van Alstyne, William, 18
Vatican Council I, 187
Vatican Council II, 106, 114, 123, 137, 165, 195; autonomy of culture, 89, 90–92; Catholic press and, 178; Code of Canon Law and, 131; church and, 87–88; Declaration on Christian Education, 130; ecumenism and, 82, 89; freedom and, 87, 89–91; Grisez and, 115; NCCB and, 118; religious liberty, 58, 90, 91, 94, 178; theology and, 85–92, 171, 196
Vaughan, Austin, 208
Vietnam War, 94, 105
Villanova University, 141

Walsh, John E., 77
Walsh, Michael, 97–98
Washingtonian, 200
Washington Post, 233

118; religious liberty, 58, 90, 91, 94, 178; theology and, 85–92, 171, 196
Vaughan, Austin, 208
Vietnam War, 94, 105
Villanova University, 141

Walsh, John E., 77
Walsh, Michael, 97–98
Washingtonian, 200
Washington Post, 233

Webb, Robert K., 207, 218, 224
Weisberg, Frederick (judge), 234, 236–38, 241n. 39, 244n. 85
Weston School of Theology, 129
Whalen, John P., 203, 205, 206
Williams and Connolly, 221, 234, 235
Woodward, Kenneth, 208
Wuerl, Donald W. (bishop), 122

Yale University, 49
Yanitelli, Victor, 207